Seductive Reasoning

Seductive Reasoning

PLURALISM AS THE PROBLEMATIC
OF CONTEMPORARY LITERARY THEORY

by Ellen Rooney

Cornell University Press

Ithaca and London

First published 1989 by Cornell University Press.

International Standard Book Number 0-8014-2192-6
Library of Congress Catalog Card Number 88-47917

Printed in the United States of America

*Librarians: Library of Congress cataloging information
appears on the last page of the book.*

*The paper in this book is acid-free and meets the guidelines for
permanence and durability of the Committee on Production Guidelines
for Book Longevity of the Council on Library Resources.*

FOR KHACHIG, WITH GOOD REASON

The master's tools will never dismantle the master's house.
—Audre Lorde, *Sister Outsider*

Whomever one seeks to persuade, one acknowledges as master of the situation.
—Karl Marx, *The Eighteenth Brumaire*

CONTENTS

ACKNOWLEDGMENTS

This book has been a long time in the making, and I owe debts of every order to the many people who helped make it possible. To begin at the beginning, Wesleyan University's English Department and its Center for the Humanities provided me with an environment both tolerant and stimulating and introduced me to the pleasures of theory. Karen Boklund first showed me the possibilities of a marxist semiotics; James Kavanagh pointed me in the direction of Althusser; Hayden White gave me the benefit of his liberating irony and read my first effort to assess Marx's suspicions about the rhetoric of persuasion; I remain grateful to each of them. I have since been most fortunate in all my readers. I particularly thank Stanley Fish, who read the manuscript in its earliest form and projected a future for it, which is the first, best gift of any reader, and Neil Hertz, who gave me the benefit of his scrupulous critical attention, shared his questions, and, on a few points, extended me the benefit of his doubts as well. Lawrence Scanlon, Andrew Gelber, Amy Barrett, and Carl Freedman all read portions of the manuscript; their comments guided my revisions. The final form of this essay owes a great deal to Christina Crosby, Mary Ann Doane, Karen Newman, and Naomi Schor, the members of a feminist reading group that welcomed me when I arrived at Brown University; they have given me intellectual and personal support, both by the sympathetic rigor of their questions and by the example of their own work. I do not expect to find better comrades anywhere. Neil Lazarus is a constant source of energy, ideas and encouragement, and I am thankful to him for pointing out my many blind spots. I benefited from the intellectual generosity of the members of the Pembroke Seminar of 1986–87, whose questions sent me back to revise again, and I am especially grateful to Elizabeth Weed, whose insights, objections, and friendship made this book easier to write. I am also indebted to the students at Brown University who attended my seminars in feminist theory and shared their insights, and whose exuberant and uncompromising struggles, both inside and outside class, are a vivid reminder that the university need never be an ivory tower. Ruth Santos, Virginia Polselli, Arnold Sanders, and Eliel Mamousette extended to me their patience and friendship and helped me to shape the material environment in which I worked. Paul Smith, Richard Ohmann, W. J. T. Mitchell, and James E. Ford provided forums for portions of this work and helpful comments along the way, as did the anonymous referee for Cornell University Press. A portion of Chapter 4 appeared in the *Dalhousie Review* 64 (Summer 1984), and I am grateful for permission to make use of this material. I owe a large debt to Bernhard Kendler; his care and patience as an editor were matched only by his persistent encouragement, which helped bring this book to press. Kay Scheuer's meticulous editorial advice brought home to me once again the limits of every critic as a reader of her own text. My thanks to Carole Doberstein and Lisa Giancola for their many gifts. My family—my parents, Lucy Hayes (the godmother we all need), and my brothers, Michael, John, Peter, and Paul—have been waiting for these pages to appear between hard covers for a combined total of forty-two years. The force of their humor, support, and love dwarfs that or any figure, and I am as grateful to them as I am hesitant to mention the next book. Finally, I am grateful to Khachig Tölölyan. He is a relentless inspiration and a tireless critic, and sometimes sings me that old tune about all work and no play. He has warned me away from unnecessary compromises and the temptation to please everyone, which is to say, he has reminded me of the seduction of pluralism, and he is one of the reasons writing is a seductive part of the life I live. It is a great pleasure to dedicate this book to him.

Ellen Rooney

Providence, Rhode Island

ABBREVIATIONS OF FREQUENTLY
CITED TEXTS

AR   Paul de Man. *Allegories of Reading*. New Haven: Yale University Press, 1979.

B   Wayne Booth. "'Preserving the Exemplar': or, How Not to Dig Our Own Graves." *Critical Inquiry* 3:3 (1977), 407–23.

BI   Paul de Man. *Blindness and Insight*. 2d ed., revised. Minneapolis: University of Minnesota Press, 1983.

CU   Wayne Booth. *Critical Understanding*. Chicago: University of Chicago Press, 1979.

F   Stanley Fish. *Is There a Text in This Class?* Cambridge: Harvard University Press, 1980.

FM   Louis Althusser. *For Marx*. London: New Left Books, 1977.

G   Suzanne Gearhart. "Philosophy *before* Literature: Deconstruction, Historicity, and the Work of Paul de Man." *Diacritics* 13:4 (1983), 63–81.

H   E. D. Hirsch, Jr. *The Aims of Interpretation*. Chicago: University of Chicago Press, 1976.

K   James Kavanagh. "'To the Same Defect': Toward a Critique of the Ideology of the Aesthetic." In *Literature and Ideology*, ed. Harry R. Garvin. East Brunswick, N.J.: Associated University Presses, 1982.

KM   Steven Knapp and Walter Benn Michaels. "Against Theory." *Critical Inquiry* 8:4 (1982), 723–42.

LP   Louis Althusser. *Lenin and Philosophy*. London: Monthly Review Press, 1971.

M   Pierre Macherey. *A Theory of Literary Production*. London: Routledge & Kegan Paul, 1978.

NA   Garry Wills. *Nixon Agonistes*. New York: Signet, 1971.

OD   Jonathan Culler. *On Deconstruction*. Ithaca: Cornell University Press, 1982.

PR   M. H. Abrams. "How to Do Things with Texts." *Partisan Review* 46:4 (1979), 566–88.

PU   Fredric Jameson. *The Political Unconscious*. Ithaca: Cornell University Press, 1981.

R   Paul de Man. "The Resistance to Theory." *Yale French Studies* 63 (1982), 3–20.

RC   Louis Althusser and Etienne Balibar. *Reading Capital*. London: New Left Books, 1979.

RW   Raymond Williams. "Marxism, Structuralism and Literary Analysis." *New Left Review* 129 (September/October 1981).

S   Gayatri Spivak. *In Other Words*. New York: Methuen, 1987.

SC   Louis Althusser. *Essays in Self-Criticism*. London: New Left Books, 1976.

Seductive Reasoning

INTRODUCTION

> Criticism is not an "homage" to the truth of the past
> or to the truth of "others"—it is a construction of the
> intelligibility of our own time.
> —Barthes, "What Is Criticism?"

> We must completely reorganize the idea we have of
> knowledge, we must abandon the mirror myths of
> immediate vision and reading, and conceive
> knowledge as a production.
> —Althusser, *Reading Capital*

The subject of this book is pluralist discourse in contemporary Anglo-American literary theory. My argument challenges both the common sense definition of pluralism as an affable form of methodological eclecticism and the consensus that literary pluralists are a relatively small and easily identifiable group of critics, centered at the University of Chicago and positioned as the heirs to R. S. Crane and Richard McKeon. I will argue instead that a hitherto unarticulated pluralism dominates American literary theory, penetrating even those discourses that seem antithetical to it. Indeed, at present, pluralism seems endowed with an infinite capacity to recuperate the potentially anti-pluralist discourses that have appeared in literary theory.

In my analysis, this hegemonic pluralism emerges as a double strategy—for reading and for writing—structured around the problem of persuasion. I shall show that the pluralist's invitation to critics and theorists of all kinds to join him in "dialogue" is a seductive gesture that constitutes every interpreter—*no matter what her conscious critical affiliation*—as an effect of the desire to persuade. As we shall see, pluralistic forms of discourse first imagine a universal community in which every individual (reader) is a potential convert, vulnerable to persuasion, and then require that each critical utterance aim at the successful persuasion of this community in general, that is, in its entirety. This demand ensures a conversation in which every critic must address a general or universal audience. This theoretical generality marks the limit of the pluralist's humanism, and it is the only absolute pluralism requires to sustain its practice.

Defined in these terms, pluralism has relatively little to do with an individual critic's lack of dogmatism or his tolerance of diverse views. On the contrary, as we shall see, the pluralist may be a partisan of *any* faction within the critical field, from intentionalist to feminist, myth critic to marxist, so long as she practices (and of course preaches) a contentious criticism founded on the theoretical possibility of universal or general persuasion. Pluralism, then, is not a practical commitment to methodological eclecticism, but an ensemble of discursive practices constituted and bounded by a problematic of general persuasion. As we shall see, the symptomatic moment of pluralist discourse arrives when the theoretical problem of the position of the reader is displaced, rewritten as a question of logic, ethics, or rhetoric. To interrogate the status of the general audience is to risk discovering the interests of readers as a theoretical limit to persuasion, and this is a possibility pluralists must consistently evade, whatever their other critical commitments.

Seductive Reasoning offers a reading of pluralism that both stresses its real discursive flexibility and heterogeneity and seeks to articulate the unacknowledged presuppositions, the limits, and, most critical, the exclusions that give it ideological coherence. Previous discussions have failed to uncover this pluralist problematic in part because most analysts have committed their energies to describing the explicit agendas of prominent and self-identified pluralists; the figure of Wayne Booth is a favorite exemplar. In contrast, the texts I have chosen are not drawn solely from the writings of recognized pluralists; most of the critics I address in fact present themselves as (more or less) active opponents of pluralism. My counterargument unfolds across close readings of five theoretical texts, the products of various hands: E. D. Hirsch, Wayne Booth, Stanley Fish, Paul de Man and Fredric Jameson, and it begins by rejecting the view that Booth is the sole pluralist in the group.

I by no means intend to suggest that the theorists just named share identical critical biases or form a homogeneous school. This book is neither a synoptic introduction to their varied theoretical *oeuvres*, nor a survey of current developments in literary theory, nor a history of the vicissitudes of the word "pluralist" in twentieth-century North American literary studies. My argument is not structured as a proof that the theorists I read are prototypical pluralists or that their works consistently display the *essence* of pluralism. In fact, my own reading is grounded in theoretical assumptions which reject the notion that a text or a career can be properly said to have an essence. Rather than trace the history or the meaning of the word "pluralism," I hope to establish the pervasiveness of pluralist ideology and to disclose that ideology's effects and limits. Thus, the individual texts I will examine are the occasion and not the final object of my analysis. The real object of my analysis is this ideological struc ture, the problematic of general persuasion.[1]

[1]A critical analysis of the relationship between the pluralism of R. S. Crane and Richard McKeon and the work of "second-generation" pluralists such as Booth is certainly needed, but I will not perform this task of intellectual history in the present essay. Crane wrote that the "critical philosophy" characterizing the Chicago school of critics was an "attitude toward criticism . . . which they have called 'pluralism,'" but he also noted that "the term may be unfortunate" and explained that "what they meant it to convey was simply their conviction that there are and have been many valid critical methods . . . each of which has its characteristic powers and limitations. They have stated this as a middle position between the extremes of dogmatism and skepticism": *Critics and Criticism: Ancient and Modern*, ed. R. S. Crane (Chicago: University of Chicago Press, 1952), p. iv. Whether the philosophical term was fortunate or unfortunate is a question I will not address. My analysis aims to treat pluralism as a contemporary discursive practice, *not* as a philosophical stance. Accordingly, I will also bracket the question of the formal parallels that may exist between contemporary forms of critical pluralism in literary theory and the philosophical speculations of such figures as Stephen C. Pepper or Nelson Goodman. Such a "history of ideas" approach fails to account for the specificity of pluralism's instantiation in the academic discourse of literary theory, and it has led some critics into confusion rather than away from it. Bruce Erlich, for example, undertakes to

4 *Introduction*

My immediate aims are thus theoretical: to demonstrate the hegemony of pluralist discourse in literary theory and clarify the nature of that pluralism's contemporary "crisis"; to trace the problematic that constitutes pluralist ideology; to suggest, at least in relief, the lineaments of certain anti-pluralisms. It is best to say at the outset that this last intention remains only partially achieved here and that this partiality is deliberate. This essay aspires to be an instance of anti-pluralist practice, to break with pluralism in the very act of disclosing its ideological ground, but my primary focus is not prescriptive. I am concerned, rather, to delineate as sharply as possible the structure of a hegemonic pluralism, a discourse of power, of the center, or (as pluralists like to think) of the mainstream. *Seductive Reasoning* is thus emphatically a critique, an effort to disclose the enabling conditions of pluralist discourse, to reveal its ideological effect, and, finally, to denaturalize its most characteristic (and all-too-familiar) gestures.

Such an approach is necessary at this stage of inquiry precisely because the pluralist problematic is now so deeply engrained in the dominant discourses of literary studies that it is generally regarded as a natural rather than a social fact. As a consequence, it retains a massive and largely invisible power; pluralism is that which goes without saying.[2] By positing a crit-

---

expose the "self-contradictions" of critical pluralism by means of a description of its "philosophic pedigree." The resulting foray into the history of ideas assumes that the problem of pluralism is a problem of *meaning*. Erlich ranges across the history of philosophy, and the result is typology gone haywire, taking in Kant, Nelson Goodman, Marx, Russell and Moore, Pepper, James, Leibniz, Locke, Aristotle, Anaxagoras, Empedocles, and the Sarvāstivādins; critical distinctions between philosophers, traditions, and whole cultures collapse. See Erlich, "Amphibolies: On the Critical Self-Contradictions of Pluralism," *Critical Inquiry* 12:3 (1986), 521–49.

[2] Indeed, as a result of its remarkable success at naturalizing its critical assumptions, pluralism has made some inroads into critical discourses such as marxism, feminism and ethnic studies, all of which offer at least implicit resistance to pluralist assumptions. Despite such incursions, pluralism remains overwhelmingly a discourse of dominant groups; it would be a serious misrepresentation of its ideological significance to confuse an analysis of its hegemonic articulations with a reading of its inscription in alternative discourses. Hence my focus here on prominent theorists of the (so-called) mainstream. A typology of

ical community unified by the assumption that every reader is theoretically amenable to persuasion, pluralisms inevitably re-inscribe traditional notions of the reader and the author as uni-fied subjects, transparently equals, at work in a homogeneous critical field. These assumptions make an irreconcilable diver-gence of interests *within* the critical community an unthinkable form of discontinuity. Armed with this strategy, pluralism can hope to recuperate any critical account (feminist, minority, marxist) that emphasizes otherness, difference, conflict, or dis-continuity: within the problematic of general persuasion, the absent or excluded term is exclusion itself. No discourse that challenges the theoretical possibility of general persuasion, no discourse that takes the process of exclusion to be necessary to the production of meaning or community and asserts, with Al-thusser, that it is the definition of a field which, "by excluding what it is not, makes it what it is," can function within plural-ism.[3]

In practice, the critics who would necessarily be excluded from the pluralist community are those who defy the problemat-ic of general persuasion, those who do not make the theoretical assumption that every reader is available to be persuaded. As Richard Ohmann suggests, these critics refuse to "lift the dy-namic of argument out of the lives of the arguer and the au-dience" or to view persuasion as a "formal matter of shoring up a proposition with the right kinds of support."[4] Such critics

---

anti-pluralisms, which are radically heterogeneous, remains a project for the future.

[3]Louis Althusser and Etienne Balibar, *Reading Capital*, tr. Ben Brewster (Lon-don: New Left Books, 1979), p. 27. Further references to this volume (*RC*) will be given in parentheses in the text.

[4]Of the many essays and books attempting a radical critique of the institution of "English," Ohmann's *English in America: A Radical View of the Profession* (New York: Oxford University Press, 1976) is the most compelling. My citation is drawn from a section entitled "English 101 and the Military-Industrial Com-plex," in which Ohmann offers a powerful critique of the protocols and assump-tions governing the teaching of freshman English. He stresses that the student, conceived as an individual "without a history and without a place in society," is taught that there is "no prior alignment of people and forces in society that cannot be overcome by a well-conducted argument" (155). This view of persua-

exclude some group or school, some class of readers from their audience, in the sense that they do *not* seek to persuade them to the (universal) "truth" of their views. This emphasis on the gesture of exclusion is based on a critical awareness that historically irreducible interests divide and define reading communities; that interests and reading are inextricably bound together. To recognize exclusion is to respect the limits that interests impose on the very possibility of persuasion and, in Gayatri Spivak's phrase, to mark "the irreducibility of the margin in all explanations."[5] The anti-pluralist marks exclusions and only thus escapes the problematic of general persuasion.

This structure is not entirely stable. As my definition suggests, the boundaries that distinguish particular pluralisms from particular anti-pluralisms are always being redrawn. At present, critical pluralism is both defensive—troubled and in some ways discredited—and resurgent, re-emerging in new and often unexpected forms.[6] This contradiction remains opaque so long as it

---

sion is quintessentially "pluralist" in my sense of the term. Ohmann's work is exceptional in its rigorous exposure of pluralist strategies. See especially "Arguing," "The Reader," and "How to Argue in Liberal," pp. 155–60, 163–66, 182–83.

[5] The phrase appears in a passage that draws attention "to a feminist marginality, . . . not to win the center for ourselves," but to insist on this irreducibility. See Spivak, "Explanation and Culture: Marginalia," *In Other Worlds: Essays in Cultural Politics* (New York: Methuen, 1987), p. 107 and passim, for an extended discussion of the logic by which "all explanations . . . claim their centrality in terms of an excluded margin" (106) and of the "feminist deconstructivist's" ability to "use herself (assuming one is at one's own disposal) as a shuttle between the center (inside) and the margin (outside) and thus [to] narrate a displacement" (107). Further references to this volume (S) will be given in parentheses in the text. Bell Hooks makes a similar argument in *Feminist Theory: From Margin to Center* (Boston: South End Press, 1984). Hooks defines marginality as a form of living "on the edge," which enables one to look "both from the outside in and from the inside out," "to be part of the whole but outside the main body" (p. ix). She argues that "it is essential for continued feminist struggle that black women recognize the special vantage point our marginality gives us and make use of this perspective to criticize the dominant racist, classist, sexist hegemony as well as to envision and create a counter-hegemony" (15).

[6] Thus, *Critical Inquiry* devotes a special issue to pluralism but entitles it "Pluralism and Its Discontents." Although the essays collected therein originated at a conference carried out in a celebratory mood, editor W. J. T. Mitchell observes : "The original working title for this issue was 'The Foundations of Critical Pluralism,' a rubric which assumes that something called 'pluralism' has foundations,

is understood as the result of purely logical confusion, a sign that literary theory has perhaps finally undone itself in a frenzy of deconstructions. In fact, the paradoxes of literary critical pluralism signal a continuity between the theoretical debate within literary studies and other, more obviously political and historical struggles in the United States, struggles in which contradiction is immediately recognized as a condition of social life rather than a logical dilemma. Acknowledging this continuity enables us to observe that insofar as literary theory, like literature itself, is a socially symbolic act, its contradictions, lacunae, and even its tropes are also social.[7] If one is concerned to trace the effects of the pluralist problematic in literary studies, it is essential to comprehend the apparent paradoxes of pluralist theory in these terms, as social contradictions; a rigid opposition between the theoretical and the practical or the theoretical and the sociopolitical is an insurmountable barrier to analysis.

Just such an opposition figures prominently in the work of many critics who address pluralism in literary theory. It can take various forms, but, as we shall see, it frequently appears in the guise of a systematic neglect of the colloquial meaning of plural-

---

or (more strongly) that it *provides* foundations for critical thought. A less explicit assumption was that this topic was uniquely fitted to a journal that is widely identified as pluralist in orientation, edited and published at an institution that is associated strongly with pluralism. The presumption was that pluralism would be treated as an object of historical inquiry, theoretical refinement, and critical celebration. All of these things are present in this issue, but something else as well: a determination to treat pluralism as an object of critical scrutiny from the standpoint of assumptions which are hostile to pluralism": "Introduction: Pluralism and Its Discontents," *Critical Inquiry* 12:3 (1986), 467.

[7]See Fredric Jameson, *The Political Unconscious: Narrative as a Socially Symbolic Act* (Ithaca: Cornell University Press, 1981). Further references to this volume (*PU*) will be given in parentheses in the text. As Cornel West observes in a note to an extremely interesting analysis of Jameson: "the major difference between Adorno and Derrida (or de Man), between a dialectical deconstructionist and a poststructural deconstructionist, is that the theoretical impasse the dialectician reaches is not viewed as an ontological, metaphysical, or epistemological aporia, but rather as a historical limitation owing to a determinate contradiction as yet unlodged because of an impotent social praxis or an absence of an effective historical revolutionary agent": "Ethics and Action in Fredric Jameson's Marxist Hermeneutics," in *Postmodernism and Politics*, ed. Jonathan Arac (Minneapolis: University of Minnesota Press, 1986), p. 142.

ism. This elision is an index of a general reluctance to consider literary theory in terms other than strictly epistemological ones; when the colloquial is overlooked, one frequently discovers that critical consideration of the social relations of literary theory is also foreclosed. As we shall see, such omissions consistently undermine, even paralyze, efforts to theorize literary critical pluralism. Contradiction is reified, and every theoretical impasse takes on the character of the absolute.

To traverse this impasse, we must acknowledge that the new defensiveness of certain pluralisms, their recent polemical assertiveness, and critical readings of both, have been engendered by events in literary studies that are not "purely" theoretical, events that put the opposition between theory and practice into question. The analysis I offer here would be unthinkable, literally, were it not for a series of theoretical *and* practical developments within the institutions of the humanities and the university in general over the past twenty years.[8] Most prominent among them are: the re-emergence of feminism and the establishment of women's studies; the ongoing struggle to revise the canon, exposing and correcting its ethnocentric and class biases; the growth of interdisciplinary ethnic and area studies, of Afro-American and Native American studies; the reintroduction of

[8]Because I began my undergraduate studies in 1975, these years of transformation coincide with the entirety of my academic life. I mention this not for the sake of introducing anecdotal evidence, but because the critical expectations of literary scholars trained in a period marked by wide-ranging political agitation from the left in concert with disciplinary upheaval, the fall into theory, and a number of consciously politicized critical and theoretical movements are undoubtedly molded by that experience; the critique of pluralism that *Seductive Reasoning* participates in is a product of this recent history. Scholars of my "generation" will unavoidably rewrite the history of this period as they attempt to redefine the nature of their intellectual work. To cite an example from the field of feminist literary studies, the distinctions between "feminist critique" and "gynocritics" (Elaine Showalter) or between an Anglo-American emphasis on practice, experience, and politics and a French emphasis on theory, the unconscious, and the signifier (Toril Moi) are often written into a narrative of stages, early and late, innocent, then knowing; these narratives simply do not apply in the same way to feminist critics who apprenticed themselves to women's studies and literary theory at the same time—who, indeed, sometimes fruitfully confused the two in their own theoretical and political practices.

marxist analytical tools into critical discourse; the radical critique of literary studies, especially "English," and of the university as an institution. All these developments are in a significant way local; their site is the university. In that arena, they are in the first instance intellectual practices—disciplinary, pedagogical, theoretical—and any analysis must attend to their discursive specificity. At the same time, these transformations are all also clearly political, contestatory efforts to effect changes in our social formation; indeed, all explicitly raise the question of pluralism in its colloquial (which is also one of its political) sense(s). The first successful assault on the liberal myth of the university's political neutrality in the postwar period was the work of the civil rights movement; as segregated schools and universities across the country were compelled, sometimes by the force of arms, to admit black children and black women and men to study, the notion that the university (or any classroom) stood above political questions or outside the structures of power was discredited. The institutional and intellectual developments I name above reiterate this point in various idioms, and they frequently challenge pluralist assumptions.

Revisions in canons, disciplines, and interpretative paradigms cannot be understood simply as "contexts" for theoretical interventions. Nor do such developments represent, for the purposes of this book, the "cultural pluralism" of American society, the background of an analysis that assumes literary theory "reflects" social contexts. These methodological models imply that social contradictions determine and ground theory, rather than conceiving of theoretical contradictions as themselves social. In contrast, I will argue that reading pluralist literary theory as one element of the pluralist conjuncture (rather than as its reflection) engenders a conception of social contradiction as *internal* to theory, indeed, as constitutive of its structure, and only thus enables us to identify pluralism's literary critical problematic in its *specificity*.

Negotiating the question of the relationship between the pluralism frequently invoked in the general sociopolitical discourse of the United States and the pluralist problematic within literary studies preoccupies my next chapter. The project of theorizing literary critical pluralism is threatened at its inception by the sheer heterogeneity of the word, the apparently trivial fact of its extraordinary range of connotations. This threat, which is an index of pluralism's ideological power, must be confronted at the outset. Its dangers can be suggested simply by observing that the very intellectual/institutional/political developments I cite as potentially disruptive of pluralism are seen by some critics as pluralism in practice.[9]

It is perhaps the insistent and eager recourse to the notion of practice which should attract our attention. The repeated failure of various critics to *theorize* the pluralist problematic is a striking feature of pluralist discourse and discourse about pluralism. Most analyses work well within the discursive boundaries that pluralists have established for themselves. Commentators rely on the testimony of self-identified pluralists to define pluralism as such, and analysis remains on the level of description and, most important, retains the *form* of pluralist discourse. Thus, the pluralist problematic remains intact. Such interventions extend rather than interrogate pluralist ideology, and never more so than when they conclude that pluralist theory is "impossible."

Predictably, the collapse of the theoretical project has as one of its corollaries frequent misreadings of literary theoretical pluralism, misinterpretations that are regularly denounced by plu-

---

[9]For example, at my university, a visiting committee on minority life and education entitled its majority report to the president and the trustees "The American University and the Pluralist Ideal." The committee defined the "social condition" of pluralism as a "state of affairs in which several distinct ethnic, religious, and racial communities live side by side, willing to affirm each other's dignity, ready to benefit from each other's experience, and quick to acknowledge each other's contributions to the common welfare" (p. ix). Obviously, no one could oppose this homage to cultural harmony (though one panelist did offer a dissenting report), and the committee's definition of pluralism is entirely different from my own. It is worth observing, however, that courses and programs in "Third World and ethnic-related materials," an Ethnic Studies concentration and an Ethnic Studies Research Institute are prominent among the recommendations the committee offers to enable the university to move beyond "diversity" into "pluralism." See The American University and the Pluralist Ideal, A Report of the Visiting Committee on Minority Life and Education at Brown University and a Dissenting Opinion by Lerone Bennett, Jr. (1986).

ralists themselves. But these misapprehensions of the meaning of pluralism are not aberrant, not simply mistakes, random errors of inattention or sloppiness. As we shall see, they persist, dogging even the best efforts of critical pluralists to clarify their theoretical views, because they are symptomatic both of the status of pluralism in the general discourse of our culture and of the position of pluralists in relation to their own *specifically theoretical* concerns. These misreadings stage a typical moment in the discourse on pluralism in literary theory. Pluralism is thus characterized by its constant—and constantly unsuccessful—efforts to correct an apparently fundamental misunderstanding about its character. This persistent ambiguity in the concept is an essential and irreducible element of the discourse.

To observe that this impasse is an irreducible feature of pluralist discourse is in effect to claim that pluralism cannot name its own problematic. As we shall see, even the consciously theoretical efforts of a pluralist such as Wayne Booth finally lead him to assert that pluralism is an "untheoretical" practice; with this gesture, he reasserts pluralism's power precisely by naturalizing it, that is, by opposing it to theory. Booth's analysis is extremely self-reflexive, but his pluralist's account of pluralism necessarily returns to the problem of how to regulate and reproduce certain established social relations—what he calls "our life together" as a "community of readers."[10] His discourse is explicitly motivated by his desire to sustain the life of his community. What is unthinkable from within this "community" is the determined outsider invoked by Audre Lorde, the oppositional critic who seeks to "dismantle the master's house."

As a pluralist, Booth thinks with/in the problematic of pluralism rather than of it. This positioning of the pluralist as the one who both knows and does not know he knows requires explica-

[10]Wayne Booth, "'Preserving the Exemplar': or, How Not to Dig Our Own Graves," *Critical Inquiry* 3:3 (1977), 420. Further references to this essay (B) will be given in parentheses in the text. As we shall see, this retreat into the persuasiveness of common sense and practice links contemporary pluralism both to cold war pronouncements concerning the "end of ideology" and to more recent polemics "against theory" and on behalf of pragmatism.

tion, and, in the chapters below, I draw on Louis Althusser's *Reading Capital* for the notion of symptomatic reading that serves as a model for my analysis. For the moment, I will only observe that to propose a "symptomatic" reading of any text is to claim a different position vis-à-vis that text, a new relation, which enables a heretofore unthinkable reading. Barthes indicates the necessity of this difference (and his own distance from pluralism) when he insists that "criticism is not an 'homage' to the truth of the past or to the truth of others,'" but a "construction of the intelligibility of our own time." Folding back upon itself, our time informs this construction in unavoidable ways; to escape back to homage, to the truth of the past, is not possible. Criticism thus inevitably claims authority over the objects of its analysis; yet at the same time it can hardly hope to escape its own limits, which are the historical limits of interpretation itself. To conceive of this process as a construction or production is, as Althusser argues, to refuse to ground reading in an essential distinction between homage and critique. Our own time engenders a productivity that shatters the illusion of interpretation as an ideal insight, a revelation on the order of a vision, and criticism emerges as a concrete and often dissident practice.

This book attempts to break with the ideology of pluralism, to think *of* it, rather than with it, and thus to make intelligible the structure of assumptions that constitute what I have named the problematic of general persuasion. This project is one that can never be completed. As Althusser observes, theory emerges from its ideological prehistory not once, at its inception, but repeatedly, and it "continues endlessly to do so (its prehistory remains always contemporary)."[11] The very productivity and flexibility that I will be at some pains to attribute to pluralist discourse prove to be obstacles to any final and totalizing account of its instances. There are, then, many pluralisms that I have not been able to examine or to anticipate here. But this empirical limitation is not a crippling one; symptomatic analysis,

[11]Louis Althusser, *Essays in Self-Criticism,* tr. Grahame Lock (London: New Left Books, 1976), p. 114. Further references to this volume (*SC*) will be given in parentheses in the text.

precisely because it takes as its object the problematic of an ideology, produces effects that do not depend on the compilation of an encyclopedic list of instances. At the same time, my essay does not pose the essentially idealizing question "what *is* pluralism?" As James Kavanagh points out, this is "a form of interrogation that takes everything, namely the existence of [pluralism], for granted with its 'What is . . .?' "[12] To formulate the question in such a way is to assume that pluralism is a thing, a substance or unified totality with an unchanging essence. *Seductive Reasoning* is an effort to put these assumptions into question, to insist that ideology has no essence, while paying scrupulous attention to its real and present effects. I will offer not a descriptive analysis of pluralism as a given object, but a theory of the "production and consumption of those ensembles of effects we experience as" pluralism, a theory that might "displace that experience with its explanation" (K 102–3).

My analysis thus seeks to be definitive but not exhaustive, to name the pluralist problematic and to identify its effects without closing the question of its future forms. Its aim is to uncover the ideological problematic that enables and constrains the heterogeneous work of critics as diverse as Hirsch, Fish, and Jameson, providing the ground for both their agreements and their conflicts. As the metaphor of terrain suggests, the structure in question cannot be interpreted as a center or an essential core; a problematic establishes the limits of a discourse, its boundaries and conditions of possibility. Within the field, a diversity of positions is the rule, and no single content characterizes all the players. Hence the claim that critics as different from one another as Fish is from Jameson and Booth from de Man may all engage the problematic of general persuasion.

Hence also the possibility that an equally diverse group of

---

[12]James Kavanagh "'To the Same Defect': Toward a Critique of the Ideology of the Aesthetic," *Literature and Ideology*, ed. Harry R. Garvin (East Brunswick, N.J.: Associated University Presses, 1982), p. 102. Further references to this essay (K) will be given in parentheses in the text. See also Louis Althusser, "Marxism and Humanism," *For Marx*, tr. Ben Brewster (London: New Left Books, 1977), pp. 219–47. Further references to this volume (*FM*) will be given in parentheses in the text.

critics may break with the pluralist problematic, step beyond its boundaries, and refuse the assumptions of general persuasion. Although my primary concern is to offer a critique of pluralism, my own interpretative efforts obviously entail a theory, or perhaps theories, of reading, and a politics of anti-pluralisms. At present—that is, in retrospect—this book appears to me to offer a reading indebted equally to feminist criticism and to Althusser and a politics rooted in that same feminist discourse, in western marxism, and in the texts of Roland Barthes. This "discovery" is not entirely a matter of an after-the-fact self-consciousness; obviously, there is no innocent beginning and I am not posing as one who stumbled into her affiliations. At the same time, writing is a practice that takes one elsewhere, and the theoretical consequences of that practice must be honored. "At the limit everyone writing is thus taken by surprise."[13]

The surprise of *Seductive Reasoning* for its author was the submerged relationship between pluralism and feminism, a relationship I could finally articulate only by addressing the ambiguous relation between pluralism and anti-pluralism; I will return to just that topic below. I am aware of the additional irony of finding in Barthes a political model and in Althusser a concept of textual production. While Barthes's text remains for me among the most adamant we have in its insistence on the necessity of exclusion, of difference, of the partisan, Althusser's reading of *Capital* provides me with a vocabulary to specify the nature and the political effect of the discontinuities I have tried to produce in my analyses. It is somewhat more difficult to name what first drew me toward this theoretical emphasis on the cut, the break, that is, what led me to what I now call a politics of anti-pluralisms. In a sense, only the readings below can adequately answer such a question, but both feminism and marxism figure in the narrative. If becoming a feminist critic taught me the inescapable partisanship of the critical enterprise, my inchoate sense that the

[13]Jacques Derrida, *Of Grammatology*, tr. Gayatri Chakravorty Spivak (Baltimore: Johns Hopkins University Press, 1976), p. 160.

problem of persuasion lay in the path of any effort to engage in political criticism first found its theoretical footing in *The Eighteenth Brumaire*. Marx's analyses there—of the *failures* of persuasion and representation and of the mastery that cloaks those whom we undertake to persuade—are in fact the origin of my argument, if arguments can be said any longer to begin in a single place. These references are admittedly little more than hints; the details of my many intellectual debts will come into sharper focus in the readings to come.

My analysis in the chapters to follow focuses not on forms of anti-pluralism, but on the problematic of general persuasion and the heterogeneity of its instantiations. I have chosen as my proof texts essays by five well-known and influential critics, men (all) whose work has had a major impact on what we commonly call the "mainstream" of literary studies in the past twenty years.[14] This emphasis is not meant to endorse a reading of literary theory as the private preserve of pluralists; on the contrary, the growing strength of insurgent anti-pluralisms has aroused pluralist polemics and thus thrown the pluralist problematic into sharp relief. Insofar as the texts I have chosen demanded to be included here, it is in part because of their prominence in the dominant discourse of North American literary theory, and in part because of the way they both address and depart from one another, dramatizing the unity and the diversity of pluralist practice. Yet other theorists might have served as concrete examples of pluralism as well as those I have chosen; certainly, many others are available, and the *individual* histories of the figures I consider have only a relative privilege in my argument. The passages I emphasize—from E. D. Hirsch's remarks on persuasion in *The Aims of Interpretation* to a startling footnote in Fredric Jameson's *Political Unconscious*—were chosen as particularly symptomatic of the strategies and displacements of pluralist ideology. The texts I draw on are thus in no sense meant to

---

[14]The inclusion of a marxist critic, Fredric Jameson, complicates this in a manner which is precisely to the point and which we will consider below.

constitute a uniquely pluralist canon; rather, they serve the strategic purpose of enabling me to disclose the structure of the problematic of general persuasion.

More precisely, the particular texts I examine below enable me to read the problematic of general persuasion as a logic (Hirsch), an ethics (Booth), a double rhetoric, of persuasion (Fish) and of trope (de Man), and, finally, as a politics (Jameson). Reading these texts as *figuring* stages in a pluralist discourse evolving under a certain pressure enables me to disclose the pluralist problematic as historically contingent; the heterogeneity of the texts and the topoi of pluralism is the mark of its positioning in the contested critical and political field of the contemporary university. Pluralism is not here conceived as an idea that might be discredited and thus put aside. Rather, it is an immensely productive discourse, and the struggle to displace it has barely begun.

1 READING PLURALISM
SYMPTOMATICALLY

> The age of pluralism is upon us. It does not matter
> any longer what you do, which is what pluralism is.
> —ARTHUR C. DANTO, "The End of Art"

I

The colloquial meaning of the term "pluralist" shadows all our
theories of pluralism. Paradoxically, those very critical discourses that set themselves the task of explicating the pluralist
project in literary studies have most successfully eluded recognition of this fact. The resulting elision has the quality of an eloquent absence, a necessary silence, which enables pluralism to
persist and develop even while thwarting efforts to break with
its problematic. To attend to this silence is to begin to trace the
limits of pluralism, to mark the colloquial as figuring that which
literary critical pluralism cannot contain.[1]

In the American idiom, pluralism is an ordinary word, a non-
technical term, an integral part of ordinary language and popular consciousness. Despite its current appeal to some literary
theorists, it is most characteristic of the quotidian cultural and
social discourses of the mass media. Americans commonly
speak of ethnic and religious pluralism, pluralist economies,
and the virtues of their own pluralistic society. In all these uses,
"pluralist" is an honorific. The very notion of pluralistic society

[1]See Pierre Macherey, *A Theory of Literary Production*, tr. Geoffrey Wall (London: Routledge & Kegan Paul, 1978), p. 60 and passim. Further references to this
volume (M) will be given in parentheses in the text.

is often identified with the United States as such, and, simultaneously, it is consistently associated with U.S. foreign policy. One can gloss this colloquial usage in a personal inflection as: "This is a free country. I can do (or say or believe) whatever I please." But the idiom also appears in presidential speeches on the need for "political pluralism" in Central America and in *New York Times* articles describing the National Endowment for Democracy with headlines that announce: "Missionaries for Democracy: U.S. Aid for Global Pluralism" and "U.S. Pays for Pluralism."[2]

I begin with the colloquial both in order to introduce the question of exclusion and to signal a certain historical conjuncture as the place of the analysis to follow. The exclusion of the colloquial from both celebratory elaborations and critical evaluations of pluralism is in fact only the first in a series of strategic exclusions or repressions: of the political, and of marxism in particular, of discontinuity, of resistance, of the possibility of exclusion itself, which together constitute the problematic of pluralist discourse in American literary studies. These elisions and the subsequent collapse of pluralism's theoretical project actually promote the pluralist agenda; these are essential oversights, the enabling conditions of pluralism's persistent ideological power. The practical and theoretical consequences of these silences, the determinate manner in which what is absent or not said structures what is or can be said, occupy a pivotal position in the argument that follows.

The difficulties that trouble any effort to discuss pluralism in literary theory can be glimpsed in the following exchange. In a 1980 interview, Ken Newton put this question to Derrida:

> It might be argued that *deconstruction inevitably leads to pluralist interpretation* and ultimately to the view that any interpretation is

[2]*New York Times*, 1 June 1986, pp. 1 and 16. As we shall see, the politics of pluralism are frequently cold war politics. W. J. T. Mitchell points to pluralism's function "as a code word for American hegemony" in "Pluralism as Dogmatism," *Critical Inquiry* 12:3 (1986), 502.

as good as any other. Do you believe this and how do you select some interpretations as being better than others?

Derrida replied:

> *I am not a pluralist,* and I would never say that every interpretation is equal, but *I* [JD] do not select. The interpretations select themselves. I am a Nietzschean in that sense. You know that Nietzsche insisted on the fact that the principle of differentiation was in itself selective. The eternal return of the same was not repetition, it was a selection of the more powerful forces. *So I would not say that some interpretations are truer than others. I would say that some are more powerful than others.* The hierarchy is between forces and not between true and false.[3]

The ironies of this particular dialogue are certainly not lost on those literary theorists who call themselves pluralists. It would come as no surprise to Wayne Booth, for example, that Derrida declines to join his company. In fact, contemporary pluralists frequently accuse *others*—Derrida prominent among them—of championing just the brand of interpretative irresponsibility Newton's question identifies with pluralism itself.

Indeed, it would be difficult to exaggerate the number of self-described pluralists who seem to view Derrida as the chief representative of that critical practice which is the antithesis of pluralism.[4] Their most energetic polemics are directed against him and his epigones, as they are called, and against everything that can be made to answer to the name he let loose into critical discourse: deconstruction.[5] To cite only a few examples: Booth,

---

[3]James Kearn and Ken Newton, "An Interview with Jacques Derrida," *The Literary Review* 14 (18 April–1 May, 1980), 21, my emphases.

[4]It is typical of the pluralist problematic that this antithesis is seen as "monism" rather than as a form of resistance to pluralism, that is, as an anti-pluralism. Obviously, the opposition monism/pluralism does not govern my analysis; I will return to this matter below.

[5]Derrida suggests that he did not anticipate that the word itself would become the focus of such polemical energy: "the word 'deconstruction' has always bothered me. . . . when I made use of this word (rarely, very rarely in the beginning—once or twice—so you can see that the paradox of the message transformed by the addressees is fully in play here), I had the impression that it was a

though openly reluctant to post "the limits of pluralism," readily informs us that "pluralism is not . . . Derridaesque *glasisme*" (B 407). In a similar gesture, M. H. Abrams opposes his historicist's pluralism to Derrida's and Nietzsche's "deconstructionist principles." He names deconstruction as "one limit to what, according to [his] pluralist views, [he] would accept as a sound alternative history to [his] own," insisting, "I would not accept a history genuinely written according to radically deconstructionist principles of interpretation." E. D. Hirsch derides the "decadence," "anti-rationalism," "extreme relativism," and "cognitive atheism" he associates with the names Derrida and Foucault. These instances are typical, and the list might be extended almost indefinitely. To cite only one second generation commentator: Paul Armstrong argues that pluralism must "chart a middle way between the anarchists and the absolutists," but anarchism and (what Armstrong sees as) nihilism are unquestionably his main concerns. He vigorously opposes the view he paraphrases as "all interpretations are necessarily misinterpretations—that no criteria exist, within the text or outside, for judging any reading the 'right' one." He adds: "I have in mind, obviously, the Yale deconstructionists and their mentor, Jacques Derrida, but Norman Holland and Stanley Fish hold similar views."[6]

---

word among many others, a secondary word in the text which would fade or which in any case would assume a non-dominant place in a system. For me, it was a word in a chain with many other words—such as trace and differance. . . . It so happens—and this is worth analyzing—that this word which I had written only once or twice (I don't even remember where exactly) all of a sudden jumped out of the text and was seized by others who have since determined its fate in the manner you well know. Faced with this, I myself then had to justify myself, to explain, to try to get some leverage. . . . For me, 'deconstruction' was not at all the first or the last word, and certainly not a password or slogan for everything that was to follow": *The Ear of the Other: Otobiography, Transference, Translation*, ed. Christie V. McDonald, tr. Peggy Kamuf and Avital Ronell (New York: Schocken, 1985), pp. 85–86.

[6]See M. H. Abrams, "Rationality and Imagination in Cultural History: A Reply to Wayne Booth," *Critical Inquiry* 2:3 (1976), 456–58. Further references to this essay (A) will be given in parentheses in the text. Abrams is responding to J. Hillis Miller's review of *Natural Supernaturalism*, "Tradition and Difference," *Diacritics* 2:4 (1972), 6–12. E. D. Hirsch, *The Aims of Interpretation* (Chicago: University of Chicago Press, 1976), pp. 13, 147 and passim. Further references to this

Given the evidence of these pluralist readings, one could conclude that Newton's suggestion that "deconstruction" might lead to pluralism, may in fact be a form of pluralism, is simply absurd, an index of his unfamiliarity with the current critical use of the terms. But Derrida answers "I am not a pluralist" without questioning Newton's premise. In fact, the breezy gloss of pluralism as "the view that any interpretation is as good as any other" is bound to seem plausible to large numbers of readers for whom the word denotes only a generalized tolerance of diversity, the view that any opinion (or individual) is "as good as any other." Thus, in contemporary literary theory, a self-conscious pluralism has positioned itself, in part, through its polemical opposition to deconstruction; and yet it remains possible to consider the proposition that Derrida may be a pluralist. We enter here a terrain wherein it is not unusual to discover that some critics apply the term "pluralist" to figures and practices that others—critics in the "same" field—regard as the incarnation of the evil pluralism resists. The discrepancy between these two perspectives discloses a critical question: what are the limits of pluralism? Where—and how well guarded—is the border that separates the pluralist from his others? This is not a strictly empirical problem to be settled by means of a survey of the content of pluralist discourses. What is at stake is the principle of exclusion, and, not surprisingly, exclusion is both a practical and a theoretical problem for pluralism.

Pluralists, that is, self-described pluralists, have of course attempted to define their position, to correct this discrepancy. The most widely disseminated definition of pluralism within literary theory foregrounds a commitment to methodological eclecticism and an ethic of tolerance and intellectual openness. This view is

---

volume (H) will be given in parentheses in the text. Hirsch declines, by and large, to name other "decadent" critics; as we shall see, this kind of reticence toward one's adversaries is typical of pluralist discourse. Paul Armstrong, "The Conflict of Interpretations and the Limits of Pluralism," *PMLA* 98:3 (1983), 341. Ihab Hassan argues that pluralism is an effort to "contain" the "radical relativism, the ironic indetermanences, of the postmodern condition in "Pluralism in Postmodern Perspective," *Critical Inquiry* 12:3 (1986), 503–20.

drawn to a surprising extent from the work of one critic: Wayne Booth. Among those figures consciously elaborating a pluralist theory, Booth emerges as its most eloquent advocate. He conceives of pluralism as the generous and ultimately pragmatic pursuit of "critical understanding" and resolutely opposes "the view that any interpretation is as good as any other," or, as Arthur Danto puts it, that it "does not matter any longer what you do." According to Booth, the literary critic, working as she does with texts that can manifestly bear the burden of more than one "correct" interpretation, must avoid the fanatical and dogmatic rigidity of "monism," without falling into the anarchic free-play of "relativism."[7] Pluralism, in Booth's texts, is a compromising reaction formation; it endorses a plurality of interpretations and methods, but stops well short of infinite textual dissemination. This "limit" is never, however, conceptualized as a monism. On the contrary, in Booth's view, "the limits of pluralism are plural" (B 423). (It is worth noting here that Booth's vision is informed by a political metaphor. He sees the critical field as a "commonwealth" in which "my continued vitality as a critic depends finally on yours, and yours on mine" [B 420]. This commonwealth bears a striking formal resemblance to the classic liberal polity, and this should alert us to the discursive register Booth shares with U.S. newspaper editorialists and politicians, the register of the colloquial.)

Booth's sustained polemic against lapses in critical understanding (reductive "monisms" such as *"glasisme"*) and in favor of a diverse and inclusive pluralism has led many to identify pluralist literary theory wholly with his work or with the work of critics who acknowledge his influence. My argument is directed to unsettling this identification. At the same time, the fact

---

[7]See *Critical Understanding: The Powers and Limits of Pluralism* (Chicago: University of Chicago Press, 1979). Further references to this volume (*CU*) will be given in parentheses in the text. An extended analysis of these terms and Booth's project appears in Chapter 3 below. For the moment, we can schematically render "monism" as the view that a single true interpretation (method) exists, and "relativism" as its mirror opposite, the claim that an infinite number of equally true (and thus "relative") interpretations are available or, in fact, necessary.

that Derrida can be asked to dissociate himself from something called pluralism (and that he complies) is symptomatic of the profound confusion surrounding the use of the term in literary critical discourse. The "misreading" of pluralism that construes it as mere relativism, the absence of principled constraints, is pervasive, and pluralists are compelled to defend themselves against it regularly; it is thus very frequently acknowledged, even if only to be rejected. As I suggest above, these misreadings are an irreducible element of pluralist discourse; the impossibility of overcoming the ambiguity of the concept seems to define pluralist theory as such.

Given this apparently fundamental ambiguity, the *theoretical* usefulness of the concept of pluralism cannot be taken for granted. This formulaic warning is itself very nearly a cliché of contemporary criticism, which finds its quintessential gesture in the claim that no theoretical position can simply be assumed, taken for granted. Obviously, I do not want to shield my observation from its resonances with the larger difficulties confronting literary theory, even supposing such a thing were possible. But in the case of pluralism, this remark has a double meaning. Before we can consider the significance of the uncertainties engendered by any theoretical effort whatsoever, we must address a problem that appears to be entirely practical.

When I suggest that the theoretical usefulness of the concept of pluralism cannot be taken for granted, I have a mundane, even banal, reference in mind: pluralism means so many things. I have already observed that this heterogeneity of usage may threaten or derail theoretical projects. The word echoes across enormous discontinuities in the public discourse of the United States, and this resonance inevitably suggests a practical alibi for the frustration pluralists meet as they attempt to refute or correct commentators like Newton, Derrida, and Danto, theorists who take pluralism to sanction the absence of principled (we might say, theoretical) restraints.

The sheer volume of material possibly relevant to an inquiry into pluralism is undeniably dizzying; anyone not inclined to produce an encyclopedic anatomy must make some deliberate exclusions, thus confronting the astonishing range of references, if only by negation. Booth, for example, explains in the opening pages of *Critical Understanding: The Powers and Limits of Pluralism*: "But I have had to resist, for obvious reasons, the temptation to complicate matters with illustrations (which of course I have 'in my files') from the fields of sociology, psychology, linguistics, political science, anthropology, law, history, philosophy, or rhetoric" (xii). This is a fairly exhaustive catalog of that which is not to be touched upon. But conspicuous by its absence from Booth's list is any reference to the pervasive colloquial use of the word "pluralism" in its political sense, which, as I have observed, in the United States is not confined to the disciplinary discourse of political science. Booth's remarks do not reveal whether or not he maintains files illustrating these more colloquial, essentially honorific uses of the term, but his text obscures what we might call the ordinary politics of pluralism by making no reference to this colloquialism.

Considerations of the vicissitudes of ordinary language, of efforts to include or exclude the shades of colloquial meaning, may seem remote from the theoretical matters with which we should immediately be concerned. After all, the opposition between the colloquial and the technical, the (allegedly) vulgar and the elite, is essential to the conventional practice of scholarship. The work of the academic critic is skewed toward isolating the conceptual force of such terms as "pluralist" and "critical pluralism." To give these terms the kind of precision we demand of theory is inevitably to set certain rigorous limits on their use, to discipline them, by fixing them as elements in a technical vocabulary. This scholarly project can typically be distinguished by the rigor with which even (or especially) the most pervasive "ordinary language" sense of pluralism—the colloquial meaning operative in the discourse of presidential speeches or the editorial pages of our newspapers—is excluded or forgotten.

I do not invoke the colloquial as a prelude to the suggestion that we abandon our theoretical project to (what seem to be) its ambiguities. My account of the pluralist problematic is articu-

lated in terms that doubtless seem remote from the common-
sense significance of pluralism; my texts are drawn from technical works of literary theory, rather than from products of mass
culture or the rhetoric of the U.S. State Department. But disciplinary projects are always haunted by the impurity of academic
discourse itself. Ken Newton and Derrida are in a sense only
speaking colloquially when they associate pluralism with the
view that any interpretation is as good as any other. Certainly,
their exchange could be cited as evidence that the appropriation
of the term pluralism by "ordinary language" disables all efforts
to define it with a rigor sufficient to our theoretical needs. From
this perspective, the refusal to confront directly the colloquial
discourse of pluralism would be viewed as a strictly practical
matter. As is often the case, however, this practical exclusion
has a striking effect at the theoretical level. The seemingly casual
inscription of the colloquial within theory discloses an unexamined conjuncture, which in its turn can be read to reveal a
theoretical impasse. The colloquial is a clue to the exclusions
that lend theory the grounds for rigor.

Those who "misread" critical pluralism as a loose tolerance, a
rejection of both limits and standards, are assimilating literary
discourse to the ordinary colloquial and political uses of the
word in the United States. The myth of political pluralism as
sheer freedom has been subjected to various and fairly numerous critiques, but its social power echoes in the misreadings of
those who consistently mistake pluralism for the absence of restraints on interpretation, thus reading the critical pluralist colloquially. Yet the pluralist critic cannot afford to broach the politics of this mésalliance. Booth goes so far as to omit the
colloquial even from his list of omissions (thus offering us an
allegory of pluralism's exclusion of exclusion). Pluralism's defenders seem curiously unwilling to accuse those who claim
pluralists are relativists of thinking pluralism in its colloquial
(and thus political) sense.

The pluralist critic is paradoxically caught between his desire
to delineate pluralism as a concept and, thus, necessarily, to
limit its significance, and the equivocal value of the colloquial or,

rather, the value of the equivocation of the colloquial, which enables him to advocate a pluralism that names no limit. To honor the conventional opposition between the theoretical and the colloquial is to escape responsibility for addressing another opposition, one which structures the theoretical *and* the colloquial discourse of and on pluralism, that is, the opposition between pluralism and marxism. Any adequate theory of the pluralist problematic in literary studies must acknowledge the critical historical relation between pluralist and marxist discourse in the United States. In this relation, the problems of exclusion and persuasion surface as both political and theoretical issues.[8] The elision of the relation established between marxism and pluralism by the colloquial discourse of democratic capitalism, which is effected by the wholesale repression of the colloquial, allows critical pluralists to evade the problem of marxist theory and with it the urgent question it asks, the question of exclusion.

The world-historical opponent of pluralism is often named totalitarianism; but figures such as Jeane Kirkpatrick (an academic and a diplomat), Elliott Abrams, and Ronald Reagan have recently clarified the series of substitutions whereby "totalitarian," instead of referring to a range of state practices from Nazism to apartheid to stalinism, has come to signify any "marxist" state—and only marxist states. This reduction of heterogeneous marxisms to a monolithic stalinism is always achieved in the name of pluralism. Thus, the *Times* editorializes on "The Sandinista Road to Stalinism" with the narrative of pluralism betrayed: "By these incremental steps, the pluralist revolution seems hopelessly betrayed. Instead of responding to the contra attacks by broadening their support, the Sandinistas use the war to justify breaking their promises to respect a vital private sector of the economy and to coexist with a lively political opposition.

[8]These questions are touched upon in Bruce Erlich's "Amphibolies," and directly addressed in my "Who's Left Out? A Rose by Any Other Name Is Still Red; Or, the Politics of Pluralism," *Critical Inquiry* 12:3 (1986), 550–63, and in W. J. T. Mitchell's "Pluralism as Dogmatism," *Critical Inquiry* 12:3 (1986), 494–502.

They are well down the totalitarian road traveled by Fidel Castro."[9]

This "pluralist" rhetoric accuses its opponents (the Sandinistas and Castro and Stalin) of a monolithic totalitarianism—the exclusion of pluralism—precisely in order to exclude them; it recalls the cold war decades, a period characterized by a liberal consensus against communism and marxist thought and one of enormous productivity for the first generation of pluralist thinkers. There are parallels between those decades and the 1980s, parallels which pass unremarked so long as we retain a narrow definition of critical pluralism, but which become obvious once we allow the colloquial to resonate in our analysis. To speak in the vernacular, we once again find ourselves in a period of reaction. In the dominant political discourse of the United States, as the president recently reminded the world, the "problem of evil" is marxism-leninism. The absolute incompatibility of marxism and democracy is an article of faith; political pluralism, "American-style," is nothing but the exclusion of marxisms, both in domestic politics and abroad.

In *Nixon Agonistes,* Garry Wills describes the cold war period as an era when an "American *consensus,*" what Booth might term an "understanding," coalesced around the dominant view that "our 'tradition' was a response to the 'givenness' of the American situation; realistic contact with the land's given things has made theory *unnecessary* and downright evil."[10] He observes

[9]10 July 1986, p. A22.
[10]Garry Wills, *Nixon Agonistes: The Crisis of the Self-Made Man* (New York: Signet, 1971), p. 509; see especially the chapters on the intellectual marketplace. Further references to this volume (*NA*) will be given in parentheses in the text. See also Louis Hartz, *The Liberal Tradition: An Interpretation of American Political Thought since the Revolution* (New York: Harcourt, Brace, 1955) and Wills's analysis, pp. 508–18; Daniel Boorstin, *The Genius of American Politics* (Chicago: University of Chicago Press, 1953); William E. Connolly, ed. *The Bias of Pluralism* (New York: Lieber-Atherton, 1973); Theodore J. Lowi, *The End of Liberalism,* 2d ed. (New York: Norton, 1979). There are, of course, extensive bibliographies within the disciplines of political science and history which treat the problem of democratic pluralism, where the term pluralism refers to a political system characterized by some form of interest-group politics. While I strongly suspect that politi-

that this consensus evolved as the "theorists of the fifties launched an effort to describe America in terms that preclude theoretical conflict" (508) and proceeds to a brilliant analysis of the crisis that accompanied the disintegration of this view in the face of the intellectual and political rebellions of the sixties. Wills argues that "to understand what happened, we must watch the currents of 'mainstream' thinking converge—in history (the consensus historians), in political science (the end-of-ideology movement), in social psychology (the status-politics school of thought), in sociology (the reconsideration of individualism)" (508). The fifties consensus thinkers defended their claim that theoretical conflict was irrelevant in the United States on the grounds that the political (and social) field was "united by a common (and laudable) *lack* of philosophy. America has had no great political theorists because it has had no political theory at all" (509). The categories of philosophy, theory, ideology, and dogma merge in this discourse, and the rejection of theory is represented as an escape from ideology as such; "ideologies are 'universal systems'" and "all *systems* of thought are 'bad'" (314–15). Those celebrating the end of ideology characterized it as essentially nonideological; the anti-theory intellectuals of the fifties claimed to exclude the theoretical for ideologically neutral reasons: "These [totalist systems] are not, notice, excluded because they are false but *because they are exclusionary*. Their fault is a methodological one, and can be detected and condemned on grounds of procedure, without value prejudice.[11] *The only things*

cal scientists in the North American academy (like anthropologists, historians, linguists, and others) are pluralists in my sense of the term, that is, that they operate within the problematic of general persuasion, a detailed analysis of the specificity of this problematic in the discourse of political science is beyond the scope of my argument here.

[11]These lines, like Wills's claim that the consensus thinkers saw theory as "unnecessary," provide a proleptic description of the terms used by Steven Knapp and Walter Benn Michaels in their polemic "Against Theory," *Critical Inquiry* 8:4 (1982), 723–42. Knapp and Michaels assure us that their "discussion of [belief and intention] is thus directed not only against specific theoretical arguments but against theory in general. Our examples are meant to represent the central mechanism of all theoretical arguments, and our treatment of them is meant to indicate that all such arguments will fail and fail in the same way. If we

that can be excluded are things that would exclude" (318, my emphases).

Nixon Agonistes captures pluralism's paradoxical effort to exclude exclusion, especially as it concerns dissent within the university, and Wills underscores the connections between this
pluralist posture, the rejection of theory, and certain political
exclusions, specifically the exclusion of marxism. The "consensus" insistence on the exclusion of exclusion masked a deeper
consensus concerning the correctness of the status quo: " 'consensus' and 'the end of ideology' made it possible to say that
one should neither accept *nor reject* capitalism as an ideology.
Therefore 'tough-minded' pragmatism could sneak free-market
thinking back onto the 'Left' side of American politics" (525). As
Wills observes, "anyone who would submit gracefully was
being herded into the great cleared space in the Middle" (518).

The emphasis on givenness and the concomitant reluctance to
enter into theoretical practice, as well as the contradictory polemic that enforces exclusions in defense of inclusiveness, are
revived by contemporary pluralism. Wills's book focuses primarily on politics, the student activism of the sixties, and the
career of Richard Nixon, but it nevertheless provides the immediate context for my essay in that it links the political turmoil
within the university, which generated many of the critical discourses, programs, and fields of study I cite above as essential to
the critique of pluralism, to more general political questions and

---

are right, then the whole enterprise of critical theory is misguided and should be
abandoned" (724). Further references to this essay (KM) will be given in parentheses in the text. See also Stanley Fish, who identifies liberalism with pluralism
in "Interpretation and the Pluralist Vision," *Texas Law Review* 60:3 (1982), 496. For
a discussion of Louis Hartz and the problematic of exclusion as it functions in
American liberalism, see Samuel Weber, "Capitalizing History: *The Political Unconscious," Institution and Interpretation* (Minneapolis: University of Minnesota
Press, 1987), pp. 40–59. Weber echoes Wills, describing liberalism as that "form
of exclusion which, whenever possible, denies its own exclusivity," and marxism as "the name of what liberalism most seeks to exclude, the inevitability of
exclusion itself" (45, 46). Weber's reading of *The Political Unconscious* foregrounds
psychoanalysis and doesn't address the question of persuasion, but his conclusions about the problematics of inclusion in Jameson's work are similar to my
own.

to the twin issues of theory and of exclusion. Wills's discussion of the "intellectual marketplace" emphasizes the discontinuity that the radical critique of the liberal academy opened up between students and faculties. The practical hegemony of the pluralist problematic within the university was first genuinely shaken by the radical movements—intellectual and political (though that distinction was not much respected)—of the sixties and seventies. These movements questioned received canons, and, as Wills makes clear, these interrogations could not avoid the questions of theory and of exclusion. Theory threatens to force pluralism to announce its own systematic exclusions; on those grounds alone, it must be avoided if at all possible. As I write, twenty-five years after the initial fracture in the pluralist facade, the reaction, which began in earnest with the Age of Reagan, is very active, powerful, and committed to reasserting pluralism's anti-theoretical consensus and the problematic of general persuasion.

Contemporary pluralist neglect of the question of the colloquial is an expression of pluralism's resistance to theory. Of course, when the very existence of theory as such is under attack, to question the theoretical usefulness of a particular concept such as pluralism is a minimal gesture, possibly even a conservative one. In a period of pervasive hermeneutic suspicion and vigorous theoretical polemic, such an interrogation echoes with sterner warnings from a wide spectrum of theorists. Paul de Man has observed that "the possibility of doing literary theory, which is by no means to be taken for granted, has itself become a consciously reflected-upon question." Terry Eagleton's recent work illustrates de Man's point. At the close of an extraordinarily popular "introduction" to literary theory, Eagleton concludes that his "book is less an introduction than an obituary" because literary theory is in fact an "illusion." Working in a rather different critical idiom, Stanley Fish shies away from the notion of illusion; but even in the very act of theorizing, he insists that theory has no practical consequences whatsoever, which is certainly one way to suggest that the connection between literary theory and critical practice is illusory.[12] Perhaps the most extreme expression of this tendency to regard literary theory, shall we say, skeptically, is Steven Knapp and Walter Benn Michaels's polemic "Against Theory," which concludes that "theory is nothing else but the attempt to escape practice. . . . It is the name for all the ways people have tried to stand outside practice in order to govern practice from without. Our thesis has been that no one can reach a position outside practice, that theorists should stop trying, and that the theoretical enterprise should therefore come to an end".[13] From this apocalyptic perspective, the narrower question of the theoretical usefulness of pluralism as a concept would simply cease to be an issue.

In the case of the resistance to theorizing pluralism, the empirical difficulty and the theoretical one cohere. The contemporary avatar of literary critical pluralism generally contributes to a subtle anti-theory polemic, and its resurgence coincides with the spread of (no longer subtle) attacks on the possibility of doing theory at all.[14] An awkward if not troubled relation to theory is

---

[12]Paul de Man, "The Resistance to Theory," *Yale French Studies* 63 (1982), 7. Further references to this essay (R) will be given in parentheses in the text. Terry Eagleton, *Literary Theory: An Introduction* (Minneapolis: University of Minnesota Press, 1983), p. 204. Stanley Fish, *Is There a Text in This Class? The Authority of Interpretive Communities* (Cambridge: Harvard University Press, 1980), p. 370. Further references to this volume (F) will be given in parentheses in the text. See also Fish, "Consequences," *Critical Inquiry* 11:3 (1985), 433–58.

[13]See *Critical Inquiry* 9:4 (1983) for responses to "Against Theory" by Jonathan Crewe, William C. Dowling, E. D. Hirsch, Jr., Steven Mailloux, Daniel T. O'Hara, Hershel Parker, Adena Rosmarin, and, of course, a Knapp-Michaels "reply to our critics." The argument continues in *Critical Inquiry* 11:3 (1985), with Fish's "Consequences," a piece by Richard Rorty, and yet another reply by Knapp-Michaels. The entire proceedings have been collected as *Against Theory: Literary Studies and the New Pragmatism*, ed. W. J. T. Mitchell (Chicago: University of Chicago Press, 1985). For a very interesting marxist view of similar issues, see Steven Shaviro, "From Language to 'Forms of Life': Theory and Practice in Wittgenstein," *Social Text* 13/14 (Winter/Spring 1986), 216–34. See also Bruce Robbins, "The Politics of Theory," *Social Text* 18 (Winter 1987/88), 3–18, and Peggy Kamuf, "Floating Authorship," *Diacritics* 16:4 (1986), 3–14.

[14]*Critical Inquiry* has been the site of both influential "theory debates" and crucial exchanges on pluralism, including the Booth-Abrams-Miller colloquy published under the title "The Limits of Pluralism." Several chapters of Booth's

central to the pluralist problematic. Ironically, despite its protestations of pragmatism, pluralism can appear as the most exaggerated instance of the theoretical will to govern practice that such "theorists" as Knapp and Michaels would condemn to oblivion. In fact, in a certain reading, one based on the work of a Chicago pluralist like Wayne Booth, pluralism is *nothing but* the desire to adjudicate other theories and thus other practices from above.[15] And even Booth grumbles about the spectacle he presents writing "a long book of what current jargon might well call meta-meta-meta criticism" (*CU* xii).

But even the meta-meta-meta-critical pluralist polemic returns inevitably to a pragmatic argument, to Booth's suggestion that "common-sense untheoretical pluralism works" (197). It is not Booth's explicitly *theoretical* discourse that strains most visibly "to govern practice from without." Rather, it is his antitheoretical, or pragmatic, discourse that produces "an account of interpretation in general" that is meant to apply universally to the interpretation of particular texts. The effects Knapp and Michaels want to assign to the theoretical enterprise are here generated from within (as) practice, or, as Booth puts it, from a position that cannot distinguish theory from practical values, from what I will designate as an *ideological* position. To assert that it is impossible (or unnecessary) to distinguish a theoretical moment is to assume that the problems before us are in a certain sense "given" rather than constituted by specific (theoretically interested) inclusions and exclusions. Both assumptions work to enable pluralism to continue to govern critical practice and to ground interpretation in the problematic of general persuasion.

Ultimately, the refusal to recognize pluralist literary theory as an element in a dominant social/political discourse undermines

Critical Understanding first appeared there and a 1986 issue, "Pluralism and Its Discontents," contains the proceedings of the Foundations of Critical Pluralism conference, which took place at the University of Nebraska in March 1984. Editor W. J. T. Mitchell observes that "the ideology usually associated with *Critical Inquiry* is that of 'pluralism'": "*Critical Inquiry* and the Ideology of Pluralism," *Critical Inquiry* 8:4 (1982), 612.
15See Mitchell, "Pluralism as Dogmatism."

any effort to describe the structure of its problematic—its theoretical limits—and thus ensures its continued force. Pluralism stubbornly retains all its honorific significance, the trace of the colloquial, while efforts to disclose its ideological effects are blocked by the term's astonishing social authority. What is at issue here is exactly the question of power and efforts to theorize that question. The exclusion of the resonances (and the history) of ordinary pluralist politics in the United States has immediate consequences for attempts to grasp the formal structure of the pluralist problematic; the peculiar inconclusiveness that attends contemporary efforts to theorize pluralism is due to this exclusion, which thwarts theorists' efforts to disentangle their practice from this very colloquialism. The most common result is an analysis that stalls at the claim that critical pluralism betrays its own ideals primarily because it neglects to reflect on its political situation.[16]

The call for a merely contextualizing reading in fact disables any symptomatic analysis of the pluralist problematic as such. Rather, the current deployment of critical pluralism is rigorously condemned for its political myopia while a commitment to its basic structure is reaffirmed; the so-called critique amounts to nothing more than the complaint that pluralism is not pluralistic enough. This approach issues in a polemical demand for reform; pluralists are asked to correct their oversights by becoming more inclusive, by making additions: the solution to the inadequacy of pluralism is to extend its scope.[17] This scenario discloses one of pluralism's primary strategies for recuperating its critics. Such a "critique" repeats the form of pluralist discourse and cannot even conceive of an analysis that would expose the systematic and concrete affiliations that bind critical and political pluralism together as the elements of a heterogeneous yet hegemonic dis-

---

[16]A typical instance was enacted at the Foundations of Critical Pluralism conference. Bruce Erlich's lecture, "The One and the Many: The Ethics and Politics of Pluralism," urged pluralists to attend to the "influence of social power upon the [critical] encounter of voices." See Erlich's "Amphibolies," p. 541.

[17]Here the literary critical argument repeats precisely the arguments of the State Department.

course. Rather than exposing pluralism as a discourse that mystifies the irreducibility of exclusions, this would-be reform actually deepens that mystification.

The difficulty cannot be overcome by subjecting pluralism in literary studies to a more sustained political analysis. This strategy often produces an uncritical blurring of the distinctions between a literally political terminology and the concepts necessary for a political critique of pluralism as a discursive practice. Fredric Jameson argues forcefully that the political interpretation of literary texts constitutes "the absolute horizon of all reading and all interpretation" (*PU* 17), but he is always acutely aware that undoing the opposition between theory and practice or between the academy and politics is not a matter of asserting that everything is political. When we talk about the politics of pluralism in the university, we must talk about what Hayden White describes as "that politics which is endemic to the pursuit of truth—the striving to share power amongst interpreters themselves."[18] This discursive strife can no longer be conceived in ethical terms which pertain to individuals (e.g., "irresponsibility"); nor can it be explained solely as a side effect of the "larger" reality of power. Rather, we must conceptualize the political as an internal or structural feature of literary critical discourse.

I am not belittling the importance of power relations broadly conceived. The critique of pluralist discourse demands an analysis of all the social and political constraints on discursive power. But the insight that we must acknowledge the force of social power can lead us to impute a kind of irreality to the academic practice of pluralism: the analysis never touches the specificity of pluralist discourse in the university. Pluralism remains opaque, even faintly mysterious, in such an interpretation. We can trace the theoretical consequences of this opacity in the tendency of some commentators and even some practitioners of pluralist theory to draw away from the concept *qua* concept.

---

[18]Hayden White, "The Politics of Historical Interpretation: Discipline and Desublimation," *Critical Inquiry* 9:1 (1982), 114.

This partially explains the difficulty pluralists have theorizing their own project. W. J. T. Mitchell, for example, suggests that "pluralism is not a coherent philosophy," and he recommends, as one solution to the intellectual contradictions of pluralist theory, that we simply "stop using the term 'pluralist' as the name of a position, a theory, a philosophy," reserving it for use "only as an adjective, signifying an attitude of amiable tolerance toward other positions, an attitude of curiosity, openness, and liberality."[19] This view abandons the possibility of theorizing pluralism while endorsing its programmatic claims about its practical effects. In a similar gesture, Booth himself carries the argument of *Critical Understanding* to an apparently definitive theoretical impasse and concludes (half-way through his text): "Surely, then, my quest for a pluralism has failed. And since few are likely to work harder at it than I have, it seems probable that there really can be no such creature as a true pluralist in my sense" (210). Nevertheless, he refuses to allow this failure to close down his project. Booth discovers that his theoretical problems, "viewed properly," are "evidence for pluralism, not against it" and proceeds to abandon not pluralism but his putatively theoretical project, concluding: "I cannot distinguish pluralistic theory from the practical value of pluralism" (211, 218). He presents his practice as a kind of embarrassment to theory: "common-sense untheoretical pluralism works, regardless of our theories" (197).

I would call Booth's position "anti-theoretical," though it predates recent polemics "against theory." Mitchell describes it as "pragmatic" (I 4), and Booth places this discussion in a section entitled "The Pluralist as Pragmatist." Pluralists tend to become nominal "pragmatists" on the question of theory, which they regard as always engaged in a flirtation with dogmatism; their "anti-theory" polemics complicate subsequent attempts to theorize pluralist practice from the outside or to defend the specifically theoretical usefulness of the concept of pluralism. The fail-

[19]W. J. T. Mitchell, "The Ideology of Pluralism," unpublished ms., p. 2. Further references to this essay (I) will be given in parentheses in the text.

ure to distinguish theory from practice functions to shield theoretical commitments from analysis; they can thus operate as if in the state of nature. Hence the ambiguous term "value." Theoretical effects are never achieved so securely as when they come naturally, that is, in the form of common sense, values, or "mere" practice, and this is nowhere more evident than in the contemporary debate on reading.

For pluralists in literary studies, the problem of theory is frequently figured as a problem of reading. From this perspective, the recent critiques directed at the possibility of theory are only a special case of a more generalized anxiety of interpretation, an anxiety captured in de Man's stricture that "the possibility of *reading* can never be taken for granted."[20] This anxiety of reading has a special relevance to my analysis; in part, pluralism has been aroused from its relative quiescence since the cold war period to respond to—or rather to resist—the suggestion that reading is "impossible." This is one way to gloss the apparent agreement among pluralists that deconstruction is not pluralism; deconstruction is targeted for censure because it is associated with the claim that reading may be impossible. In the analysis that follows, I will argue that the polemics on the question of the possibility of reading actually mask anxieties concerning the possibility of *persuasion*. Pluralism's contention that its primary antagonist is a Derridaesque *glasisme* is a serious one, but it does not tell the whole story.

In certain pluralist scenarios, the resistance to theory is explicitly linked to resistance to the view that reading is impossible. (Both are seen as contravening common sense.) But Wills's argument suggests that what is at stake in the peculiarly American consensus against theory, against "the evil of system," and for the exclusion of things that would exclude, is not the possi-

---

[20]Paul de Man, *Blindness and Insight: Essays in the Rhetoric of Contemporary Criticism*, 2d ed., rev. (Minneapolis: University of Minnesota, 1983), p. 107, my emphasis. The context for this remark is the question of theory: "Prior to any generalization about literature, literary texts have to be read, and the possibility of reading can never be taken for granted." Further references to this volume (*BI*) will be given in parentheses in the text.

bility or impossibility of reading *per se*. The pluralist focuses debate on the question of the possibility of reading in order to displace the problem of exclusion and, with it, any questions concerning persuasion. Wills demonstrates that the question of reading can never be addressed innocently; he insists that the exclusions that make reading *practical* were and still are political. Reading is thus neither possible nor impossible, but practical under certain political and theoretical conditions; it is here that the question of the limits of persuasion becomes critical. The politics of the colloquial lead to the question of reading; the distance is much shorter than we might have imagined.

II

> As there is no such thing as an innocent reading, we must say what reading we are guilty of. . . . a philosophical reading of *Capital* is quite the opposite of an innocent reading. It is a guilty reading, but not one that absolves its crime on confessing it. On the contrary, it takes the responsibility for its crime as a "justified crime" and defends it by proving its necessity. It is therefore a special reading which exculpates itself as a reading by posing every guilty reading the very question that unmasks its innocence, the mere question of its innocence: *what is it to read?*
>
> —ALTHUSSER, *Reading Capital*

> When no known language is available to you, you must determine *to steal a language*—as men used to steal a loaf of bread. (All those—legion—who are outside Power are obliged to steal language.)
>
> —BARTHES, *Roland Barthes by Roland Barthes*

In her essay "Man on Feminism," Nancy Miller asks a "speculative question" about Denis Donoghue's "lurid representation of feminist critical theory as massively Derridean": "to what extent is Donoghue's attack on feminism as bad literary criticism,

and feminism as the theory of phallocentrism not about feminism at all, but instead an attack on 'Deconstruction' and [on]
political criticism in the name of common sense?"[21] I would like
to suggest that this displacement may (also) run in the opposite
direction: pluralist attacks on deconstruction may in fact have
less to do with the play of the signifier than with the problem of
sexual (or racial or class) difference. Although certain forms of
deconstruction can undeniably be read as threatening the pluralist problematic, post-structuralism often appears in pluralist
polemics as a screen for less exotic but more immediately threatening critical developments, specifically, the appearance of feminist, marxist and minority movements in criticism and in theory.[22] All these critical movements have the potential to bring the

[21]Nancy Miller, "Man on Feminism: A Criticism of His Own," *Men in Feminism*, ed. Alice Jardine and Paul Smith (New York: Methuen, 1987), pp. 140–41.
As Miller's remarks suggest, she does not think feminist criticism in the United
States is overwhelmingly indebted to post-structuralism. Her description of the
heterogeneity of feminist criticisms seems to me absolutely correct, although I
would perhaps place more emphasis on the possibilities of positive connections
between feminism and post-structuralism than she does in her most recent
work. See her "Changing the Subject: Authorship, Writing, and the Reader,"
Feminist Studies/Critical Studies, ed. Teresa de Lauretis (Bloomington: Indiana
University Press, 1986), pp. 102–20, and "Arachnologies: The Woman, The Text,
and the Critic," *The Poetics of Gender*, ed. Nancy K. Miller (New York: Columbia
University Press, 1986), pp. 270–95.
[22]Possible relationships between these developments and deconstruction—
which would explain a certain slippage in pluralist attacks—have been observed
by many critics. As a marxist, feminist, deconstructivist, Gayatri Spivak speaks
very forcefully for the interconnections among these positions. See her *In Other
Worlds*. In *Resistance Literature* (New York: Methuen, 1987), Barbara Harlow suggests that "given . . . the current intensity of the debate and the rapid developments in contemporary literary critical theory in the West (structuralism, deconstruction, psychoanalysis, Marxism, etc.), it is important to examine the
applicability of these theoretical structures and modalities outside the cultural
tradition which produced them. Can they be deployed in analyzing the literary
output of geopolitical areas which stand in opposition to the very social and
political organization within which the theories are located and to which they
respond? Is there, to take just one example—that suggested by the Moroccan
writer Abdelkebir Khatibi in his book *Maghreb pluriel*—more than chronological
coincidence to connect 'deconstruction' and 'decolonization'? Khatibi, at any
rate, claims ideological affinities for the two movements and sees critical potential in developing their association" (p. xvii). In *Breaking the Chain: Women, Theory
and French Realist Fiction* (New York: Columbia University Press, 1985), Naomi

pluralist problematic into crisis, to expose the limits of general persuasion; the pluralist polemic responds primarily to this threat, and Althusser's account of the guilt of reading can help us trace this displacement. If there is no innocent reading, how does the guilty reader justify her crimes?

Jonathan Culler marks the connection between the so-called crisis in criticism (often associated by its interpreters with the advent of deconstruction) and theories of reading by opening *On Deconstruction: Theory and Criticism after Structuralism* with a chapter entitled "Readers and Reading." Culler takes feminist criticism as his example, thus acknowledging that the appearance of women's studies and feminist literary theory have contributed to the current crisis of interpretation (and of pluralism).[23] He observes that critics and theorists across the ideological spectrum "have concurred in casting the reader in a central role, both in theoretical discussion of literature and criticism and in interpretations of literary works" (31) and argues that the "impact" of feminist criticism is "in part due to its emphasis on the notion of the reader and her experience" (42).

Schor writes: "It is difficult but I think important—if only to 'bear witness'—to communicate to younger critics, especially the feminist, who have come of age in the relatively permissive intellectual climate of post-structuralism, the subtle oppression exercised by structuralism at its least self-critical and most doctrinaire on a reader who bridled at bracketing herself, who felt stifled in a conceptual universe organized into the neat paradigms of binary logic, and who ultimately found it impossible to accept the claims to universality of models of intelligibility elaborated without taking gender into account. It was not until Derrida began to deconstruct the major paradigms/hierarchies of Western metaphysics at their linguistic foundations that feminist criticism became possible in the context of departments of *French* in American universities. The fact that, as is becoming increasingly obvious, the relationship of deconstruction and feminism is complex and fraught with controversy, should not obscure the immense significance of early Derrida for French neo-feminisms and, by the same token, their American spin-offs" (p. ix–x). The most ambitious and interesting examination of this controversial conjuncture is Alice Jardine's provocative analysis of the "woman-effect" she calls "gynesis," the problematization or putting into discourse of "woman" in the texts of modernity/post-modernism. See *Gynesis: Configurations of Woman and Modernity* (Ithaca: Cornell University Press, 1985).

[23]Jonathan Culler, *On Deconstruction* (Ithaca: Cornell University Press, 1982), pp. 31–83. Further references to this volume (*OD*) will be given in parentheses in the text. Culler marks the link between deconstruction and feminism in part by

In a similar gesture, though this time from the side of a self-conscious pluralism, M. H. Abrams names our critical epoch the "Age of Reading"; he then denounces Derrida, Stanley Fish, and Harold Bloom specifically in their roles as "Newreaders," practitioners of "Newreading," "a principled procedure for replacing standard meanings by new meanings."[24] This overthrow of standard meaning, of consensus, is extremely disturbing to pluralism. In an earlier essay, "Rationality and Imagination in Cultural History," Abrams explains the centrality of the problem of reading to the pluralist polemic when he warns that "if one takes seriously [J. Hillis] Miller's deconstructionist principles of interpretation, any history which relies on written texts becomes an *impossibility*. . . . the elementary assumption that a cultural historian must make is that he is able to understand, in the sense that he is at least able to approximate, the core of meanings that certain writers at certain times expressed in their writings" (A 458, my emphasis). For Abrams, this elementary assumption depends on the possibility of right reading or understanding.

> the authors cited wrote, not in order to present a verbal stimulus (in Roland Barthes' term, *un vide*) to the play of the reader's interpretive ingenuity, but in order to be *understood* . . . . though the sentences allow a certain degree of interpretive freedom, and though they evoke vibrations of significance which differ according to the distinctive temperament and experience of each *reader*, the central core of what they undertook to *communicate* can usually be *understood* by a *competent reader* who knows how to apply the norms of the language and literary form employed by the writer. [A 457, my emphases]

Communication and understanding are theoretically the achievements of any (and every) competent reader, defined here as a

---

citing Peggy Kamuf's "Writing like a Woman" (*Women and Language in Literature and Society*, ed. Sally McConnell-Ginet, Ruth Borker, and Nelly Furman [New York: Praeger, 1980], pp. 284–99) as an example. For an interesting contribution to the argument about women's reading, see Robert Scholes, "Reading like a Man," *Men in Feminism*, pp. 204–18.

[24]M. H. Abrams, "How to Do Things with Texts," *Partisan Review* 46:4 (1979), 566, 568. Further references to this essay (*PR*) will be given in parentheses in the text.

critic committed to the possibility of reading. Allegedly speaking for the critical opposition, and in direct response to Abrams, Hillis Miller concedes that "deconstructionist principles" could reveal that "a certain notion of history or of literary history, like a certain notion of determinable reading, might indeed be an impossibility," and he agrees that "'the impossibility of reading should not be taken too lightly.'"[25]

The significance of this claim hinges on the meaning of the term "(im)possible." The resurgence of critical pluralism coincides with the anxiety of reading in the age of the newreaders; it also coincides with the appearance of a powerful, new kind of theoretical practice closely associated with speculation on the impossibility of reading. On one level, pluralism thus appears as a form of resistance to the claims "deconstruction" allegedly makes about reading.[26] This account is not flatly wrong; pluralists are indeed responding to the challenge of certain post-structuralisms. As we shall see, some of the pluralist polemics of recent years can be read as strategic interventions that attempt to assimilate post-structuralism to the pluralist paradigm that dominates North American literary studies. But a significant portion of the anxiety of reading stems from the interpretative practices of those newreaders not generally named in lists that mention Derrida, Fish, and Bloom as incarnating the threat to pluralist harmony (hegemony). These resisting newreaders[27] also suggest a certain impossibility of reading, but their interventions are often obscured, screened, in fact, by polemical debates that *appear* more purely theoretical and therefore more fundamental, while they are in fact only less immediately threatening to the pluralist.

[25]J. Hillis Miller, "The Critic as Host," *Critical Inquiry* 3:3 (1977), 440.

[26]In philosophy "proper," the debate on pluralism also concerns itself with the question of right "reading." See Nelson Goodman, *Ways of Worldmaking* (Indianapolis: Hackett, 1978), especially chap. 7, "On Rightness of Rendering." See Jacques Derrida, "The Principle of Reason: The University in the Eyes of Its Pupils," *Diacritics* 13:3 (1983), 3–20, for a discussion of Leibniz and the principle of rendering reason: "'*Omnis veritatis reddi ratio potest.*' Or, to translate . . . literally, for any true proposition, *reason can be rendered*" (7).

[27]The phrase refers to the title of Judith Fetterley's feminist study, *The Resisting Reader* (Bloomington: Indiana University Press, 1978).

Critics on both sides of the debate seem careful to address the (im)possibility of reading as a strictly formal or epistemological problem. (Both sides in this argument are ultimately pluralist.) When theorists confine the question of the (im)possibility of reading to epistemological terms, they displace the local, historical, political and theoretical crises that enable and limit both possibility and impossibility. Their efforts to cast the question of reading in terms of the binary possible/impossible, rewrite a generalized and extremely unsettling debate about what reading *should* be—rather than what it is—and about what exactly we should read, a debate engendered in large part by a powerful critique of the history and canons of literary studies and engendering an explicitly political program, as an epistemological struggle between those who believe reading is possible and those who believe it is not. This formulation of the argument elides precisely the critical role of the resisting newreaders, black literary critics, marxist literary critics, feminist literary critics, and others, who suggest an impossibility of reading by exposing the interests that ground "standard meanings." (I think Derrida belongs with this group, but he is not its leader.) This elision necessarily reaffirms the possibility of pluralism, that is, of general persuasion; indeed, this reaffirmation may be the most significant effect of the entire debate. The Anglo-American pluralist rewrites (or misreads) his indigenous opponents' challenges to the possibility of *persuasion* as an "imported" poststructuralism's insistence on the impossibility of reading. The difference between these two formulations is a political difference. In the work of those critics who represent a potential break from the pluralist problematic, those whose work can be read as refusing the imperatives of general persuasion, determinate limits and the irreducibility of the discontinuities within the critical community are political *and* theoretical facts; reading is neither possible nor impossible, but interested or, as Althusser would insist, guilty. And guilt is associated with persuasion. The possibilities and impossibilities of persuasion reveal the play and struggle of interests.

The model of reading I employ in *Seductive Reasoning* originates in the work of Louis Althusser. The response to Althusser's work has been both slow and uneven in the United States, particularly when contrasted with the reception accorded other French theorists of his generation, including some of his students.[28] Recently, references to his work on ideology and theoretical practice have become more common, in part thanks to the work of such British feminists as Michèle Barrett,[29] but it is still relatively rare for commentators in the United States to observe the degree to which his earliest work emphasizes a theory of reading: "I dare maintain that only since Marx have we had to begin to suspect what, in theory at least, *reading* and hence writing *means (veut dire)*" (*RC* 16). Although his subject matter is remote from my own, in the course of *Reading Capital* Althusser generates the concepts that are critical to my analysis of pluralism: problematic, symptomatic reading, theory and ideology. In fact, his account of the relation between Marx and his predecessors in political economy stands as a model for the relationship I hope to establish between my discourse and the discourse of critical pluralism, a relationship *produced* by the practice of symptomatic reading.

[28]See Andrew Parker, "Futures for Marxism: An Appreciation of Althusser," *Diacritics* 15:4 (1985), 57–72, for a discussion of Althusser's reception in the United Kingdom. Althusser's oeuvre has been the subject of considerable critical commentary by British and continental theorists, and it is not my intention to enter into a polemic in his defense here. Although the criticisms (some of which I incorporate below) directed at his theory have exposed weaknesses and wrong turns, I largely agree with John Frow's assessment: "Althusser's critique of the empiricist position and indeed his general critique of economism and historicism seem to me to remain more powerful than any countervailing response": *Marxism and Literary History* (Cambridge: Harvard University Press, 1986), p. 56. See Ted Benton, *The Rise and Fall of Structural Marxism* (New York: St. Martin's, 1984); Simon Clark et al., *One-Dimensional Marxism* (London: Allison & Busby, 1980); Gregory Elliot, *Althusser: The Detour of Theory* (London: Verso, 1987); Michel Pêcheux, *Language, Semantics and Ideology* (New York: St. Martin's Press, 1982); Göran Therborn, *The Ideology of Power and the Power of Ideology* (London: New Left Books, 1980). James Kavanagh's work has been indispensable to my understanding of Althusser. See Kavanagh, "Marxism's Althusser: Toward a Politics of Literary Theory," *Diacritics* 12:1 (1982), 25–45; "Interview" with Etienne Balibar and Pierre Macherey (conducted with Thomas E. Lewis), *Diacritics* 12:1 (1982), 46–52; "'To the Same Defect': Toward a Critique of the Ideology of the Aesthetic,"; "The Jameson Effect," *New Orleans Review* 11:1 (1984), 20–28. See also Thomas E. Lewis, "Reference and Dissemination: Althusser after Derrida," *Diacritics* 15:4 (1985), 37–72.

[29]See Michèle Barrett, *Women's Oppression Today: Problems in Marxist Feminist Analysis* (London: Verso, 1980).

Althusser argues that Marx founds a radical theory and practice of reading by refusing the ideology of innocent *"reading* which makes a written discourse the immediate transparency of the true, and the real discourse of a voice" (16). He claims that "this immediate reading of essence in existence expresses the religious model of Hegel's Absolute Knowledge," and he aligns it with "all the complementary religious myths of the voice (the Logos) speaking in the sequences of a discourse; of the Truth that inhabits its Scripture;—and of the ear that hears or the eye that reads this discourse, in order to discover in it (if they are pure) the speech of the Truth which inhabits each of its Words" (17). The myths of the Logos and of Truth support the fiction of transparent expression, of a meaning that can be read "at sight," innocently.

Many contemporary literary theorists have advanced critiques of the ideology of innocent reading. This position against innocence is, for example, essential to the work of feminist criticism, where I first encountered it in Mary Ellmann's *Thinking about Women.*[30] Yet, the fiction of first reading returns again and again in pluralist discourse, as the figure of innocence is constantly revised. "Critical understanding" in the pluralist commonwealth requires the innocent eye of a reader defined only by his competent sight reading. The pluralist polemic against theory is ultimately a defense of the innocence of reading.

Althusser argues that the Marx of *Capital* abandons both the posture of innocence and the theory of expression and, with these renunciations, establishes historical materialism as a theory of history.

> Marx could not possibly have become Marx except by founding a theory of history and a philosophy of the historical distinction between ideology and science. . . . this foundation was consummated in the dissipation of the religious myth of *reading.* The

---

[30]Mary Ellmann, *Thinking about Women* (New York: Harcourt Brace Jovanovich, 1968). Roland Barthes offers a strong version of this view in *S/Z*, tr. Richard Miller (New York: Hill & Wang, 1974): "We must further accept one last freedom: that of reading the text as if it had already been read. . . . rereading . . . contests the claim which would have us believe that the first reading is a primary, naive, phenomenal reading . . . there is no *first* reading" (15–16).

Young Marx of the *1844 Manuscripts* read the human essence at sight, immediately, in the transparency of its alienation. *Capital*, on the contrary, exactly measures a distance and an internal dislocation *(décalage)* in the real, inscribed in its *structure*, a distance and a dislocation such as to make their own effects themselves illegible, and the illusion of an immediate reading of them the ultimate apex of their effects: *fetishism*. It was essential to turn to history to track down this myth of reading to its lair. . . . the truth of history cannot be read in its manifest discourse, because the text of history is not a text in which a voice (the Logos) speaks, but the inaudible and illegible notation of the effects of a structure of structures. [*RC* 17]

This passage posits the young, "pre-marxist" Marx as a humanist, at once an idealist and an empiricist.[31] According to Althusser, the author of the *1844 Manuscripts* believed in a universal human essence, an idealized humanity, alienated by its fall into history. Alienation appears as a transparent fact, a truth spoken in the manifest discourse of history; one has only to look in order to see it. "In Marx's early works . . . the proletariat in its 'alienation' represents the human essence itself" (*FM* 221). For Althusser, this "illusion of immediate reading" remains the "apex" of bourgeois ideology: fetishism.

He contrasts this young humanist to the Marx of *Capital*. The "break" in Marx's work entails his rejection of the religious myth of *reading*. Indeed, in Althusser's account, the question of the possibility of reading—and of newreading—marks the crisis of historical materialism as vividly as it now highlights the crisis of literary studies. Reading ceases to be an innocent act at the very moment that history enters a new theoretical problematic. The rejection of the myth of innocent reading opens a chasm between "Logos and Being; between the Great Book that was, in its very being, the World, and the discourse of the knowledge of the world; between the essence of things and its reading"; "once we have broken these ties, a new conception of *discourse* at last becomes possible" (*RC* 17). A new practice and theory of reading

---

[31]"An empiricism of the subject always corresponds to an idealism of the essence (or an empiricism of the essence to an idealism of the subject)": Althusser, "Marxism and Humanism," p. 228.

and of history emerges, in which reading is an anti-essentialist (and anti-pluralist) practice. Althusser employs the vocabulary of vision, blindness, and oversight to describe this new theory; or, rather, he defines the break Marx inaugurates as a critique of the epistemology in which "all the work of knowledge is reduced in principle to the recognition of the mere relation of *vision*" (19).

Althusser embraces the terms in which M. H. Abrams attacks the "newreaders": Marx's reading of Adam Smith in *Capital* is a "double reading." The first remains trapped within the illusory metaphor of vision. "Marx very often explains [Smith's] omissions by [his] distractions, or in the strict sense, his *absences:* he did not *see* what was, however, staring him in the face, he did not grasp what was, however, in his hands" (*RC* 19). Althusser insists this reading finally produces nothing but a "summary of concordances and discordances"; rather than explaining the oversights in Smith's text, Marx's first reading obliterates them, filling in the lacunae. This process "reduces Marx to Smith minus the myopia" (19). This "logic of sighting and oversight" also

> reduces every weakness in the system of concepts that makes up knowledge to a psychological weakness of "vision." And if it is absences of *vision* that explain these *oversights,* in the same way and by the same necessity, it is the presence and acuteness of "vision" that will explain these "sightings". What Smith did not see, through a weakness of vision, Marx sees: what Smith did not see was perfectly visible, and it was because it was visible that Smith could fail to see it while Marx could see it. We are in a circle—we have relapsed into the mirror myth of knowledge as the vision of a given object or the reading of an established text, neither of which is ever anything but transparency itself. [*RC* 19]

This is the religious myth of expression and of reading at first sight, reasserting the transparency of the text, the *givenness* of the object of knowledge. This ideology of "givenness" reappears in pluralism's consensus against theory.

Althusser argues that the Marx of *Capital* discloses a second quite different reading when he reveals that the "combined ex-

istence of sightings and oversights in an author poses a problem, the problem of their *combination*" (*RC* 19). The combination
of insight and oversight is not random; on the contrary, their
interrelation is a "symptomatic" effect of the problematic that
structures the text as a whole. When this "combination" is the
focus of analysis, the status of both insight and oversight is
fundamentally transformed. Reading must account for the determinate relation between absence and presence. Oversight is
no longer an accidental omission, but an *essential* repression, a
determinate exclusion, the "necessary effect of the structure of
the visible field" (20). The first reading, the disclosure of concordances and discords, is abandoned. Instead, the text must be
compared with itself, "its non-vision with its vision," in order to
discover the "connexion between the field of the visible and the
field of the invisible" (21, 20). As Francis Barker suggests (in
another context): "the point is not to supply this absence, to
make whole what is lacking, but to aggravate its historical significance."[32]

Althusser pinpoints Marx's break with political economy at
the moment when he identifies a *question* in Smith's text.

> In the course of the questions classical economics asked about the
> "value of labour" something very special has happened. Classical
> political economy has "*produced*" (just as Engels will say . . . phlo-
> gistic chemistry "produced" oxygen . . .) a correct answer: the
> value of "labour" is equal to the value of the subsistence goods
> necessary for the reproduction of "labour." A correct answer is a
> correct answer. Any reader in the "first manner" will give Smith
> and Ricardo a good mark and pass on to other observations. Not
> Marx. For what we shall call his eye has been attracted by a
> remarkable property of this answer; *it is the correct answer to a
> question that has just one failing: it was never posed.* [*RC* 22]

This "remarkable property" has been the object of considerable
theoretical speculation since the sixties.[33] What transforma-

---

[32]Francis Barker, *The Tremulous Private Body* (London: Methuen, 1984), p. 38.
[33]Derrida's work provides just one example. Irene E. Harvey points to passages such as the following from *La voix et la phénomène* (Paris: Presses Univer-

tions—of the myth of reading and our concept of knowledge—
result from the claim that a text answers a question that it never
asks? How does this possibility redirect the question of the impossibility of reading?

In his first reading of Smith, Marx exposed what was "perfectly visible" but somehow overlooked, in order to "make
whole" the argument. In his new reading, the not seen, the
invisible, is an absence *within* Smith's work; it is both present
and (although this metaphor is no longer adequate) invisible.
Althusser describes this new problematic as follows:

> what classical political economy does not see, is not what it does
> not see, it is *what it sees;* it is not what it lacks, on the contrary, it is
> *what it does not lack;* it is not what it misses, on the contrary, it is
> *what it does not miss.* The oversight, then, is not to see what one
> sees, the oversight no longer concerns the object, but *the sight*
> itself. The oversight is an oversight that concerns *vision:* non-
> vision is therefore inside vision, it is a form of vision and hence
> has a necessary relationship with vision. [*RC* 21]

The paradoxes of this passage revolve around the notion that
one may see something and not see it, simultaneously: blindness is not pure lack but a form of vision. It is precisely this form
of "vision" at work in the pluralist texts I read below: general
persuasion is what every pluralist sees but does not see.

This argument overturns the conception of knowledge that
rests on the metaphor of vision, of seeing or not seeing objects
of knowledge which are simply given: "we must abandon the
mirror myths of immediate vision and reading, and conceive
knowledge as a production" (*RC* 24). The model of production

---

sitaires de France, 1967): "When *empirical life* or even the pure psychic region is
placed in parenthesis, it is again a *transcendental life . . .* that Husserl discovers.
And thus he thematizes this *unity of the concept of life* without however posing it
as a question" (9–10, Harvey's translation), and she argues that Derrida "tends
to focus on what he calls the 'unasked questions,' which seem to necessarily
arise in the arguments he analyzes but which seem to have been 'hidden from
the view' of their respective authors. The significance of the 'unasked questions'
is always revealing for Derrida." See Harvey, *Derrida and the Economy of Différance*
(Bloomington: Indiana University Press, 1986), pp. 45, 48.

allows us to conceptualize the process by which a discourse can shift terrain, change the very terms in which a problem is articulated, and produce new objects of knowledge, new answers, without acknowledging the process of knowledge production itself (without posing questions). Such a discourse enacts a production, without reflecting upon or theorizing it, and *"it is the classical text itself which tells us that it is silent: its silence is its own words"* (22). Althusser observes:

> what political economy does not see is not a pre-existing object which it could have seen but did not see—but an object which it produced itself in its operation of knowledge and which did not pre-exist it: precisely the production itself, which is identical with the object. What political economy does not see is what it *does:* its production of a new answer without a question, and simultaneously the production of a new latent question contained by default in this new answer. . . . It made *"a complete change in the terms of the"* original *"problem,"* and thereby produced a new problem, but without knowing it. . . . it remained convinced that it was still on the terrain of the old problem, whereas it has *"unwittingly changed terrain."* Its blindness and its "oversight" lie in this misunderstanding, between what it produces and what it sees, in this *"substitution,,"* which Marx elsewhere calls a *"play on words" (Wortspiel)* that is necessarily impenetrable for its author. (RC 24).[34]

[34]Althusser's position differs in interesting ways from the apparently similar view Paul de Man puts forward in *Blindness and Insight*. The problematics of reading and vision also intersect in Derrida's texts: "The reading must always aim at a certain relationship, *unperceived* by the writer, between what he commands and what he does not command of the patterns of the language that he uses. This relationship is not a certain quantitative distribution of *shadow and light*, of weakness or force, but a signifying structure that *critical reading should produce* [my emphases]. . . . To produce this signifying structure obviously cannot consist of reproducing, by the effaced and respectful doubling of commentary, the conscious, voluntary, intentional relationship that the writer institutes in his exchanges with the history to which he belongs thanks to the element of language; "if it seems to us in principle impossible to separate . . . the signified from the signifier, . . . we nevertheless believe that this impossibility is historically articulated. It does not limit attempts at deciphering in the same way, to the same degree, and according to the same rules . . . what we call production is necessarily a text, the system of a writing and of a reading which we know is ordered around its own *blind spot": Of Grammatology*, pp. 158, 159, 164. Deconstruction might be described as the unveiling of a word play that is similarly impenetrable to its author.

This account of the production of knowledge as an "unwitting" shift in terrain provides the crucial figures for Althusser's account of reading. Political economy obscures "production itself," the (theoretical) operation that engenders a new object of inquiry and a new *problematic*. This term designates the historically determinate structure of presuppositions that constitutes a discourse, its enabling conditions. The problematic of a discourse is a conceptual matrix that defines objects within the field, fixes lines of inquiry, sets problems, and thereby determines the "solutions" that can be generated within its limits. According to Althusser, any given discourse "can only pose problems on the terrain and within the horizon of a definite theoretical structure, its problematic, which constitutes its absolute and definite condition of possibility, and hence the absolute determination of *the forms in which all problems must be posed*, at any given moment" (25). This definition suggests how remote his position is from pluralism. For Althusser, the appearance of an object of knowledge is determined by the structure of its theoretical problematic. "Vision" ceases to be a "religious privilege" of mysterious insight: "it is literally no longer the eye (the mind's eye) of a subject which *sees* what exists in the field defined by a theoretical problematic: it is this field itself which *sees itself* in the objects or problems it defines" (25). Ideology is characterized above all by its refusal to confess to the theoretical work that produces the objects of its inquiry and thus robs it of its innocence.

Althusser models the process by which a critic discloses a text's problematic on "the 'symptomatic reading' with which Marx managed to read the illegible in [Adam] Smith" (28). My analysis of pluralism will take this form. Just as the problematic defines and structures the visible terrain of a discourse, so it "structures the invisible," that which is "defined as excluded by the existence and peculiar structure of the field of the problematic" (26). The excluded is no longer conceived as a random set of objects that were overlooked. On the contrary, "the invisible is the theoretical problematic's non-vision of its non-objects, the invisible is the darkness, the blinded eye of the theoretical problematic's self-reflection when it scans its non-objects, its non-problems without seeing them, *in order not to look at them*" (26). Exclusion is determinate and determining: "the invisible is defined by the visible as *its* invisible, *its* forbidden vision: the invisible is not therefore simply what is outside the visible (to return to the spatial metaphor), the outer darkness of exclusion—but the *inner darkness of exclusion*, inside the visible itself because defined by its structure" (26). Thus, a given problematic is defined as much by what it *excludes*, by its "outside," as it is by its content: "the field of the problematic . . . defines and structures the invisible as the defined excluded, *excluded* from the field of visibility and *defined* as excluded" (26). To break with the pluralist problematic is to identify its unposed question, the symptomatic absence that structures its discursive field and the objects therein as given, precisely by rendering its "non-objects" invisible. In the case of pluralism, this unarticulated question inevitably concerns the possibility of general persuasion.

The articulation of the unposed question inaugurates an "epistemological break," a definitive shift in the theoretical terrain. This break produces the controversial relation between ideology and theory (or science) which is so important in Althusser's work and which has been criticized by both marxist and non-marxist readers. Althusser argues that a science emerges from an ideological prehistory and "continues endlessly to do so . . . by *rejecting* what it considers to be *error*, according to the process which Bachelard called the 'epistemological break'" (*SC* 114). "Every science, in the relationship it has with the ideology it emerged from, can only be thought as a 'science of the ideology'" (*RC* 46). In his later work, especially in *Essays in Self-Criticism*, he cautions that the term "science" should not be taken as the sign of a "relapse into a theory of *science* (in the singular). . . . *Science* (in the singular) does not exist," and insists that the epistemological break cannot be understood in the "rationalist terms of science and non-science" (*SC* 112, 119); it offers no new epistemological guarantee. On the contrary, it must be explained precisely as a "*historical* fact in all of its dimensions—social, political, ideological and theoretical"

(*SC* 106). In *Reading Capital*, Althusser warns that we must protect "the decisive distinction between science and ideology . . .
against the dogmatic or scientistic temptations which threaten
it" (*RC* 45). We must not "make use of this distinction in a way
that restores the ideology of the philosophy of the Enlighten-
ment, but on the contrary, . . . treat the ideology which constitutes the prehistory of a science, for example, as a real history
with its own laws and as the real prehistory whose real confrontation with other technical practices and other ideological or
scientific acquisitions was capable, in a specific theoretical conjuncture, of producing the arrival of a science, not as its goal,
but as its surprise. (*RC* 45). For my purposes here, theory is this
symptomatic analysis of the problematic of a "precursor" text, a
text which is thus *produced* as ideological. My book takes the text
of pluralism as just such a precursor. To claim either innocence
or a purely *epistemological* priority for this reading would be to
ignore the main thrust of the Althusserian intervention.

The relationship between ideology and theory bears critically
on my efforts to read the pluralist problematic. In Althusserian
terms, ideology does not name an articulated world view or set
of ideas or consciousness in general. Althusser stresses that the
problematic of a discourse is unconscious: "one thinks in it
rather than of it" (*RC* 25). Ideology is not false consciousness, or
illusion, or error (*SC* 119–25); rather, it designates a profoundly
unconscious, "lived" relation to the real. Ideology works practically, within institutions or ideological state apparatuses. It
spontaneously constructs "reality" for the "subject," including
the reality of subjectivity itself, without requiring the support of
self-conscious reflection. As Althusser puts it, "ideology represents the imaginary relationship of individuals to their real conditions of existence."[35] This imaginary relation has as one of its
effects the production of subjects, subjects bathed in ideology,

[35]See Louis Althusser, "Ideology and Ideological State Apparatuses," *Lenin
and Philosophy,* tr. Ben Brewster (New York: Monthly Review Press, 1974), p.
162. Further references to this volume (*LP*) will be given in parentheses in the
text.

who "innocently" see the objects of ideology as given, as objects in the world. "Men 'live' their ideologies as the Cartesian 'saw' or did not see—if he was not looking at it—the moon two hundred paces away: *not at all as a form of consciousness, but as an object of 'their' world*, as their *world* itself" (*FM* 233). Its practical functions make ideology "a structure essential to the historical life of societies, . . . an organic part of every social totality" (232). In the case of pluralism, as we shall see, this process of ideological "interpellation," whereby pluralist "ideology hails or interpellates concrete individuals as concrete subjects" (*LP* 173), produces a particular kind of reading and writing subject. The subject of pluralism assumes an infinitely persuadable (general) audience even as he neglects to theorize general persuasion.

This view of ideology installs a new concept of science or theory. If ideology is neither a lie nor an error, it will not be swept away in some utopian future. The relationship between the ideological and the theoretical thus lacks the drama of a simple opposition, with theory taking the part of Truth. Rather, ideological and theoretical practices are different "social instances," distinct operations in the production and reproduction of social relations. The relation between a particular ideology and its theory is thus always a matter of determinate historical practices. James Kavanagh observes that "the difference between ideological and scientific practices is the difference between those [practices] which re-produce and re-adequate the subject's '"lived" relation to the real,' and those which install the subject . . . in a process of production of knowledge."[36] Ideological practice aims to reproduce some aspect of social life as a set of practices and structures of feeling; in contrast, theoretical practice aims at the production of knowledge (of ideology). "An ideological concept . . . really does designate a set of existing relations, [but] unlike a scientific concept, it does not provide us with a means of knowing them" (*FM* 223). Neither theory nor ideologies exist "in general"; specific theoretical practices work

[36]Kavanagh, "Marxism's Althusser," p. 28.

in determinate relationships with the specific ideological practices they take as objects of knowledge.[37] Althusser's work thus
suggests that theory is not an epistemologically or ontologically
privileged Archimedean point; rather, it is a strategy of reading,
a strategy pluralists fiercely resist, particularly when it emphasizes exclusion and threatens their innocent notion of the given
as (merely) common sense. Theoretical practice "breaks" with a
particular ideology by interrogating the apparently spon-
taneous, lived relation ideology constructs and, ultimately, by
exposing the "problematic" that structures the ideological and,
in turn, is concealed by it.

This book is an instance of "theoretical practice" precisely in
the sense that it works to break with the ideology of pluralism
and thus to produce the problematic of general persuasion. My
aim is not to "govern" pluralist practice (in the sense Michaels
and Knapp condemn) but to theorize it, to deprive it of its innocence and, thus, to disable it, to disrupt the ideological effects by
which pluralism reproduces its social practice and the subjects
appropriate to that practice. This undertaking requires that we
pose *as a question* what pluralism consistently offers as a solution: we must pose the problem of persuasion.

III

> The cry goes up that one is murdering history whenever,
> in a historical analysis . . . one is seen to be using in too
> obvious a way the categories of discontinuity and
> difference, the notions of threshold, rupture,
> transformation. . . . One will be denounced for attacking
> the inalienable rights of history and the very foundations
> of any possible historicity. But one must not be deceived:
> what is being bewailed is the development that was to
> provide the sovereignty of the consciousness with a safer,
> less exposed shelter than myths, kinship systems,
> languages, sexuality or desire; . . . It is as if it was
> particularly difficult, in the history in which men retrace

---

[37]See Althusser, "Marxism and Humanism," and "Ideology and Ideological
State Apparatuses."

their own ideas and their own knowledge, to formulate a
general theory of discontinuity, of series, of limits. . . . As
if, in that field where we had become used to seeking
origins, . . . and to having constant recourse to
metaphors of life, we felt a particular repugnance to
conceiving of difference, to describing separations and
dispersions. . . . As if we were afraid to conceive the
Other in the time of our own thought.

> —MICHEL FOUCAULT, *The Archaeology of Knowledge*

Abrams . . . claims that deconstructionist readings will
destroy history. His test at that point is not primarily
cognitive but pragmatic. Stop, you're killing me!

> —WAYNE BOOTH, "'Preserving the Exemplar': Or, How
> Not to Dig Our Own Graves"

There is never a rupture in the practice of literary
criticism. Changes are always produced and perceived
within the rules of the game. . . . Continuity in the
practice of literary criticism is assured not despite but
because of the absence of a text that is independent of
interpretation. Indeed, from the perspective I have been
developing, the fear of discontinuity is an incoherent one.
The irony is that discontinuity is only a danger within the
model erected to guard against it; for only if there is a
free-standing text is there the possibility of moving away
from it.

> —STANLEY FISH, *Is There a Text in This Class?*

Seductive reasoning appears to be an oxymoron. But as the
phrase itself signals, appearances, words in this case, are treacherous and can deceive us, especially if we are innocent or inex-
perienced. If an oxymoron is a figure that conjoins contradictory
terms—makes marriages of odd bedfellows—but nevertheless
frequently makes sense, indeed, is "more pointedly witty for
seeming absurd," as the Greek *oxy* (sharp) and *mōros* (stupid)
suggest, then seductive reasoning is not an oxymoron; nor is it
used as such in the ordinary idioms of English. Unlike the
obscurity of a darkness visible or the monstrousness of the fiend
angelical or even the common bitterness of the bittersweet, the

contrary epithet "seductive" is generally understood to over-power and thus negate the rationality of the word "reasoning": seductive reasoning is not reasoning but seduction. Worse yet, it is seduction disguised in reason's garments, a hypocritical seduction.

Seductive reasoning, then, is an epithet in the secondary, narrow, and disputed sense of "an abusive or contemptuous word or phrase."[38] Some would suggest that the word "seductive" is always already an epithet in this narrow and disputed sense, that is, always already a term of contempt. In this perspective, seduction is always hypocritical and always distinguished from reason for this very fault; seduction is by definition duplicitous. Even in a period of relative sexual freedom—as tenuous and embattled as that freedom may be at this moment, it is still relatively real—"seductive" is not yet a common term of praise or celebration. Those rare occasions when it is used in a positive sense seldom involve questions of intellectual argument or analysis; only fictions seem genuinely praised when reviewers invoke their seductive powers.[39] Even those who take "seductive" to be a neutral or affirmative term hesitate to praise a critical text for its seductive reasoning. On the contrary, this epithet commonly announces a demystifying project; it nods in the direction of the cunning with which wrong-headed if not flatly false arguments are introduced, but remains uncompromisingly committed to exposing the pretense, the sham of reasoning, that seduction tries to work. Seductive reasoning, then, is an epithet that inscribes a reluctant and ambivalent admiration for the scam we didn't fall for, the confidence trick we have successfully exposed.

There have been attacks on this devaluation of seduction, attacks that insist alternatively on the omnipresence of seduction and its value or power. In *The Daughter's Seduction*, Jane

---

[38]My citations are from the *American Heritage Dictionary*. The definition proper names oxymoron "a rhetorical figure in which an epigrammatic effect is created by the conjunction of incongruous or contradictory terms."

[39]See Ross Chambers, *Story and Situation: Narrative Seduction and the Power of Fiction* (Minneapolis: University of Minnesota Press, 1984).

Gallop figures the mutual seduction of psychoanalysis and feminism, the father and the daughter, as "the introduction of heterogeneity (sexuality, violence, economic class conflict) into the closed circle of the family."[40] Gallop argues that this heterogeneity undermines resistances and reveals the father's "impassive self-mastery" as a cloak for his desire; the operation of seduction makes static and rigid roles "more complicated, more equivocal, more yielding" (xiv). In her analysis, the disavowal of seduction is a disavowal of desire that grounds the imposture of phallic mastery and authority; the ostentatious refusal of seduction "gains [the father] another kind of seduction (this one more one-sided, more like violation), a veiled seduction in the form of the law" (70).[41] Thus, the law masks its own omnipresent seduction; feminist discourse must both unveil and embrace seduction, including "the seductive function of the law itself" (75), in order to undermine and disrupt that law.

Gallop's analysis is very suggestive, but I want to take a slightly different tack concerning the figure of seduction. Seductive reasoning is the practice of pluralism: the problematic of general persuasion imposes a regime of general seduction or seductive reasoning which is in a certain sense *not* veiled. Indeed, Althusser's insistence that we abandon the metaphors of vision implies that the figures of veiling and unveiling may not account for the way in which pluralism *produces* seductive reasoning, that is, produces reason as a universal seduction. Pluralism defines reason itself as the assumption of the theoretical

[40]Jane Gallop, *The Daughter's Seduction: Feminism and Psychoanalysis* (Ithaca: Cornell University Press, 1982), p. xv. See also Gallop, "French Theory and the Seduction of Feminism," *Men in Feminism*, pp. 111–15, for a discussion of Jean Baudrillard's *De la séduction* and the seduction of seduction.

[41]Gallop is reading and revising the "phallic proportions" of what she calls "Lacanian conceit" (15–32). In her analyses of theorists ranging from Juliet Mitchell and Ernest Jones to Lacan, Irigaray and Kristeva, she stresses the subversive power of seduction as a strategy of unveiling and argues that what must be unveiled is seduction itself. Throughout, Gallop's readings turn on Lacan's account of desire and his claim that the phallus is a privileged signifier that "can play its role only when veiled." See Lacan, "The Signification of the Phallus," *Ecrits: A Selection*, tr. Alan Sheridan (New York: Norton, 1977), pp. 287–88 and passim.

possibility of general persuasion, that is, of the possibility of absolute seduction, seduction without exclusions, without contingencies. To refuse the seductive, to decline to attempt to persuade a universal audience, to assume veils, is thus the unmistakable sign of irrationality; as Booth puts it, "criticism stops and reductive vilification begins." Within the problematic of general persuasion, reasoning is always already seductive; indeed, it must be uniformly or consistently seductive, seductive without exception. An unseductive reason is a contradiction in terms.

In the pluralist idiom, then, "seductive reasoning" is redundant rather than oxymoronic. But to escape the pluralist problematic is neither to celebrate seduction, revising its connotations, nor to reverse the current pluralist problematic, refusing seduction entirely, thus returning to what Gallop describes as the rigidity of veiled, phallic roles. Such an escape would be nothing less than a reversal, a mirror image of pluralism's assertion of general persuasion. Anti-pluralisms do not embrace so much as displace the play of seduction, engaging in partial, contingent, and interested seductions, playing favorites.[42]

Feminist criticism provides an example of critical practice which resists the claims of seductive reasoning without falling into simple opposition to them. In "Iconoclastic Moments: Reading the *Sonnets for Helene,* Writing the *Portuguese Letters,*" Elizabeth Berg defines "iconoclastic" or "partial" reading and writing. She argues that "a writing project based on identity sets up one of two possible relationships to the reader: one of seduction or one of confrontation. That is, the reader may accept what is set down by the writer and be seduced (or persuaded) over to the writer's side, or else the reader may refuse the writer's determination and set himself up in opposition to the text. In either case, the relationship is one of specularity, where the reader can

[42]In this field of displacements, the veil no longer figures an abstract, phallic bar to the universal subject's gaze. Rather, veiling reappears as one of many figures for social and political discontinuity; the opposition veiling/unveiling is displaced by the concept of the veil as a partial strategy, one that marks the place of the subject who gazes *out* from behind it.

only mirror the writer."[43] In contrast, Berg argues for reading and writing "as iconoclastic activities, as activities that undo images of identity, of truth and of authority" (208). She advocates a deliberate refusal to grant the authors of texts the authority they seek to control interpretation. Berg refuses to be seduced, even when the text demands the reader's seduction; but she also refuses to refuse to be seduced—in other words, she reserves the right to follow her desire elsewhere, to pursue some other path. In the terms I will be developing in my argument, Berg rejects general persuasion.

Faced with a group of students who refuse, as she puts it, to take Baudelaire seriously, Berg first chastizes them; but she eventually acknowledges the force of their "frivolous" reading. She concludes: "a writer's power resides only in the referential aspect of his or her work: only in its claim to represent and affect reality. In refusing that referential aspect, the reader disarms the text. . . . The authority of literature is grounded in a pact between writer and reader to read the text *as if* it were real; in reading the text as fiction the reader reclaims his or her power to determine the meaning and significance of the work" (212–13). Fiction is the term that allows Berg to assert (to produce, in fact) a *discontinuity* between her discourse and that of the text she reads. Her refusal to grant the referential power of the text is also a refusal of its persuasiveness and of its authority. Berg refuses to take up the position of the reader of general persuasion. She defines the difference or discontinuity she effects by abandoning the "pact" between writer and reader as the "partiality" of her reading.

Partial reading "undermines the power of the text simply by reading it as fiction, by not taking it seriously, *by displaying . . . indifference to what is being said*" (219, my emphases). Indifference, as we shall see, is a stance that the pluralist problematic must disallow: the indifferent are not vulnerable to persuasions. Berg's "frivolous reading neither accepts nor rejects the image

---

[43]Elizabeth Berg, "Iconoclastic Moments," in *Poetics of Gender*, ed. Miller, pp. 219–20.

put forth by the text; instead it ignores the rules set down by the text in order to extract from it what it wants. *It eliminates confrontations as well as seductions* by displacing the relationship, by stepping out of the reader's appointed place in order to defy fixed battlelines" (214, my emphases). This different relationship is not a simple reversal because the partial reading makes "no claim to exclusivity, truth or universality." This is the quintessential gesture of anti-pluralism. The very possibility of positing a general audience, that is, of pursuing the project of general persuasion, requires that the reader/critic assert the truth *and* universality of her views. Without this grounding, the specular process that universalizes both author and reader is interrupted—a veil is tossed across the mirror. As Berg observes: "in the absence of a universal, transcendent standard, their relationship is also transformed: they are no longer in opposition, seeking to impose the universal for themselves" (213).

The "partiality" of this positioning of the reading subject allows for unanticipated "exchanges, intersections, possible congruences." Berg's partial reading exposes the myth of impartiality and acknowledges both difference and indifference in its interpretative practice. Partial reading reveals a certain desire, but it resists the problematic of general persuasion; it asserts discontinuities and in that respect resembles symptomatic reading. Its seductions can never be universal. *Seductive Reasoning* is a partial reading in so far as it argues that pluralism's claim to impartiality can never be realized; it is an iconoclastic reading in its insistence on the discontinuity between the identity pluralism espouses and the partial one it is assigned herein; it is an anti-pluralist reading in its effort to acknowledge the irreducibility of its margins, to read beyond the problematic of general persuasion.

As a partial or anti-pluralist reading, this book must recognize the limits of its own persuasiveness. The power of pluralism is not simply or even primarily a question of the suppression of a particular voice or content, much less of a specific interpretation. On the contrary, pluralism's power lies in its extraordinary *productivity* and in the form this productivity takes. Pluralism's hegemony is due in part to its broad, generous invitation to all comers to join the "dialogue," that is, to try to *persuade* all the other members of the pluralist community. Thus does the problematic of general persuasion screen both the pluralist and the subject (object) of her criticism from the impolitic knowledge that *all* discourses, in the very process of establishing significance, *necessarily* exclude not only some readings but also some readers. This distinction is the location of a key evasion in a text such as Booth's. He does observe that every way of speaking excludes certain readings and meanings: "Every mode of speech and thought can be said to forbid certain kinds of further speech and to invite certain other kinds" (B 419). But he is interested in and therefore conscious of the "proscription of meanings" only because this is the first step in the process of establishing the existence of a core of determinate meaning. Paradoxically, he manages to evade the necessary corollary: every mode of speech forbids certains kinds of speakers and invites certain other kinds. As we shall see, pluralism inevitably retreats into a humanistic account of the subject to avoid this unacceptable conclusion, and it encourages everyone who writes to fall back beside it.

The double-edged mystification or screening of writer and reader does not produce uniformity or "monism" (as Booth would call it) in the content of critical practice. The substance or content of one's critical position does not guarantee immunity to pluralism's seductions. But an explicitly theoretical inquiry into the operations of pluralism risks turning its attention to the problem of failures of persuasion. The ideology of an essentially undifferentiated critical community is thus endangered, not by the fact that persuasion frequently fails, but by the theoretical analysis that threatens to reveal the systematic and determinate lines of that failure. To *theorize* that failure, in Althusser's sense, is to disclose its problematic.

Practical agreements are elusive, but the generality or universality of the pluralist invitation is reinscribed elsewhere, in the theoretical imperative that every critic attempt to persuade the community in general. Anti-pluralism must do more than point to individual cases where persuasion fails. In the pluralist community, gender, race, class position, sexuality, nationality, and material interests are all accidents to be excluded in the construction of the general reader/writer. Booth actually identifies efforts to theorize exclusion in critical discourse as a form of "critical killing": "When I reduce your effort to discuss reasons to a mere expression of irrational forces (your id, your class, your upbringing, your inherited language), I make it impossible for you to reply—except, of course, with similar charges. Criticism stops and reductive vilification begins" (*CU* 259). Notice the gap where race, gender, and religion might appear on the list. (Class is an easy concept to exclude from our critical discourse since so few North Americans believe in it, much less write seriously about it.) Critical killing is defined here as a reductive emphasis on "irrational" or accidental differences among readers, differences *within* the critical community, partiality. All forms of political discourse are by definition guilty of this reductive obsession with irrational forces or accidental differences, simply because all the myriad types of political interpretation assume that interests play as significant a role as reasons in the production of powerful interpretations. Predictably, Booth warns against the temptation to politicize the discourse of literary studies. In *Critical Understanding,* he opposes "prophetic" polemics in pursuit of "*the* function of criticism *at the present time*"; such criticism "risk[s] turning critical battles into politics or even open warfare" (5).

In a certain sense, my aim here is to "open" what has been a secret war—not by an unveiling, but by a partial indifference, which begins by reading against the grain and against the interests of the text. The contradiction that threatens contemporary pluralism is its coupling of a polemic for *inclusion* with a commitment to essential *exclusions,* in particular, the exclusion of exclusion, and, as Garry Wills argues, of those who would exclude. As Barthes might observe, it is precisely at the moment of its greatest generosity, in its most *persuasive* mode, that pluralism "reinforces this relation of exclusion."[44] To take the example that has historically been most significant in the United States, the exclusion of marxist theory (which defined pluralism in its earliest articulations) is theoretically essential because marxism itself theorizes the necessity, indeed, the inevitability, of exclusions; but it must be practiced by means of a discursive strategy that privileges inclusion in the form of general persuasion and denies the very possibility of exclusion, of partial seductions. The problematic of general persuasion struggles at this conjuncture to inscribe all discourse within the boundaries of pluralism's commonwealth.

Anti-pluralist discourses attend to the partiality of persuasion and to the exclusions partiality implies. As I have suggested, marxism is a discourse that privileges exclusions; class is one of the many limits to general persuasion. In this regard, marxist discourse is paradigmatic of the kind of critical intervention that most threatens pluralist hegemony, and, in the United States in particular, it has long served as the major target of pluralism's polemic. But more recently the possibility of general persuasion has been attacked and the necessity, really, the inevitability, of making exclusions affirmed in texts from sources as diverse as Foucault and Afro-American studies, radical feminisms and Derrida. These anti-pluralisms are not distinguished primarily by what a pluralist such as Booth might call metaphysical or methodological monism; indeed, as we shall see, monism is no threat to the problematic of general persuasion. The recognition of the irreducibility of the margin in all explanations, the foregrounding of *interests*, with *exclusions* as the inevitable and clearly articulated consequence—these are the marks of anti-pluralisms.

[44]Roland Barthes, "Taking Sides," *Critical Essays*, tr. Richard Howard (Evanston: Northwestern University Press, 1972), p. 170.

2 PERSUASION AND THE PRODUCTION OF KNOWLEDGE

> Yet, with the critical cat now so far out of [the] bag
> that one can no longer ignore its existence, those who
> refuse the crime of theoretical ruthlessness can no
> longer hope to gain a good conscience. Neither, of
> course, can the terrorists—but then, they never laid
> claim to it in the first place.
> —PAUL DE MAN, "The Return to Philology"*

Within the problematic of general persuasion, difference is never theorized as a matter of irreducible dispersions or discontinuities; the "metaphors of life" Foucault alludes to are taken literally, and the category of the human (reader) quietly obscures the "murderous" difference of the other(s). So long as pluralist hegemony is assured, critics work confidently within the problematic of general persuasion and rarely address persuasion as such. Instead, various strategies are employed to recast the traditional opposition between rhetoric and logic, each yielding a more or less summary identification of merely rhetorical persuasiveness with mechanical niceties, formalities that can then be quickly dismissed. Some critics prefer to distinguish logic from rhetoric in explicitly moral terms, often proffered in a tone more generally associated with fear of the mob. In the liberal tradition, they regard rhetoric as a close cousin of

*"The Return to Philology" was first published as part of "Professing Literature: A Symposium on the Study of English," *Times Literary Supplement*, 10 December 1982, pp. 1355–56. When the essay was reprinted in *The Resistance to Theory* (Minneapolis: University of Minnesota Press, 1986), after de Man's death, "terrorists" was amended to "theorists," p. 26.

demagoguery; even its appearance is to be avoided. Argument is a matter of right reasoning, not flattery or cajoling; the persuasiveness of logic is wholly immanent, that is, not rhetorical. Other critics, moving in the opposite direction, ignore the putatively ethical question and underscore the mechanical or "technical" issue. Rhetoric is identified with poetry, and poetry is the object of criticism; criticism, therefore, must be radically opposed to poetry and poeticisms. Criticism and theory deal in propositions, not in rhetoric.[1] The traditional opposition is elevated to a scientific distinction grounded in the essential qualities of language. The problem of critical persuasiveness is entirely forgotten in this rush to science, which is precisely the end pluralism requires. Demurring that poetry is not "persuasive," the critic is free to move on to the question of what poetry is. The nature of persuasion is not the object of literary criticism.

Since the early seventies, diversionary tactics like these have come under extraordinary pressure. For (both practical and theoretical) reasons we shall consider, pluralists cautiously began to broach the issues of persuasion and persuasiveness, though their interests were clothed in a vocabulary of understanding or belief that conceals the stubborn problems of how belief is constituted, understanding verified, or understanding distinguished from belief (from being persuaded to the truth of any given understanding). As their traditional postures become more and more untenable, reluctant critics are swept into the defensive polemics characteristic of pluralism's contribution to contemporary critical debate. These efforts treat persuasion as a theme rather than venturing into a discussion of the logic of persuasion, as the latter would expose the structure of the pluralist problematic. But such work nevertheless reveals more than it conceals; the contradictions that now press upon the problematic of general persuasion demand some gesture toward resolution. The lapses and confusions that plague both the initial efforts to subdue those contradictions and later recuperative

---

[1]This is not, of course, a new position. Cleanth Brooks proposes just such a distinction in "The Heresy of Paraphrase," *The Well Wrought Urn* (New York: Harcourt, Brace & World, 1947).

projects are symptomatic of the weaknesses in the problematic as a whole, and they enable us, as Macherey argues, "to read the ideological contradictions within the devices produced to conceal them, to reconstitute the contradictions from the system of their concealment."[2] The pluralist polemic is an unwittingly revelatory "system of concealment."

E. D. Hirsch's *Aims of Interpretation* can serve to illustrate the pattern of the earliest stages of this (somewhat grudging) pluralist examination of persuasion. There are those who might refuse Hirsch the honorific "pluralist" on the grounds that he harbors a "monistic" commitment to authorial intention. This exclusion fails for several reasons that I will sketch here and argue over the course of my analysis. First, practically speaking, Hirsch's notion of "significance" allows for at least as large and diverse a plurality of interpretations as any pluralist conception would permit.

> Meaning is the stable object of knowledge in interpretation, without which wider humanistic knowledge would be impossible. The chief interest of significance, on the other hand, is in the unstable realm of value. The significance of meaning in a particular context determines its value in that context. For significance names the relationships of textual meaning, and value is a relationship, not a substance. Value is value-for-people. Textual meaning has wide interest only when it has actual or potential value for a number of people. And this value changes. A poem may have a very different value for me at age twenty and age forty. It may possess different values for people in different cultural contexts. A poem has no absolute value. [H 146][3]

In terms of pluralism's own articulation of its ideal, Hirsch's theory encourages pluralistic multiplicity. This observation, combined with a close reading of a paradigmatic pluralist polemic such as Booth's "'Preserving the Exemplar,'" leads to the more pointed observation that pluralism—via the problematic

---

[2]"An Interview with Pierre Macherey," *Red Letters* 5 (Summer 1977), 7, cited in Tony Bennett, *Formalism and Marxism* (London: Methuen, 1979), p. 162.

[3]See Hirsch's "Introduction: Meaning and Significance," pp. 1–13, and his concluding discussion of knowledge and value, pp. 146–58.

of general persuasion—in fact works to impose a Hirschian notion of intention, expressed as respect for authors, on all participants in the pluralist "dialogue." Hirsch's (apparently monistic)
position as an intentionalist does not conflict with his pluralist
position; it is merely a particular species of pluralism. Its practical effects are pluralistic, and, as we shall see, the logic of
Hirsch's intentionalist account entails the pluralist view of persuasion. Ultimately, this reading of the Hirschian element in
pluralist discourse leads to a critique of pluralism's opposition
between "monism" and "pluralism" in my discussion of Booth
in Chapter 3. This opposition cannot be sustained; monisms are
necessary to the theory and the practice of pluralism. In fact, as
we shall see, pluralism, in Booth's terms, is a monism. In my
reading, the charge that Hirsch is a monist *rather than* a pluralist
loses its coherence.

Hirsch's work reveals the trajectory that carries an essentially
theoretical text toward the problem of persuasion and, in the
process, transforms it into a pluralist polemic. This transformation is dramatized in Booth's work when he abandons his effort
to distinguish pluralist theory from its practical values. *The Aims
of Interpretation* contains ample evidence of the moral indignation characteristic of those who see persuasive rhetoric as a gau-
dy paint that renders even the most questionable postures
tempting to some. But Hirsch is also committed to the scientistic
model typical of those who dream of a pure language, a neutral
instrument of communication, systematically cleansed of rhetorical excrescences, of seductive linguistic tricks meant to persuade the recalcitrant or the unwary. In the case of *The Aims of
Interpretation*, both evasive strategies fail. Hirsch is left struggling to locate persuasion deep in the margins of his discourse.
The silences and strains which hinder this effort mark the whole
of *The Aims of Interpretation*. And the contradiction of the pluralist polemic so deforms Hirsch's argument that persuasion paradoxically reappears at the very center.

Predictably, Hirsch defers the subject of persuasion until his
"Afterword." (Even here the pluralist reluctance to speak directly to the question lingers.) Then, he concedes only that "the

communal acceptance of hypotheses has much to do with persuasion, and persuasion in doubtful matters requires attention to rhetoric" (153). The vague, guarded word "much" never acquires more substance, and Hirsch has already assured his reader that "obviously, the consolidated knowledge within a discipline has nothing directly to do with rhetoric" (153). Persuasion thus occupies an embarrassingly compromised position; it bears the double burden of an unseemly intimacy with rhetoric—which must cut it off from knowledge—and of "much" of the responsibility for the "communal acceptance" of this same knowledge in its original (not yet consolidated) form as hypothesis.

Hirsch senses some problem here, but he attempts to solve it with a semantic distinction and, in the process, overlooks the real difficulty with his position. He argues that in a discipline, once a hypothesis has been communicated (persuasively, one must assume), it "must be used, tested, and expressed by others *in a different form*" (154, my emphases). This formal transformation yields *"what* is communicated (that is, propositions)" (154), which are distinct from the persuasive rhetoric that first brought the hypothesis to the community's attention (and, apparently, inspired its subsequent use and testing).[4] Hirsch concludes: "If this condition is not met, the hypothesis is not really subject to criticism at the level of the discipline and has nothing to do with knowledge" (154). Propositions alone can be said to have any relation whatsoever to knowledge, and a proposition is a hypothesis divested of its rhetoric, the *how* of its communication. This interlude has the tone of a final clarification, and Hirsch's last, knowing remark confides that it is "easy" for a critic "to express with eloquent persuasiveness what is in fact nonsense" (154). The concept of eloquent persuasive nonsense remains murky and faintly redundant. In fairness, one must concede that this notion of persuasive nonsense is very widely accepted, and it is quite possible that Hirsch, were he to offer an example or an explanation of the term, would be scolded from some

---

[4]Cf. his discussion of synonymity, pp. 53–73.

quarters for belaboring the obvious. At any rate, he dismisses, with apparent relief, the issue of the relationship between persuasion and knowledge and closes his argument with a reprise of his central point, the distinction between value and knowledge, art and discipline *(scientia)*.

It is perhaps extreme to suggest that these distinctions are so urgently pursued largely to obscure the problems surrounding the nature of persuasiveness. Hirsch seems not at all perturbed that eloquence can give nonsense the tone and character of "persuasiveness." He rather leaves the impression that this is simply the state of our fallen nature. And he appears convinced that the step from hypothesis to proposition genuinely purges "what is communicated" of all rhetorical impurities and, thus, erases the ambiguities of persuasion's role in the constitution of knowledges and the disciplines elaborated around them.

Under some circumstances, this kind of treatment of a concept like persuasion might go unremarked. The distrust of rhetoric and the fear of "bad" persuasion, of seductive reasoning, are pervasive cultural tropes; they appear in political and social as well as intellectual avatars, and their traditions are so well established that, generally, one may simply allude to them and trust any audience to fill in the lines of the argument. But Hirsch himself makes it quite impossible to allow these remarks to pass without comment. He avoids any theoretical analysis of the unresolved issues crowded around his treatment of persuasion. Nevertheless, he betrays his consciousness of its problematical importance by placing this flawed and untrustworthy concept of persuasion at the heart of his larger project, the defense of literary studies as a discipline. Defending the possibility of knowledge in literary criticism is one of the central aims of Hirsch's enterprise. "One purpose of this book, then, is to give encouragement to those who are still willing to entertain the belief that knowledge is possible even in textual interpretation" (12). For him, the suggestion that reading may be "impossible" translates directly into a threat to the scientific or disciplinary status of criticism, and it generates his strongest condemnation: "Some of my colleagues are indignant at the present decadence in literary scholarship, with its anti-rationalism, faddism, and extreme relativism. I share their feelings. Scholars are right to feel indignant toward those learned writers who deliberately exploit the institutions of scholarship—even down to its punctilious conventions like footnotes and quotations—to deny the whole point of the institutions of scholarship, to deny, that is, the possibility of knowledge" (13). Hirsch's effort to respond to this threat leads him willy nilly to the problem of persuasion.

Hirsch approaches the question by way of a discussion of "the sociology of knowledge." He rejects Thomas Kuhn's concept of the paradigm and replaces it with a strikingly similar notion. His own theory of "cognitive inquiry" is based on the "logical relationship between evidence, hypothesis, and probability," but he claims that this relation is a "stable and *permanent* paradigm" (my emphasis) that "transcends" the ephemeral paradigms Kuhn defines (H 152). This transcendent paradigm is a kind of ultimate proposition; its logic is permanent, that is to say, not historically relative. Hirsch presents this argument without reference to rhetoric or persuasion, and it stands quite well, unsupported, for a moment. Then he adds:

> Now this is a very abstract and simplified model for inquiry, but it is the *kind* of model that every serious inquirer assumes. Furthermore, it is an accurate model to the extent that it is widely assumed. For I have referred not only to the logical relationship between evidence, hypothesis, and probability, but also to a communal enterprise that exists only to the extent that this logical relationship remains the paradigm (or ideology!) for the members of a community of inquirers. . . . Thus in a special sense, there *is* a sociology of knowledge on which inquiry depends, on which all *scientia* depends. And to the extent that this sense of the communal enterprise collapses, so does the discipline itself collapse as a discipline. . . . The health of a discipline as a discipline is entirely dependent upon the devoted allegiance of its members to the logic of inquiry. [H 152, 154]

The tendency toward repetition here is characteristic of Hirsch's treatment of the issue of communal allegiance. He insists that the centrality of community, indeed, of devoted allegiance, be acknowledged. The transcendent, permanent paradigm of the logic of inquiry is an accurate model of disciplinary enterprise only "to the extent that it is widely assumed," that is, "only to the extent that this logical relationship remains the paradigm (or ideology!) for the members of the community of inquirers." It is thus a social fact in the most profound sense. And what is the unspoken role of persuasion in all this? Persuasion is nothing less than the originary moment in the process by which the potential (or hypothetical) community (an entity Hirsch does not discuss, as it falls outside the logic of the paradigm) comes to accept "the paradigm (or ideology!)" of a communal enterprise organized around the logic of inquiry: "Communal acceptance of hypotheses has much to do with persuasion." Hirsch's (dubious) distinction between a "proposition" and its rhetorical dress[5] does not begin to address his real dilemma: the discipline of literary studies, as a discipline, and the knowledge that it produces depend upon persuasion.

The premium placed on avoiding the questions surrounding persuasiveness in general and persuasive nonsense in particular—no matter what the cost in coherence—becomes increasingly obvious. The very roots of Hirsch's community lie in persuasion. Yet he summarily defines it as an erratic, unpredictable tool and declines to examine it further. He abandons the topic with the faintly mystical remark that "the *writing* of history is an art, or can be, but history is not an art; it is a discipline, which is to say *scientia*" (154).

Literary criticism, also a discipline, has for Hirsch a parallel relationship to art. Hirschian persuasion is a form of artfulness; it is added to something—"what is communicated"— which is located not in writing but elsewhere. The hybrid, as it is acted upon by a group of inquirers, generates devotion or allegiance, community, and then knowledge. But that elsewhere, the place

---

[5]This distinction is untenable, and it represents as grave a threat for Hirsch's position as his ultimate dependence on persuasion to found the critical community of inquirers. I pass by the opportunity to develop a critique of the opposition between "propositions" and the language in which they are "embodied" only in order to pursue the more crucial matter of persuasion.

of history and criticism which is not writing, is never named; and, curiously, it seems that art (persuasion) does the essential work, or at least, "much" of it. One wonders if that history which is not written with art (in art) can ever hope to be admitted to the discipline as knowledge.[6] Without the persuasive artifice that wins communal acceptance for the logic of inquiry (or any other hypothesis), there can be no propositions.

Hirsch's mishandling of the concept of persuasion is symptomatic. Having ignored the problem of persuasion through the entirety of his argument, he finally takes it up, then hastily discards it, after offering a contradictory definition concerned, above all, with forcing persuasion to the most remote margin of pluralist discourse. Why does pluralism shrirk so from the problem of persuasion? What is masked by this sudden and awkward silence?

What is most puzzling in the closing passages of *The Aims of Interpretation* is not its silences, but rather Hirsch's decision to place persuasion at such a crucial juncture in his argument. This is not the ideal strategy to defend his view of the logic of inquiry. And one can easily envision an "Afterword" that presents an essentially similar argument without pausing to muse about persuasive nonsense and the grave consequences of the failure of community. Why does Hirsch cloud the clarity of the logic of inquiry with a venture into the sociology of knowledge—a project he ultimately dismisses—and thus expose the weakest link in the pluralist argument?

The canniness and subtlety that marks the rest of Hirsch's essay should warn us away from any illusion that his remarks

----

[6]For a rebuttal of Hirschian scientism as it touches on historiography, see Hayden White, *Metahistory: The Historical Imagination of Nineteenth Century Europe* (Baltimore: Johns Hopkins University Press, 1973). On the question of history's status as a science, White notes: "The physical sciences appear to progress by virtue of the agreements, reached from time to time among members of the established communities of scientists, regarding what will count as a scientific problem, the form that a scientific explanation must take, and the kinds of data that will be permitted to count as evidence in a properly scientific account of reality. Among historians no such agreement exists, or ever has existed" (12–13).

on persuasion are simply misbegotten. On the contrary, he is denied the luxury of his own ideal argument; conditions within the profession of literary studies compel attention to matters he might prefer to pass over. The simple fact that *The Aims of Interpretation* exists as a polemical address to the community is only the first sign that the problematic of general persuasion and its model of a homogeneous community of general readers labor under growing inconsistencies.

Hirsch writes to forestall the dissolution of the community of inquirers, which he defines as the source of any discipline's capacity to produce knowledge. He must address this problem and, by extension, the problem of persuasion, because the community has already begun to divide. Hirsch's explicit call for allegiance to pluralism's logic of inquiry tacitly acknowledges that the "natural" homogeneity of the community can no longer sustain its traditional practices and methods, its very logic, without conscious and polemical efforts like his own; the community must now be persuaded to remain (even perhaps to become) a community.

In a sense, Hirsch's text intervenes at precisely that originary moment which his theory elides: the moment at which a potential (or hypothetical) community comes to accept "the paradigm (or ideology!) of a truly communal enterprise organized around the logic of inquiry." A process of fragmentation, or differentiation, has put the old consensus into question, and a new one has yet to be achieved; and, of course, "communal acceptance of hypotheses has much to do with persuasion." There are many ways to characterize this process of dissolution. One might begin with the simplest demographic observations. The class, race, gender, and ethnic homogeneity of the university in the United States has been crumbling since at least 1945, and since the civil rights and women's movements of the sixties, this process has been both theorized and translated into pedagogical and disciplinary/scholarly practices. Yet although the very existence of his argument concedes this fragmentation of the critical community, Hirsch does not and cannot explicitly acknowledge this development. The logic of inquiry must be a "stable and permanent paradigm." As a result, virtually nothing in his text contributes to a concrete image of the community he claims to represent. Hirsch discusses his community in strictly abstract terms, as an ethical subject operating a set of transcendent principles (the logic of inquiry) in the pursuit of knowledge (and self-reproduction). This enables him to displace his anxiety about the dissolution of the reading community away from "mainstream" scholars and onto a clique of "dogmatic relativists" (148), who can then be countered on more congenial theoretical ground, on ground at a safe distance from the problem of persuasion.

When explicit remarks about the character and makeup of the greater pluralist community or about its actual methods or what Stanley Fish will call its "interests and *tacitly* understood goals" (F 16) are unavoidable, Hirsch's argument shows the signs of enormous strain. At such moments, the pressure on his text is visible in startling passages that fail to conceal a rising panic. The logic of inquiry no longer seems wholly adequate to the task of unifying or constituting the community of inquirers.

Consider, for example, his observation that "the current *instinct* of students" suggests that they believe "more truth and value are found in underground studies than in those pursued within institutions" (H 136, my emphasis). This is an unexpectedly frank admission of the conflict and suspicion "within" the academy. Instinct is in apparent conflict with logic. This is *not*, however, cause for alarm: enterprising teachers have incorporated the underground into established courses. Hirsch's celebration of naive cooptation concludes: "Literary study is at present astonishingly heterogeneous. In some American universities little remains that the underground can call its own. I am not referring just to courses that stress or include pornography, but to the whole range of subject matters and their mixtures, historical-modal, generic-thematical, modal-generical, historic-thematical, covering, for instance, 'The Literature of Fantasy,' 'Women in Literature,' 'The Black Man in Literature,' 'Patristic Elements in Anglo-Saxon Literature'" (136). These curious comments appear in the course of the argument that "the idea of literature is not an essentialistic idea, and no critical approach [i.e., the aes-thetic] can, without distortion, make essentialistic claims upon literature" (135). Hirsch believes that the heterogeneity regis-tered above demonstrates that "the aesthetic mode of perception can no longer be considered the governing mode, and the only vestige that remains of its former potency is the continued cheerful use of the word 'literature' in the titles of these courses" (136). Rejecting the previous overemphasis on the aesthetic, he insists that literary scholars have an ethical responsibility to tea-ch "valuable books of many sorts in addition to valuable works of art" (143). Aesthetic criteria are to be suspended—or at least relaxed—in a curricular version of open admissions. But the old standards are not to be forgotten. As Hirsch observes, "the best that is thought and said is not always said well, even if it ought to be" (136).

In this context, the remarks quoted above might be inter-preted merely as an unfortunate lapse into matters of personal taste, admittedly a politically insensitive lapse, but finally an irrelevant aside. At worst, they would suggest that Hirsch's allegedly historical view of the category of "Literature" is some-what underdeveloped. But to dismiss these comments as margi-nal would be an error.

Underlying these brief remarks is the conviction that those "valuable books" which women ("Women in Literature") and blacks ("The Black Man in Literature") have recently forced into the canon—or at least, into the classroom—are aesthetically in-ferior to those chosen over the years by essentially white, male, and privileged scholars; despite "cheerful" incantations, litera-ture from the underground is not valuable as art, in other words, it is not Literature. The brackets of fantasy and patristics serve not to camouflage the central issues but to highlight them; the effort to mask the troubling matters of sex and race is extra-ordinarily transparent. (I refrain from gratuitous speculation as to the groups or individuals Hirsch has in mind as the partisans of pornography; this reference remains extremely puzzling to me.) This "critique" of the aesthetic approach to literature mere-ly reinforces the claim that the traditional canon was formed on the grounds of strictly aesthetic judgment. This claim is precisely what is at issue.

Hirsch displaces the responsibility (or the blame) for these course changes away from teacher-scholars and onto students. This creates a gap between the alleged source of the changes—wary students who *instinctively* believe truth and value are lodged in "underground" courses—and the actual sponsors of the courses—faculty members at established institutions. Hirsch bridges this gap with expediency. By representing scholar-critics solely as pragmatic teachers adjusting to the market, he reduces scholarly interest to the survival instinct. The initial displacement underpins Hirsch's assumption that aesthetic value is no longer a central criterion for the selection of course materials (after all, students are interested in "relevant" texts, not poetic ones); with the second step, the complex and key role of the scholar is reduced to that of a commodity producer accommodating a new generation of consumers.

Hirsch is struggling to account for the fundamental shifts that are slowly taking place within literary studies as a discipline *and* to read them with as little emphasis on their discontinuity with the dominant pluralist paradigm as possible. Changes in the intellectual, social, political, and economic composition of the critical community have produced his persuasive efforts on behalf of the logic of inquiry. But only if specific references to this radically changed community of readers, and especially to their astonishing heterogeneity, can be avoided or discounted can it then be called upon to ratify the logic of inquiry with one disinterested (pluralist) voice. Hirsch must locate the source of innovations in the content of literary studies (and his focus on content is significant) outside the intellectual field of the academy: in political and social developments among students, above all, in an arena far removed from critical theory and theorists. This is the characteristic interpretative gesture I referred to in my discussion of pluralist commentators above, the tendency to consign power to a field that is wholly outside the discipline as such. Social power is acknowledged, but never as an imbalance or struggle internal to "science." Naming "instinct" as the ultimate source of the new course material enables Hirsch to absolve the teachers who are involved from any lapse in aesthetic judgment; we understand that although they teach these valuable books, they do not consider them to be valuable as art. The new material is thus put in its place. This is Hirsch's first reductive maneuver.

He then proceeds to supply a "new" definition of literature which is purely empirical, essentially cribbed from the reading lists his new colleagues are posting for their courses. This step allows him to take the new content of literary studies as a given ("the present realities," [135]), rather than as a problem that has theoretical import. This gesture actually depends on another assumption: the notion that the essence of the "underground" is contained in the *content* of what can be studied there. Hirsch simply ignores the possibility that students seek "truth" and "value" outside their institutions because of the *methods* (critical and pedagogical) which prevail within them. He assumes that when we transplant "underground" material into established institutions we do not destroy or damage the very qualities that made it valuable in the first place. Conversely, and perhaps more significantly, he seems to assume that this migration does not fundamentally disrupt any of the conventional practices of literary criticism. He imagines that students and teachers form an essentially unified, pluralist community.

Hirsch simultaneously applauds the broadening of the curriculum and evaluates the new texts negatively as "works of value that have little aesthetic appeal" (136). The category of the aesthetic is not deconstructed but merely deferred, subordinated to other aims, certainly, but powerfully reasserted in the apparently acquiescent observation that we must now teach "valuable books of many sorts" as well as great works of art. In a revealing phrase, Hirsch attributes the historical predominance of the New Criticism's aesthetic-intrinsic approach to "the *natural,* centripetal impulse of the discipline" to "[define] itself over against other disciplines" (137, my emphasis), and he concedes that the result was "one-sided" (138). He can thus admit the need for a corrective expansion of the domain of literature and conclude that "the process is entirely *natural*" (136, my emphasis). Both the theoretical prestige and formal status of the New Criticism and the purely aesthetic significance of the traditional canon are strengthened by this idealist critique, and Hirsch quickly moves to a series of analogies between contemporary critical issues and those faced by Matthew Arnold. The historical leap is justified by allusions to the "recurrent tensions of literary criticism" (139).[7] Such a naturalizing account obscures the ideological and political significance of this apparently natural "process" and the deep rifts it has produced in the critical community. In this vision, not only is the reading community united, but it is essentially ahistorical, unchanged since Arnold's day. In the most obvious sense, Hirsch's is a typically bourgeois analysis, attempting to dissolve history into the natural play of timeless human tensions.

Paradoxically, Hirsch's prescription for contemporary criticism takes as a major theme the critic's role *in* history, her necessary tie to historical developments. He appears to address a fundamentally historical issue when he traces the "idea of literature" through its historical mutations. This line of analysis recalls the decidedly un-Hirschian work of such critics as Pierre Macherey and Raymond Williams. Hirsch's rejection of aesthetic criticism's claim to predominance on the grounds that it is intrinsic seems to align him even more closely with these marxist critics. Yet Hirsch's ultimate aim is not to challenge the idea of literature but to defend both it and its Arnoldian mission "to civilize and humanize" (143).

The historicism of Hirsch's account masks an essentialist project. His brief historical sketch of "how the grand, broad, and noble conception of literature as *les bonnes lettres* disappeared and was replaced by the narrower, more decadent conception of *les belles lettres*" (141) is a mythic evocation of the Golden Age of Literature. It is aimed against historical "relativism" and functions primarily to clear the ground for an Arnoldian assertion of

---

[7]Although one would not immediately think of Paul de Man and E. D. Hirsch as allies, de Man takes up a similar position in "The Resistance to Theory." See Chap. 5 below.

the transcendent mean as an ahistorical paradigm: "The aims of criticism change with history only because the deeper principle of balance is absolute and therefore requires different applications at different times. This absolute principle of balance is the antique norm of human fulfillment—the classical ideal of harmony under which all the conflicting appetences of life are nourished, with none subjected to the tyrannical domination of another" (139). This abstract image of a discourse composed of conflicting appetences but freed from the domination of hierarchy is the ideal expression of Hirsch's empirical "opening" of the category of Literature to include "just about anything in print" (143). Hirsch's vision of harmony represses the increasingly bitter process by which the disciplinary boundaries established and enforced by traditional literary studies are being disrupted.

This exclusion lies at the heart of Hirsch's text. He could not simply ignore the problems of community and of persuasion; the crisis of the logic of inquiry demands both a theoretical response and a direct appeal to the general reader. But to make that appeal successfully from within the problematic of general persuasion, he must mask the true character of the division in the critical community. Thus, Hirsch belittles and misrepresents those who have criticized the aesthetic approach as an ideology, noting that the New Criticism "had a purely intellectual success greater than anything to be hoped for by those who attack it on the grounds that it has grown boring and can no longer meet the ideological and psychological requirements of the young" (128). Again, the "young," students, it seems, are the real source of discontent. "Those" who speak for them apparently have no other argument save the growing tedium (perhaps their own as well). Of course, the very possibility of "purely intellectual success," great or small, is precisely what is at issue here, just as the possibility of pure aesthetic value was above. But with the aesthetic held in reserve and neatly balanced by "valuable books" (and courses like "Women in Literature"), Hirsch reduces the hegemony of the aesthetic approach to a formal matter of scholarly excess and the "new definition" of literature to its simplest symptom. The resulting account of the transformation of the object of literary study enables him to continue to regard the aesthetic approach primarily as *"our* most powerful programmatic idea" (127, my emphasis) and to imply that those teachers—always distinguished from theoretical "relativists"—who are responsible for expanding the domain of literature are more or less in agreement with him. Only his abstract and apolitical account of the critical community makes this collapse of contemporary critical issues and Arnold's humanist project possible.

The ahistorical argument articulated in the invocations of the classical ideal and Arnoldian balance deflects the historical inquiry that rejects even the possibility of a purely aesthetic evaluation based on some invariant set of formal properties. This form of historical analysis is often a component of the work done by scholars writing and teaching at the margins of the canon. As Tony Bennett argues, this kind of inquiry seeks to identify "the historical formation of contemporary European *belles lettres* as a new and distinctive form of writing predicated on a new set of social, political and ideological relationships."[8] Hirsch obliterates all traces of this threatening work. Scholars and teachers who introduce "works of value with little aesthetic appeal" into the curriculum are presented as Arnoldian humanists recreating the tradition of *les bonnes lettres* and reasserting the (ahistorical) golden mean. Critics currently pursuing Bennett's questions—practically and theoretically—are ignored or represented as dogmatic relativists. From the Arnoldian vantage point he erects in place of their oppositional work, Hirsch can invoke the logic of inquiry.

Hirsch's text evades the problem of critical method as it is articulated by changes in the curriculum. What is thus achieved is an evasion of theory at the site of its practice. This is paramount in a theoretical text like Hirsch's where the effort is simultaneously to isolate and discredit an allegedly small group of irresponsible theorists and to shore up and discipline the general mass of scholar-teachers. The two groups must not appear to

[8]Bennett, *Formalism and Marxism*, p. 83.

overlap. Hirsch insulates his community of inquirers from the theoretical significance of its own pedagogy by misrepresenting the enormous critical pressure which is being placed upon the concept of Literature as a reversion to the "noble conception" of *les bonnes lettres*. He separates theory from content and divides contemporary theoretical issues from the (apparently) mundane practical changes that accompany them.

But the transformation in curricula has coincided with a general cognitive crisis that Hirsch prefers to represent only in terms of "decadent" French relativists and German hermeneuts. Growing numbers of scholars (and students) take a skeptical attitude toward Hirsch's pluralist logic of inquiry and show an unmistakable interest in continental criticisms of it. These scholars are suspicious of the process whereby "hypotheses" are transformed into "knowledge," and they have suggested, in a great variety of theoretical *and* practical ways, that this process may not be the simple or rational procedure Hirsch describes. They have begun, for example, to inquire into the possibility that the canonical texts identified thus far only as "valuable works of art" may also be "works of value" in a more social or ideological sense, that is, valuable in the service of particular ideological ends—ends not necessarily favorable to the whole of the expanded community of inquiry. The critique of the logic of inquiry is one aspect of a much broader social and political analysis.

Obviously, this analysis takes many different forms. The critical spectrum that spans the work of feminist critics and Derrida is a broad one. In fact, the heterogeneity of theoretical work adds another layer of complexity to the problems Hirsch faces as he seeks to resuscitate the logic of inquiry. But he obscures the possibility that these phenomena might be related. He argues for a continuity between Arnold's critical project and the teaching of "The Black Man in Literature," but not for a link between the latter and Foucault. Denying theory to those scholars who put it to practical use, he preserves an incongruously static image of a homogeneous critical community, an image that grounds his pluralist logic.

Yet even if Hirsch were not committed to the separation of theorists and practitioners (as well as theory and practice), he would find that serious difficulties attend any attempt to describe the various scholars engaged in critical analyses of the logic of inquiry. Raymond Williams has recently remarked that in literary studies in Great Britain, the current "crisis of the dominant paradigm and of its established professional standards and methods" has a "resonance well beyond the terms of a professional dispute. It is, in the fullest sense, one of the key areas in which a very general cultural crisis is being defined and fought out."[9] This assessment applies equally to the American context. The "opposition" that refuses the blandishments of the logic of inquiry is extremely diverse, even self-contradictory, comprising, as it does according to *The Aims of Interpretation*, everyone from Kuhn and Foucault to Derrida and (shadowy) marxists (H 147). We must add feminists and scholars of Afro-American literature to better understand pluralism's anxiety; the list could be extended.

My own analysis of this heterogeneous "movement" is complicated by the fact that only some of the factions within it can be said to work outside what I will call the problematic of general persuasion, that is, to be genuinely anti-pluralist. Hirsch gives the largest part of his book over to refuting those theoreticians who are least threatening to pluralist discourse in the United States. He does not name names; as we shall see, this in itself is remarkably common among pluralists. But the "relativistic themes [of] contemporary hermeneutics" (H 13), transplanted from their original philosophical contexts and operating as handmaidens to neo-romantic, new critical analyses, that Hirsch concerns himself with do not seriously challenge the hegemony of pluralist discourse. In *The Aims of Interpretation*, those critical positions that threaten to name the problematic of general persuasion, those scholars who are examining the margins of the literary canon in order to put into question the political and

[9]Raymond Williams, "Marxism, Structuralism and Literary Analysis," *New Left Review* 129 (September/October 1981), 54. Further references to this essay (RW) will be given in parentheses in the text.

ideological function of our "discipline," are only briefly represented, posed in cooperative, noncritical tableaux as the heralds of a return to *les bonnes lettres.*

Williams observes this tendency to confuse theories and theorists, and he contributes a typology of specific positions within the critical opposition. He focuses on marxism and structuralism, stressing that even *within* these discourses there are diverging tendencies, some wholly "compatible with the paradigm and thus with established professional arrangements" and others "not so assimilable and . . . indeed quite incongruent with the received definition" of literary studies (RW 54).

Williams's clarification is necessary because of the extremely ambiguous status of marxism and structuralism within the dominant paradigm. He writes: "Now, for various reasons, both Marxism and structuralism, in their different ways, have impinged directly on the paradigm and on its anomalies. Indeed the surprising thing is that in so many of their actual tendencies they have been accommodated, or have accommodated themselves, *within* that paradigm, where they can be seen as simply diverse approaches to the same object of knowledge. They can then be taken as the guests, however occasionally untidy or unruly, of a decent pluralism" (54). Hirsch's argument follows such an unusual trajectory and ends with such a surprisingly vulnerable account of persuasion in part because he does not recognize, as Williams does, the astonishing degree to which dogmatic relativists and oppositional critics will cooperate with pluralist discourse. In his desire to establish a pure standard, he sees all deviation, however minor, from the logic of inquiry, as an irretrievable fall from rationality. He is left demanding communal allegiance to ratify his "transcendent" logical paradigm and threatening an intellectual apocalypse if the community of inquirers resists.

"Decent pluralism" assumes a more compromised and less puritanical practice than that of the logic of inquiry, and it generates more oblique strategies. The decent pluralist realizes how much room there is to bargain, and he seizes the opportunity presented by the willingness of certain critical discourses to accommodate themselves to pluralism. A paradigm is not truly in crisis until it has lost its intellectual authority, its discursive confidence, and the administrative power to impose its analysis. (Williams remarks that the crisis in literary studies is in an early stage; in the Cambridge tenure battle which was the immediate occasion for his essay the dominant paradigm prevailed, and Colin MacCabe lost his position.) But as administrative power seeps away, the discourse is diluted and even revised; as it attempts to accommodate its critics and opponents, incorporating the "underground," it increasingly runs the risk of exposing its contradictions. We see this process in microcosm in Hirsch's text: the difficulty he evidences in handling the concept of the community at close range; his empiricist program to open the category of literature; his ultimate recourse to an impotent intellectual ultimatum: either respect the logic of inquiry or the discipline as discipline will cease to exist. These stumbles in an otherwise deft and complex analysis suggest both the difficulties engendered when persuasion is treated largely by evasion and the principal issues in the current struggle. But to establish fully the pluralist stake in this critical crisis, we must turn to one of Williams's decent pluralists and to a text less centered on hermeneutic issues, more extensively struggling with the concepts of community and persuasion, which constitute the problematic of general persuasion. When the logic of general persuasion collapses, what strategies does decent pluralism adopt to pacify unruly guests? How does it seek to control or contain those discourses it finds most difficult to accommodate?

In Wayne Booth's work, decent pluralism comes into plain view, asserting its anxiety and its minimum requirements in an open polemic. Booth specifies the pluralist polemic as a response to an intruder who disrupts the ethical balance of general persuasion. As we develop an analysis of this decent pluralism, we can simultaneously uncover the contradiction of the pluralist polemic and begin to construct an image of the antipluralist, the unwelcome guest in the decent paradigm of literary studies.

3 THE LIMITS OF PLURALISM ARE NOT PLURAL

> No reading, however outlandish it might appear, is inherently an impossible one. Consider, for another example, Booth's report that he has never found a reader who sees no jokes against Mr. Collins, and his conclusion that the text of *Pride and Prejudice* enforces or signals an ironic reading. First of all, the fact that he hasn't yet found such a reader does not mean that one does not exist, and we can even construct his profile; he would be someone for whom the reasons in Mr. Collins's list correspond to a deeply held set of values, exactly the opposite of the set of values that must be assumed if the passage is to be seen as obviously ironic. Presumably no one who has sat in Professor Booth's classes holds that set of values or is allowed to hold them (students always know what they are expected to believe).
>
> —STANLEY FISH, *Is There a Text in This Class?*

> To be useful, humanistic study, like any other *study*, needs to be believed.
>
> —E. D. HIRSCH, *The Aims of Interpretation*

Pluralists have been forced to define the limits of pluralism. As distasteful and intellectually compromising as this enterprise is, the menacing growth of those discourses Booth defines as what "pluralism is not—skepticism, relativism, solipsism, impressionism, subjectivism, Derridaesque *glasisme*" (B 407), leaves them with no alternative. In "'Preserving the Exemplar': or, How Not to Dig Our Own Graves," Wayne Booth confesses his reluctance. He claims to find the very phrase "the limits of pluralism" oxymoronic. But the "true pluralist" presses on.

The problematic of general persuasion appears in Booth's work both as a "theoretical ideology," in Althusser's phrase, and as a practice. Booth's position is at once fully elaborated and extremely simple. He would like to exclude from the community of pluralists anyone who refuses to embrace the problematic of general persuasion: he would like to exclude those who would exclude others.[1]

Booth's project shares certain features with Raymond Williams's effort. Like Williams, Booth wants to identify the unruly guests who cannot be accommodated in pluralism's community of the Many as One. Williams's aim is to distinguish those strains of marxist and structuralist discourse that support the dominant paradigm of literary studies from those that are incompatible with it; his primary concern is to foster the growth and development of the strains that challenge the paradigm. Booth wants to make the same critical distinction, but he hopes to silence all discourses that prove themselves incorrigibly antipluralist. There is a fundamental flaw in this project. At the very moment that the pluralist polemic comes into existence to defend the problematic of general persuasion, it falls into contradictions.

At one level, what is at issue is the form in which "poststructuralism" will be put into the discourse of Anglo-American pluralism. This formulation necessarily introduces the problem of what post-structuralism is. A "definition" of the term will emerge with more precision in the course of my account of antipluralism, though the former cannot simply be identified with the latter. For the present, keeping in mind Josué Harari's observation that "post-structuralism—like structuralism—invites a plural spelling" and his warning that no unified definition may be possible,[2] I use the term to designate roughly the same diverse group of contemporary theorists Hirsch indicates with his

[1] See "'Preserving the Exemplar,'" pp. 419, 421, 423, and passim.

[2] "Critical Factions/Critical Fictions," *Textual Strategies*, ed. Josué Harari (Ithaca: Cornell University Press, 1979), p. 27.

term "dogmatic relativism" and Booth with his list of what "pluralism is not." The widespread perception that certain critics represent something called "post-structuralism" is more important to my analysis at this point than a rigorous conceptualization of the definitive characteristics of post-structuralism as such. What is crucial is that pluralism has identified (constructed) a theoretical intruder that seems to embody principles antithetical to the pluralist problematic; nevertheless, it is imperative that pluralism incorporate this intruder. That is to say, pluralism must read post-structuralism as a pluralist discourse, must include it.

Pluralist anxiety and the pluralist construction of post-structuralism are thus not the simple effects of an intrusion by a foreign substance that might be isolated and named as the cause of the recent intensity of pluralist polemics. Throughout my argument, I have avoided an inquiry into the justice of any critic's identification (either by others or on his own behalf) with post-structuralism, and I do not want to become involved in the search for the essential post-structuralist position. The critical controversy turning on the question of which theorists most successfully avoid "domesticating" post-structuralism's "original" formulations seems rather ill-considered, given the prominence of the critique of origins and the concept of the trace in at least some of the texts in question. I do argue that Booth, Fish and de Man construct pluralist readings of post-structuralism; I do not mean, however, to imply that these readings can then be criticized from the perspective of the true post-structuralism. The critical struggle is precisely between contending readings. The pluralist polemic only tacitly admits this point. The pluralist cannot acknowledge all those forces that constrain the production of his text; nor can he name his own project properly or fully. (I stress that in this he resembles any other critic.) Foucault has suggested that "power is tolerable only on condition that it mask a substantial part of itself. Its success is proportional to its ability to hide its own mechanisms. Would power be accepted if it were entirely cynical? . . . would they accept it if they did not see it as a mere limit placed on their desire, leaving a measure of freedom—however slight—intact? Power as a pure limit set on freedom is, at least in our society, the general form of its acceptability."[3] Booth represents his project in precisely these terms; he sets out quite frankly, though with suitable misgivings, to set the limits of pluralism. Throughout, his emphasis falls on those freedoms—our individual, "monistic" approaches to the text—which are to be left intact. The plurality of the limits to be named is meant to guard this freedom.

But this setting of limits is a more problematic undertaking than Booth is willing to confess. He owns simply that he will exclude from pluralist discourse those critics who exclude others. The mundane problem that he does not address is the *procedure* by which he (or pluralism) would carry out a sentence of banishment on any particular critic. How would pluralism prevent the spread of skepticism, solipsism, and the various forms of the Derridaesque? What legislative or administrative move could control the errant productivity of these discourses?

Foucault remarks that the paradox of the juridical model of power as repressive force, the naysaying of the Law, is that such power is "in no condition to produce; capable only of posting limits, it is basically anti-energy. . . . It is incapable of doing anything, except to render what it dominates incapable of doing anything either" (HS 85). As we consider Booth's dilemma, it is tempting to suggest that his position is even more paradoxically and radically restricted. He appears incapable of doing precisely what he claims to do, incapable even of posting limits that could render post-structuralism "incapable of doing anything." But Foucault offers an alternative to this juridical model. Perhaps Booth's posting of limits does result in something other than the paralysis of the outlaw. Perhaps in presenting himself as the patroller of pluralism's borders, Booth conceals the most substantial part of his power. Thus our question evolves: how does Booth present his project in " 'Preserving the Exemplar' "? What

---

[3]Michel Foucault, *The History of Sexuality* (New York: Pantheon, 1978), p. 86. Further references to this volume (*HS*) will be given in parentheses in the text.

is merely evoked and what actually accomplished? What are the limits of the pluralist polemic?

When pluralism initially perceived the anti-pluralist potential (or threat) of post-structuralism, two possibilities immediately presented themselves. The first was simply to ignore the intruder. This option is the only one which preserves pluralist ideology in an uncompromised form, in a form that successfully conceals its anomalies and sustains its coherence. As practice, ignoring the intruder means silence, without exception.

One might argue that this path was taken as far as possible. The penetration of "French" theory into general literary discourse in this country was certainly slow, in some ways painful, and the resistance to it is by no means dead.[4] But post-structuralism proved capable of producing a flood of texts, and because no ideology allied with democratic capital can long ignore the productive (this being capital's great strength), studied pluralist silence gave way to a second course, albeit one contiguous with the first. Pluralism proceeded to ignore the anti-pluralism of post-structuralism, that is, to treat it as though it were yet one more pluralist discourse. And, as Williams argues, certain forms of post-structuralism cheerfully lend themselves to this accommodation.

This accommodation can take at least two forms: pluralism can either adopt post-structuralism's models or oppose its critique. Jonathan Culler's *Structuralist Poetics* is a classic of the former genre, the adoption and adaptation of critical innovation for an Anglo-American audience, and I would place the work of American literary "deconstructionists" such as Geoffrey Hartman and J. Hillis Miller in the same general category, though their "translation" differs from Culler's. The elisions and contradictions that characterize these efforts reveal the difficulties of

---

[4]See Mitchell, ed., *Against Theory*, and de Man, "The Resistance to Theory." Numerous reflections on the state of the controversy in literary theory have appeared in the mass media, including *Time* and *Newsweek,* the *Washington Post* and the *New York Times.*

translating structuralist and post-structuralist discourse directly into a pluralist idiom. Coherence is forfeit.[5] But the position of those who would oppose rather than adapt is even more problematic. How can one attack a fundamentally anti-humanist account of the reader, to choose the most obvious example, without acknowledging its anti-pluralism? Most efforts of this kind quickly mutate, transforming themselves spontaneously into pluralist polemics. Hirsch's work is a fairly good example of this second type of response, slowly fading from theoretical critique into polemic as it proceeds.

But this evolution is not recapitulated in Booth's essay. He seems to surrender all possibility of convincing his theoretical opponents in argument, alleging that "no demonstration of intellectual or cognitive incoherence or unverifiability will be decisive" (B 417). In this apparently defensive move, the true pluralist polemic is constituted, for the main thrust of pluralist polemic is never theoretical, but always moral or ethical. Hirsch's text, as we saw, is especially interesting because it is literally divided on this matter; he offers a detailed theoretical refutation of his opponents, then admits that the entire edifice depends upon persuasion rather than epistemology.

Booth seems to retreat, almost to the point of simply abandoning pluralism—and the problematic of general persuasion: "Any argument we might construct to prove that texts are substantive after all, or that the author has or had a self, or that we exist in a way invulnerable to Nietzsche's critique of our substance—any such argument will easily be dismantled by any confirmed deconstructionist, revealing at the end what was known in advance: that like everybody else we haven't a leg to stand on, that all the platforms have been blasted away, down down into an infinite abyss" (B 417). But these remarks are not a white flag. Booth's first priority is to maintain the fiction that the limits of pluralism are plural. Thus, pluralism cannot openly compete with various critical monisms in defense of one master theory,

---

[5]See Terry Eagleton, "The Idealism of American Criticism," *New Left Review* 127 (May/June 1981), 53–65, and Frank Lentricchia, *After the New Criticism* (Chicago: University of Chicago Press, 1980).

its own. Pluralism must instead appear a mediator between monisms. The suggestion that pluralism is "just another complex monism, . . . one umbrella to cover the various umbrellas," appears only to be hurried offstage: "You will be glad to know that you will hear no more about this intriguing question today" (414–15).

An adequate theoretical defense of pluralism would require the exposition of the problematic of general persuasion; but this is ideologically impossible. Booth must present his argument on a plane somehow discontinuous with the discourses of literary theory. The parallel with Hirsch's recourse to the transcendent logic of inquiry is precise. In Booth's terms, pluralism as such does not defend *a* theory of the text or *a* theory of the reader, but embraces many theories, a plurality of limits. Pluralism's concerns are not "cognitive but pragmatic" (B 418). This distinction allows Booth to appear uncommitted to any ideological position. It is true that he opposes the pragmatic to the cognitive rather than to the ideological, and, indeed, the word "ideological" appears very rarely in his text. But he maintains that his are those practical questions essential to the survival of our community; this is a matter above ideology, a matter too grave for dogma.

To prepare the ground for this move, Booth construes poststructuralism itself in practical rather than cognitive terms: "Many observers have noted in the latest wave, of which Mr. [J. Hillis] Miller is today's exemplar, a shift of emphasis from cognitive to practical or actional goals, particularly the goal of intellectual or spiritual liberation" (416). This gesture is analogous to Hirsch's attempt to view the curriculum through any prism save that of post-structuralist *theory*. It makes explicit the refusal to offer a theoretical retort to post-structuralism and permits Booth to proceed on a level "above" theory as he expounds the ethical principles of general persuasion.

Booth presents a pragmatic catechism of the would-be pluralist. He poses a series of questions that develops the problematic of general persuasion in its two complimentary aspects: as a rule of writing and as a rule of reading. He first asks: "Does [the critic] invite us all into a community of inquiry, or is he simply exhibiting his own new freedom? . . . Does he, *must* he, because of his presuppositions, condescend to or exclude this or that reader or group of readers? All criticism will *accidentally* exclude some readers. But some criticism excludes on principle. How many of those who read and think are ruled out from this new enterprise necessarily, by definition? These three versions are all part of the test of whether the critic is offering life to a community of *readers*" (419–20). Booth does not elect to name this "new enterprise." His interrogation is imbedded in an analysis that claims to be primarily disquieted by post-structuralism's romance with indeterminacy, which he defines as the "claim that understanding is not in any sense possible or desirable" (B 421). One might assume that these three questions are aimed at the solitary nihilist who persists in believing that truth or right reading is impossible and thereby threatens the possibility of literary knowledge. Yet while some of the rhetoric of Booth's essay is directed at these dark figures[6] ("Derridaesque *glasisme*"), his queries are here specifically concerned with a *discriminating* discourse rather than with a solipsistic one, a discourse that systematically excludes "some readers" or "group[s] of readers" ("How many?" he demands) while including others. "Accidentally" does not simply mean inadvertently in the sense that a critic might write a text and be unaware of the fact that his reading or theory must exclude a determinate set of readers. Obviously, this happens constantly. Booth means accidentally in the sense of randomly or unsystematically. As Hirsch puts it, "If a Marxist critic construes a text differently from a formalist critic, that is an irrelevant accident. No perspectival necessity requires him to do so. Marxist *critics* and formalist critics may be equally able to understand what a text means. What they usually differ in is the significance they give to that meaning" (H 44). Hirsch's portrait of the critic conflicts with Booth's vision of

[6]To be just, the contexts of its presentation have lent a certain plausibility to this rhetoric. The MLA session, "The Limits of Pluralism," which was eventually published in *Critical Inquiry*, included J. Hillis Miller as the "exemplar" of deconstruction; both Booth and Abrams suggest that solipsism and the end of communication are the primary threats Miller's "deconstructionist principles" present to literary scholarship. Miller seems (more or less) to agree.

the post-structuralist who excludes all potential readers. His notion of accidental differences seems designed to encompass a
much larger number of critics with much less rigidly exclusive
practices, and his example, the marxist critic versus the formalist
critic, suggests a motivation for the discriminations Booth objects to.

Booth's reticence concerning this condescending "new enterprise" is actually a pluralist inversion of Williams's rigorous attempt to distinguish the diverse forms of post-structuralism.
Booth's work seems to resemble Williams's, but a clarification
such as Williams seeks would damage pluralism to the precise
degree that it would serve the ends of cultural materialism.
Booth blurs his characterization of this threatening new enterprise for a purpose.

Nevertheless, though the transgressor appears as a somewhat
shadowy figure, the sin itself is vividly drawn. When Booth asks
if the critic offers "life to a *community* (my emphasis) of *readers*"
he assumes that the fact that "we" read welds us into a single
community that the critic—to the extent that he is a pluralist—
must honor. To condescend to or exclude any reader is a violation of this community. Thus it is that the readers of Booth's
imaginary community have no determinate qualities; it is precisely their anonymous generality (suggesting homogeneity)
which makes them an adequate test of the critic's commitment
to persuasion *in general.* To discriminate among them is forbidden. In this respect, Booth's representation of the critical community closely resembles Hirsch's.

This term "reader" belongs to a familiar lexicon: "first reading," "the common reader," "the informed reader," even, sometimes, "the reader's experience." This reader has now been challenged from all sides. Barthes dissolved him (along with the
concept of first reading, "primary, naive, phenomenal reading,
which we, long afterwards, have to 'explicate,' to intellectual-
ize") into the lexias of S/Z 16. The "resisting reader" accused him
of cultural imperialism or "phallic criticism"[7] or (a new epithet)
humanism. Althusser and Foucault, Kristeva and Lacan have

---

[7]Ellmann, *Thinking about Women* pp. 27–54 and passim.

decentered and displaced him (and his author, "a man speaking to men"). Still, this reader abides and with him his community of readers; his persistence is neither accidental nor insignificant, and Booth is committed to preserving his privilege. The defense of this reader is identical to the continued dominance of the problematic of general persuasion.

At the simplest level, Booth merely demands that no discourse *confess* its exclusionary rule—to others or to itself; silence is sufficient. The reason is obvious. Once a critic defies the generality of persuasion and identifies the ideological limits of his discourse in the form of those readers who, *by definition*, fall beyond his persuasive grasp, he undermines the human community of readers which grounds the practice of critical pluralism. To name one's limit is already to declare that some are beyond it, to acknowledge that some readers have distinguishing characteristics that set them apart, qualities that are not "human" in the sense of universal, transhistorical, or general, qualities that exclude them from the community of readers Booth envisions. These readers need not form an elite to trouble pluralism. The pluralist critic must exclude no one; he must aim at the persuasion of the entire community, taking each reader as a potential convert.

This commitment on the part of the critic writing is only half of our compact. Booth's community of readers is not entirely lacking in determinate qualities, completely anonymous and therefore homogeneous. These readers are in fact uniformly marked by a singular commitment to the possibility that *they can be persuaded:* the factions they compose erect no barriers to the possibility of persuasion. Booth puts this requirement in the form of a question to the critic as a reader of texts. "I would care even more . . . about whether the critic acknowledges community with the other *authors* [poets and critics] he treats" (B 420). There are several points collapsed into this phrase, not the least of which is an identification with the authors of the "classic" texts over and against all critical ephemera. M. H. Abrams, one of the exemplary pluralists Booth cites in *Critical Understanding*, takes a similar view: "Our prepossession is that, no matter how interesting a created text of Milton may be, it will be less inter-esting than the text Milton wrote for his fit readers though few" (*PR* 581). Such an identification (appropriation) suggests ques-tions about the celebratory mode in criticism, about literary eval-uation and the cultural values "embodied" in the high art of the English canon. At present I want only to emphasize the form Booth wants the acknowledgment of community to take. No longer is it a question of the persuasive stance one assumes in one's own writing; the problem of community has now become a question of the a priori consent with which one must *read:* the pluralist must read to be persuaded.

Booth here offers a negative example. Rather than an instance of right reading, he points to the kind of reading that does not "acknowledge community." Insisting that the pages of critical journals ("*Mayhem*" and "*Sadiste*") are marred by critical knifings and blasphemies,[8] Booth ascribes to the typically bloodthirsty commentator the pose of the bad reader: "What if I find a critic who habitually assumes that the authors of all other texts are less perceptive, less generous, less politically aware, less devot-ed to truth, justice, and the enhancement of life, than he is?" (B 420). There is a certain heat in this parataxis. And, again, the "Yale School" is not the sole object of Booth's wrath. Indeed, as a group, Miller and his colleagues do not characteristically charge that other critics are less "politically aware [or] less devot-ed to truth," as Miller's response to Booth demonstrates.[9]

Yet Booth introduces this bald leading question by alluding to the "strange and destructive new contra-cogito" of the "poly-semic" reader: "'I invent new readings, therefore, you, the au-thor, are not'" (420). As the question cited above follows close

[8]Booth employs metaphors of violence in his characterizations of the negative and meaningless aspects of contemporary critical debate: "slapping down," "killed off" (409), "slashing" (410), "knifed" (420).

[9]J. Hillis Miller, "The Critic as Host," *Critical Inquiry* 3:3 (1977), 439–47. The most political remark in Miller's essay is the claim that "'the impossibility of reading should not be taken too lightly.' It has consequences, for life and death, since it is inscribed, incorporated, in the bodies of individual human beings and in the body politic of our cultural life and death together" (440). Life and death quite overcome politics as the focus of Miller's concern.

upon this remark, Booth implies that it is directed at the nihilistic critic after all. This seems even more plausible when we recall the common charge that the "polysemic" critic belongs to just such an exclusive club, a closed circle playing a cryptic, "uncanny,"[10] private game (and writing a prose that is said to be more intimidating than illuminating to the outsider).

Again, Booth's equivocation is not accidental, but strategic; it actually begins at the beginning of his essay when he offers those "Un-new Critics, Wellek and Warren," as exemplars of the "pointless" (408, 410) criticism of the bad reader. They compose an unlikely, almost idiosyncratic illustration. But Booth's preference for a historical rather than a topical or contemporary example and his choice of a pointedly pre-Derridian discourse are clues that he is not simply concerned with the narrowly construed post-structuralism embodied in the work of Hillis Miller.

We have already observed that the critic Booth addresses on the questions of exclusion and condescension is a discriminating critic, admitting some readers and excluding others according to some unspecified principle. With the negative example of the bad reader, Booth seems to present a true nihilist, an isolato damning "the authors of all other texts" for a variety of intellectual and ethical failures. But despite the force with which Booth suggests his bad reader's splendid pride and isolation, he has placed an incongruous set of charges in the creature's mouth, and they fundamentally disrupt the image. Not only does this bad reader seem an unlikely colleague of Miller and company, but finally one cannot help but doubt that such a solitary figure could possibly exist anywhere. Critics given to digressions on politics, justice, and the enhancement of life tend to travel in schools (be they New Critical or marxist), which makes them another kind of problem entirely. Booth wants to solve this "other" problem, but he can only articulate it obliquely, as a corollary to his criticism of nihilistic tendencies within post-structuralism.

Booth weaves together two arguments. One is directed at the

[10]J. Hillis Miller offers the distinction between canny and uncanny criticism in "Stevens' Rock and Criticism as Cure," *Georgia Review* 30 (1976), 5–33 (part I), 330–48 (part II).

polysemic critic (solipsist, subjectivist) conceived as a loner and (literally) represented in "The Limits of Pluralism" by Miller. I would suggest that Booth recognizes that Miller's criticism is very far from being a radical threat; it is a neo-romantic assimilation of post-structuralist themes to an essentially idealistic, New Critical model.[11] As Williams observes, this avatar of post-structuralism *is* the dominant paradigm of literary studies and not in any sense a challenge to it.

The second strand of the argument is covertly aimed at critics who cannot be adequately represented as crusaders against the possibility of understanding. They are *anti-pluralists*, and they practice "exclusive" or "condescending" criticism. These critics have abandoned the normative pluralism that disables any analysis of the antagonistic struggle by which interpretative systems are put into practice and "literary" consciousness constituted. The dominant paradigm itself has become the object of study; the analyses that result fall "outside the paradigm altogether" (RW 64). In Foucault's terms, these anti-pluralists are not "afraid to conceive the Other in the time of [their] own thought"; indeed, they are bent upon it.

Booth's attempt to refer to these anti-pluralists, without actually naming them, gives his pluralist catechism its strangely abstracted quality. (I am aware that I too have drawn these figures in general rather than specific terms; I shall repair this omission

[11]Miller employs deconstruction strictly as a method for interpreting literary texts. Perhaps the clearest indication of his unwillingness to carry deconstructive practice to his discipline itself (in a manner that might parallel Derrida's philosophical intervention) is his position on the status of the canon: "I believe in the established canon of English and American literature and in the validity of the concept of privileged texts. I think it is more important to read Spenser, Shakespeare, or Milton than to read Borges in translation, or even, to say the truth, to read Virginia Woolf": cited in Carolyn Heilbrun, "Men, Women, Theories, and Literature," *Profession* 81 (New York: MLA, 1981), p. 25. One can only ask "important to whom?" Such "beliefs" in "privilege" are precisely the object of deconstructive investigations. In his review of Miller's *Fiction and Repetition* (*Nineteenth-Century Fiction* 38:1 [1983], 97–101), Robert Scholes brilliantly anatomizes Miller's deconstructive interpretations, which conceive reading as "a process of submission to authority" (97). In Miller's model, Scholes suggests, "we are grounded. No flights of Nietzschean fancy here. No grand Deleuzeans. Miller's texts have an outside and an inside, and the outside is forbidden" (100).

as we proceed.) Booth must obscure the identities of the bad reader and the bad writer in order to represent the diverse forms of post-structuralism as a unity or rather, as we shall see, in order to represent all forms of post-structuralism as one (potentially) pluralist discourse.

Neither the "Yale School" nor Wellek and Warren represent Booth's nemesis; both Miller and the Un-new Critics are monists, critics who "hope to resolve all contests over concepts with a victory for the one true view" (B 410). Booth's real concern is the threat presented by any anti-pluralist criticism that is *not monistic.* The pluralist can tolerate (even embrace) the intolerant monist, be he a deconstructionist or an Un-new Critic. But the pluralist must exclude the faction which theorizes its practice as fundamentally and necessarily exclusive, in the sense of being irreconcilably closed to certain readers, and which, consequently, *no longer seeks to persuade them.* Such a faction is anti-pluralist precisely to the degree that it is non-monistic. The monist seeks to persuade everyone to one (his) way of seeing (reading); he is always already a pluralist because his practice assumes the possibility of general persuasion. He produces the controversy, the free and open debate in the pursuit of conversion, which *is* pluralism (in the academy as well as in the liberal democracy).

Booth attacks the critic who willingly abandons certain elements (the political overtone is apt here) of the community and theorizes their exclusion. This anti-pluralist believes general persuasion is impossible. But Booth's anger is not a matter of local sympathy for those individuals who might be excluded in this manner *(how* is a problem we will return to). The anti-pluralist endangers the entire pluralist community because she undermines the problematic of general persuasion which grounds that community.

The theoretical possibility of general persuasion rests upon a concept of the "human" (reader) as a general or universal category that escapes or transcends the incidental conditions of class, gender, race: an acontextual essence, not unlike the core of determinate meaning. The anti-pluralist claims to expose this

human reader as a creature with determinate and limited interests, "special interests" concealed in a definition of the human
that happily incorporates and generalizes them as the "natural."
She suspects the rationality of pluralist debate and the logic of
inquiry and posits hidden irrationalities and power relations as
the deep structure of the problematic of general persuasion.
"Culture" here denotes antagonistic relations of domination and
subordination rather than a canon of texts and interpretations
that celebrate the essential or the best in "man"; Hirsch's call for
humanists to "humanize and civilize" takes on an "imperialistic"
cast he did not intend when he conceded "humane studies have
a natural tendency to be imperialistic" (H 137).

This feature of anti-pluralism especially troubles the pluralist.
As long as the canon stands as a monument to traditional western values and those values enjoy an unassailable hegemony,
those who professionally disseminate and explicate literary texts
are perceived as the guardians of a common inheritance. But
now that canon and the very concepts of literature and man are
being reevaluated as part of a critique of the operations of culture in reproducing social relations; in such a context, the guardians may be accused of complicity or, worse, of playing the
leading role in what Balibar and Macherey call the "academic or
schooling practice which defines both the conditions for the
consumption of literature and the very conditions of its production as well."[12] In this context, Booth's concern about critics who
accuse others of being "less politically aware and less devoted to
truth [and] justice" begins to take on a new significance.

Booth is elusive concerning the identity of the bad reader
presented above, but candid about the distress he feels reading
such self-righteous, divisive criticism. It is a form of "injustice"
born of double standards. To restore justice, we must shun "any
critical method inviting the use of double standards" and give
each critic "his due," just the amount of critical attention "his
statements deserve as they claim a passport into the country of

[12]Etienne Balibar and Pierre Macherey, "On Literature as an Ideological
Form," *Oxford Literary Review* 3:1 (1978), 5.

debate" (421, 420). If we fail in this, we must "abandon hope for our common enterprise" (421).

Understandably, no example is offered of a method that advocates a double standard, and it is not entirely clear how a method might "invite" (an ambiguous word with its overtones of covert welcome) such a procedure. But an example would not further Booth's effort to fuse the diverse forms of post-structuralism and thus to incorporate them into his pluralist community. His benign assumption is that critical "mayhem" could only be the result of double standards applied to equally "deserving" authors. The mirror proposition, namely, that many standards are being applied in a community that is doubled and redoubled into many exclusive camps that are in no practical sense equally deserving, is simply unthinkable.

Of course, the unthinkable is a concept Booth cannot articulate within his pluralist discourse. The unthinkable implies a limit, an irreducible boundary beyond which a given reader or group of readers, burdened by historically determinate interests, can never travel. This limit is inadmissible; pluralism produces a persuasive context in which the notion of the strictly unthinkable cannot be sustained.

Booth denounces the idea of a rigid, "single standard" for criticism: "the test of the single standard does not require that all critics be judged by the same standard, only that the critic agree to be judged by the standard he himself applies to others" (421). This could be complicated. One imagines the Freudian critic, reading the "Derridian" critic, trying to judge him not by his own (Freudian) standards, but by the "Derridian's" own ("Derridian") standards, which, of course, he (the Freudian) has access to primarily in the form of the very ("Derridian") essay he is to judge, somehow justly. This is not precisely what Booth means, though literal "justice" would require just such a reading. Booth's single standard poses as a matter of mere procedure. The bad reader refuses to "acknowledge community with the other authors he treats," habitually assuming a moral and intellectual superiority (distance). He reads, but he refuses to be persuaded. Booth offers an antidote, though it falls somewhat

short of his own strictures. Presented as a neutral rule for justice, it actually embodies Booth's own critical program: "All critics, at least all who write and publish, implicitly ask us to understand them and claim that they have understood others. I
therefore have a right to be skeptical about any critic's claim that
understanding is not in any sense possible or desirable. . . .
Nothing I have said or anyone can say about vitality makes any
sense unless we all believe that people can understand each
other, sometimes, and that they should always try to understand" (421–22). Booth is elaborating the notion of persuasion as
a self-reflexive act. The pluralist must pursue general persuasion
when she addresses the community in writing, and she must
approach the authors she reads in a *self*-persuasive mode. Justice, giving "your neighbor's monism a fair shake" (423), is nothing less than the willingness to be persuaded, *to persuade oneself*,
and the reward is a role in our common enterprise.

The "sometimes" with which Booth qualifies the possibility of
understanding—"people can understand each other, sometimes"—operates as an explanation for the disagreements that
fill the pages of critical histories. Booth would surely accept the
same "some" to modify his universalizing term "people," but
the emendation would have only an "accidental" significance:
some people are "accidentally" excluded from the criticism of
Daniel Deronda, for example, because they have never read the
novel. But all such accidents are contingent and easily corrected.
The generality here is absolutely essential; "people" is a euphe-
mism for the general reader.

Booth seeks a general principle that can guarantee our common vitality. Vitality is imagined to be a necessarily common, in
the sense of equally shared, possession: "If my continued vitality as a critic depends finally on yours, and yours on mine, it
is clear that our life together is threatened whenever either of us
fails to *attempt* justice to the other" (my emphasis; B 420). The
anti-pluralist vision of antagonistic, contending systems is ignored; Booth's is not a zero-sum community.

The standard is neatly circular. Those who ask us to be persuaded by them must, in turn, agree to be persuaded by us. Of

course, success cannot be assured in every case. Nothing I have said is meant to suggest that the problematic of general persuasion requires that every individual who "reads and thinks" be convinced by every critic she encounters. On the contrary, the plural failures of persuasion in particular cases are essential because they represent the freedom of individual critics within the community. The critical commitment to the possibility of general persuasion, to the theoretical availability of each individual to be convinced in argument, is the crux. The critic who attempts justice is one who asserts the possibility of general persuasion. Failures do not bankrupt the undertaking; the effort alone produces sufficient regard, binding each reader to her fellows and sustaining our life together. Yet, despite this optimistic reading, the gap left when persuasion fails and fails, again and again, *is* problematic for pluralism. It cannot be closed; but its significance can be largely obscured by emphasizing a crucial middle term: understanding. Pluralism requires a fiction that can simultaneously guarantee the homogeneous unity of the community and account for the unbroken stream of disagreements which is the history of literary criticism. The problematic of general persuasion allows for failures of persuasion only. But by enforcing the rules of reading and writing, it assures general *understanding* without failure.

Because understanding plays a pivotal role in pluralist discourse, misunderstanding is a source of endless fascination. Booth has argued that deconstruction is "plainly and simply parasitical" on "a base of shared knowledge," the obvious or univocal reading of the text it purports to deconstruct.[13] Parasitism is a deadly dependence. But "parasitic" connotes, for Booth, a form of bad faith whereby the deconstructive critic recognizes the obvious reading, then fabricates a not obvious reading, essentially as a labored afterthought, and finally attempts to pass off the ersatz version as his reading. Booth accuses deconstruction of perversely manufacturing misunder-

---

[13]Wayne Booth, "M. H. Abrams: Historian as Critic, Critic as Pluralist," *Critical Inquiry* 2:3 (1976), 441.

standing where once there was none, of producing a distorted object, rather than accounting for the found object, the poem itself.

This productive distortion is one source of Booth's aversion to meeting the argument of post-structuralism with explicit counterargument on the level of theory. Any method, to the extent that it takes pluralism as an object, generates a discontinuity that cuts it off from debate *with* pluralism; it has begun to debate pluralism itself in terms both foreign and explicitly hostile to it. Booth's charge that certain critics "exclude this or that reader or group of readers . . . on principle" (B 419) springs from this conjuncture. The deepest trace of this discursive discontinuity is the figure of misunderstanding.

Misunderstanding is a central topos in the pluralist polemic; it marks the border where theoretical struggle meets political polemic. But it appears in two guises: one a misleading thematization, a red herring of sorts; the other a deep figure that generates the logic of the pluralist attack on post-structuralism.

Misunderstanding first appears as a minor theme of anxiety. Abrams remarks in a typical passage: "I want, in the time remaining, to present what I make out to be the elected linguistic premises, first of Jacques Derrida, then of Hillis Miller, in the confidence that if I misinterpret these theories, my errors will soon be challenged and corrected."[14] He later confesses that he expects Miller's reply will "express some natural irritation that I, an old friend, should so obtusely have misinterpreted what he has said in print about his critical intentions" (D 437). The congenial tone that belies the words and insists "we *really do* understand one another" is characteristic. This thematic invocation of misunderstanding is important insofar as it marks a real anxiety about pluralism's capacity to comprehend post-structuralist innovations and integrate them into its practice. But the anxiety of misunderstanding remains a minor theme. It sometimes degenerates into bad faith; more often a declaration of misunder-

---

[14]M. H. Abrams, "The Deconstructive Angel," in "The Limits of Pluralism," *Critical Inquiry* 3:3 (1977), 428. Further references to this essay (D) will be given in parentheses in the text.

standing is a theatrical gesture that signifies the general obscurity and arrogance of post-structuralist discourse. (This, naturally, happens less often between old friends, though very old friends can get away with it.)

Pluralism works the theme of misunderstanding into a powerful figure in which misunderstanding is seen to imply the unfading possibility of understanding, even as understanding becomes the logical pivot of general persuasion. Hirsch illustrates the leap from understanding to the ironic trap generated by the figure of misunderstanding: "Whenever I am told by a Heideggerian that I have misunderstood Heidegger, my still unrebutted response is that I will readily (if uneasily) concede that point, since the concession in itself implies a more important point, namely, that Heidegger's text *can* be interpreted correctly, and has been so interpreted by my accuser" (H 6). There are countless variations on this analysis, all built on an argument from general persuasion. It locates in post-structuralism (Derrida is the most commonly cited culprit) the argument that language does not "work," that meanings cannot be communicated, and consequently, that everything is constantly in giddy, relativistic flux. Abrams finds a great contradiction in the fact that in Derrida's "deconstruction of logocentric language he assumes the stance that this language works, that he can adequately understand what other speakers and writers mean, and that competent auditors and readers will adequately understand him" (D 573). This is not the moment to defend *Of Grammatology* as a revelation of just this "working" of language, to which Derrida is unceasingly attentive. But however inadequate Abrams's comment is as an account of deconstruction, his remarks do point (blindly) toward the real threat post-structuralist strategies can pose to pluralism's ideological problematic.

Hirsch offers an exceptionally apt illustration of the full argument. He insists (sounding uncannily like Booth—the pluralist polemic can exhibit remarkable unity) that "to treat an author's words merely as grist for one's own mill is ethically analogous to using another man merely for one's own purposes," and he reformulates Booth's theory of reading as "acknowledging community," naming it the "golden rule" at the heart of the "ethics of language" (H 91).

> "When you write a piece of criticism, do you want me to dis-regard *your* intention and original meaning? Why do you say to me 'That is not what I meant at all; that is not it at all'"? . . . It was not surprising that M. Barthes was displeased when his inten-tions were distorted by M. Picard. Few critics fail to show moral indignation when their meaning is distorted in reviews and other interpretations of their interpretations. But their sensitivity is of-ten one-way, and in this they show an inconsistency amounting to a double standard—one for their authors, another for them-selves. [H 91]

The originary moment of this theoretical move is Picard's "mis-understanding" of Barthes's work, identified here as Barthes's intention. The failure of understanding is the essential token of this argument: as one defines this failure, so one establishes orthodox pluralist practice.

We have seen that pluralism cannot tolerate the concept of the unthinkable; all the energy born of pluralist indignation strives to exclude this term. The centrality of the figure of misunder-standing is bound to this exclusion. Pluralism's reader is defined as an essential category, and the critical community is extrapo-lated from him. His community of readers provides no site for the outsider, the other, and no account of her ontology save personal caprice, deviance. Literary study seeks only to produce "a verifiable truth, what Northrop Frye calls scientific knowl-edge—that is, a knowledge sufficiently systematic both to cover the territory and *to be teachable to all who will take the pains to follow*" (B 414, my emphases).

In this context, to misunderstand is to acquire a very problem-atic status. All readers who take the pains to follow are capable of understanding; whoever fails is at fault. Picard has failed to understand Barthes. But in pluralist polemic, the theme of mis-understanding is quickly turned to advantage, working by in-version to produce understanding. In the pluralist context, ev-eryone understands. Virtually no commentator will write: I do not understand. Here are my questions. (There is of course a material constraint operating here: journals publish *answers*.)

The pluralist surmises that misunderstanding is not determinate but accidental, and in that sense, general, accidentally finding expression in a *particular* individual. Doubtless, Picard has simply not read Barthes closely enough. From an individual instance of misunderstanding, the pluralist infers the possibility of *general* understanding. The unarticulated step is from understanding as a specific (limited) achievement in a determinate setting to general understanding, universally available without limits. Hirsch's delight in finding Barthes "indignant" at Picard and his own willingness to confess a misinterpretation of Heidegger both stem from his confidence that Picard—like anyone else—*can* understand Barthes, and he Heidegger. Similarly, Abrams chides Derrida, not because his language fails and he is misunderstood, somehow "indeterminate," but because his language works, because Abrams *understands*.

Understanding always expresses a power relation, in this case, the power to accommodate certain forms of post-structuralist discourse as "diverse approaches to the same object of knowledge, . . . guests . . . of a decent pluralism"; the academy accommodates the "underground." When Hirsch attributes a hypocritical indignation to Barthes because the latter seems to want to be understood by Picard, he is simultaneously accusing him of acceding to the principle of general persuasion, accusing him of being a pluralist *malgré lui*. Pluralism incorporates the monistic text by this understanding: the pluralist takes his understanding—or the accusation of misunderstanding, as in Hirsch's encounter with the Heideggerian—as a sign that the post-structuralist does actually operate within the problematic of general persuasion. The anti-pluralist, outside this problematic, declines all indignant postures in order to claim that understanding is a limited, determinate accomplishment. That Picard misunderstood Barthes does suggest that Barthes can be understood. But it does not follow that Picard is among those who can understand him. The anti-pluralist traces the limit of his discourse across the ground of understanding as well as persuasion.

The problematic of general persuasion produces a context in which "everyone understands" by establishing an opposition between the statement "I believe" ("I am persuaded") and the statement "I understand." The grammar of pluralism can produce the statement: "I am not persuaded" because it has rendered "I do not (cannot) understand" unutterable. This structure guarantees that understanding and belief will not appear as a single action. The structure of the argument precisely reproduces Hirsch's distinction between knowledge and value. The opposition between belief and understanding makes it possible to claim "I understand but I am not persuaded." This sign marks the place of the pluralist subject and prevents the erosion of the pluralist consensus along the deep faults that separate monism from monism. As long as each critic approaches each reader in his audience as a *possible* convert, the reader will have the option to understand.

When Booth accuses the anti-pluralist of elusive, condescending discourse, of not trying to persuade, he reads the breakdown in understanding, misunderstanding, as a symptom of the critic's refusal to try to persuade. The assertion of understanding is identical to the offer to readmit the wayward into a "reconstruct[ed] critical commonwealth" (B 423). As Booth becomes the pluralist-as-host, he affirms his willingness to accommodate post-structuralism, based on a reading in which it too is a pluralist discourse, persuasively pursuing its monism, which everyone understands.

My counter to this line of reasoning will not be to reverse its founding assumption, explaining that Abrams and company do not understand Derrida and proceeding from there with an explication that will finally make them understand. Critics who undertake to make post-structuralism *lisible*, understandable and persuasive according to the terms of pluralist ideology, play into Booth's hands, reanimating the problematic of general persuasion. The figure of misunderstanding by which pluralism seeks to reconcile post-structuralism to its own paradigm—and which any pluralist effort to render post-structuralism must employ—evades the problem of reciprocity. A reciprocal agreement (or understanding) exists only when two parties have reached an understanding together, that is, when they have agreed to agree. Reciprocal understanding collapses together or weds persuasion and understanding; when a critic succeeds in bringing a reader into agreement with her own understanding of her material, she has persuaded him. Understanding and belief are simultaneous.

However, there is a form of understanding that does not attend to the matter of agreement between parties. In sharp contrast to the reciprocity among insiders who have agreed upon an understanding, we find the critical, sometimes even hostile, understanding of the outsider. This "understanding" bears no resemblance to the submissive act that Booth idealizes as finding "our freedom" by "entering someone else's mind" or "by molding our minds in shapes established by others" (422). It characteristically appears as a gesture of demystification, aggressively demonstrating that its object is not what it claims to be but something else entirely. In Boothian terms, this strategy of understanding often begins paradoxically with the assumption that the object does not (cannot) understand itself. Analysis proceeds as a symptomatic rereading that explicitly locates itself in opposition to the conclusion or understanding offered by the author of the text or by other critics allied with the author.

Such a procedure plays havoc with certain pieties concerning intention. But it also exposes the incoherence of pluralism's claims for understanding. Booth argues for the ethical priority of a *submissive* understanding. Yet the quintessential form of the pluralist polemic is that of demystification. We see this in even the briefest asides; Booth notes drily, "There is a claim to novelty in much of this that puzzles me" (417). The structure of the pluralist polemic conforms to the model of nonreciprocal understanding. Pluralism recognizes post-structuralism's theoretical protests, its uncanny attempts to decenter, its *intentions,* only to sweep them aside; despite the determined resistance of post-structuralism, pluralism *understands* it. The figure of misunderstanding is an aggressive inversion of (pluralism's interpretation of) post-structuralist theory: pluralism infers general understanding from specific (mis)understanding(s) and accuses post-structuralism of incoherence, of not understanding itself. With this constructed understanding, pluralism exposes (produces) post-structuralism as a pluralist discourse.

I have deliberately avoided locutions that might imply that pluralism only "thinks" that it understands post-structuralism; there is no delusion here. Any such opposition between true and false understanding would undermine my claim that understanding is never the neutral gesture pluralism requires it to be; it can never be evaluated on a simple scale of purity or accuracy. As Derrida points out, it is not a question of true or false but of the play of forces. Understanding is either a reciprocal act based on agreement between parties (critic and critic or critic and text)—in which case, to understand is to be persuaded, and the work of the critic locates itself in continuity with the tradition he takes as an object of study; or, understanding is a demystifying act that claims authority or power over its object—in which case, to understand is to remain unpersuaded, and the work of the critic seeks to interrupt the tradition that she takes as an object of study, to initiate a break with that tradition. The latter practice puts an end to "innocent reading."

My description may seem to imply a preference for understanding based upon persuasion; this is not the case. There is a significant distinction to be made between the two forms of understanding I have described, but at no point is it a matter of the greater truth value of one over the other as interpretation. Nor is that understanding which assumes persuasion in fact less aggressive or productive an act than the hostile understanding of the unpersuaded. The importance of contrasting them is to demonstrate that the concept of persuasion assumed in these two positions differentiates them and thus determines their relative discursive force in contemporary debate.

When a post-structuralist discourse takes the pluralist problematic as an object of study, the "understanding" produced by the analysis is often not reciprocal. And ironically, pluralism's response to post-structuralism repeats post-structuralism's critique of pluralism. My own account of Booth's essay as a pluralist polemic unconsciously exfoliating the problematic of general persuasion falls into the same category. What differentiates these analyses is their representations of their own practices. Pluralism insists on understanding as a submissive gesture in order to defend the ethics of general persuasion. Yet, under the cover of this idealized version of understanding, Booth offers a radically discontinuous reading of the post-structuralist problematic. To do otherwise, to admit that understanding is marked by reciprocity or to argue that post-structuralism is not a potentially pluralist discourse—this is to become an anti-pluralist. Understanding, detached from belief, from persuasion, must be preserved in order for Booth to generate the theoretical space that contains his reading, thus to escape the powerlessness of the merely negative censor; only this *reading* of post-structuralism can preserve the pluralist community. Booth insists that critics who in their writings exclude some readers, by definition, and in their readings take their distance and censure some of their peers rather than acknowledging community with them, will be judged by the factional standards they themselves apply and consequently excluded from the pluralist community. But he cannot inflict this ultimate penalty: it is, in practice, impossible and, equally important, it is theoretical suicide for pluralism.

The crisis of the problematic of general persuasion has produced a contradiction in the form of the pluralist polemic. First, "we" who read are defined such that we constitute a critical community that is *essentially* one. We must protect and nurture "our life together" and "our vitality." Our unproblematic respect for general persuasion renders each of us—from Abrams to Miller—a pluralist. There is no "full romping textual rapist" among us, as Booth remarks (B 413). But belying this definition of the reader and the ethical reading community, the pluralist polemic attempts to discipline and control the not-we, the other, the reader who flouts general persuasion. This legislative or administrative impulse contradicts the essentialism of the definitions from which it is paradoxically derived. In the very act of *recognizing* the anti-pluralist, pluralism begins to sacrifice its coherence. Booth is in the compromising position of destroying pluralism in order to save it, and he is not altogether unaware of his peril.

We have observed Booth's attempts to blur the faces of those critics who seem to be dangerously close to expulsion, the objects of his scolding analysis. Are they Wellek and Warren? Hillis Miller? Barthes?[15] Booth is loath to name his opponent because in the act of purifying the community, in the act of expulsion, the common enterprise is betrayed. The limit of pluralism, once it is invoked to exclude any critic, denatures pluralism itself. The equivocations and inconsistencies in Booth's identification of these critics save him another precious piece of ideological territory. He avoids the implication that any historically determinate conditions might cause a group of critics to break away from the pluralist community of readers. The sole exception is Booth's use of the word "bourgeois." It appears only twice, first in the phrase "bourgeois political control" (416) and then in the remarkable suggestion that "We can expect a criticism that is 'democratic,' anti-bourgeois in the worst sense: egalitarian, reductionist, egocentric, self-indulgent . . ." (423). Booth's vision of the bourgeois is not developed; the term is essentially a label that does very little intellectual work in the course of his analysis. Nevertheless, with these qualifications, its presence suggests that Booth has an inkling that his opponent is "anti-bourgeois." This is not a hunch he can pursue. He limits his analysis to the ethical practice of the individual critic; the inevitable result is that explanation is forced to the level of personality and, as such, in keeping with professional conventions, must be ignored. This silence implies that only irresponsibility or ego or perversity could cause the bad reading and the condescending, exclusive writing of the anti-pluralist. Still, there is no hint as to the kind of writing that can successfully exclude readers, for the obvious reason that such writing cannot

[15]The latter haunts Booth's essay, inevitably chosen to illustrate a general point, but always with the studied casualness of one who wishes to appear to be taking the example nearest to hand.

exist within the terms of the problematic of general persuasion. Finally, the anti-pluralists are as anonymous and homogeneous as the general readers who have remained within the community; Booth ends by shrugging them into facelessness: "Those critics—whoever they really are" (423). The corrosive impact of the social and political critique of pluralism inherent in the anti-pluralist's rejection of the problematic of general persuasion is tightly contained.[16] Above all, the road home is left open.

Booth finishes by propping the door open, inviting all the recalcitrant to enter a "reconstruct[ed] critical commonwealth," a commonwealth to include "deconstructionists and mysreaders [sic] and intentionalists and cognitivists and various other monists" (423), indeed, any monist, so long as she is committed to a contentious criticism founded on the generality of persuasion. But

> if they are to show *us* something they must themselves count on our sense of justice, our belief in the possibilities of understanding, and our openness to many modes[.]
> It is by no means easy to decide which new flames will fatally consume that which they were nourished by. But we can be sure that those critics—whoever they really are—who live by the sword of dysjustice [sic] and dysunderstanding [sic] will perish by that sword. If the first commandment issued by my commonwealth is "Pursue some one chosen monism as well as you can," the second is like unto it: "Give your neighbor's monism a fair shake." [B 423]

This musing over the biblical sword of injustice is slightly incongruous, a peculiarly violent image for the peacemaker and

---

[16]This is one aspect of the generally ahistorical and abstract cast of Booth's argument. In this it is typical of pluralist polemics. The most cogent illustration of this strategy appears in Booth's survey of historical skepticisms (pp. 417–18). The multiplication of skeptics from the past—Socrates, Hume, Santayana, Burke, Peirce, Dewey—serves the anti-historical claim that post-structuralist "skepticism" is simply more of the same, and, consequently, neither threatening nor politically or socially significant. We've weathered such storms before; the sky is not falling. Anything that is specific to post-structuralist discourse is painted over, and the possibility that deconstruction/post-structuralism is a determinate, coherent phenomenon of a specific historical conjuncture is ignored.

an oddly bleak note given that even the mysreaders have been welcomed into the ethical commonwealth. Ultimately, the sword seems to threaten oblivion: the anti-pluralists, "whoever they really are," will be ignored, which is death to the critic. But Booth recognizes that he cannot post the limits of pluralism with the edge of his sword. The oblivion imaged by the sword of "dysjustice" vows a return to an option pluralism long ago abandoned, the attempt to ignore the intruder. This threat depends upon a shade, the homogeneous critical community that would act with a single impulse to preserve a life together.

"'Preserving the Exemplar'" discloses the tremendous cunning and productivity of pluralism and the discursive strength inhering in its capacity for innovation. With a single creative misunderstanding—the figure of misunderstanding—it generates a place and a voice for post-structuralism *within* pluralism, a reading of post-structuralism as a monism that conforms to the problematic of general persuasion. The refusal to counter post-structuralism as a theoretical rival appears as a ploy. Booth has reinscribed the theoretical argument he seemed to disdain. His practical position as a pluralist is identical with the familiar account of the cognitive status of the reader and of the text, a traditional account absolutely challenged by many who speak in the idiom of post-structuralism. Booth regains everything he seemed unwilling even to argue, but under the rubric of pluralism's ethical community rather than than of literary theory. Booth's critical community is nestled in a tautology: the persuasive critic is the critic who has been persuaded. One demonstrates that one is willing to be persuaded by having been persuaded. By this perverse turn upon itself, the hegemony of pluralism is reasserted over the commonwealth of deconstructionists, mysreaders, and intentionalists. Pluralism reappears as a monistic insistence on the general reader, on an image of the unity and homogeneity of the critical community, and on respect for intention, which is construed as the author's original meaning.

Booth only seems to be in retreat: "If you can't beat 'em, join 'em" (418). But "to join" has a transitive use: to put or bring together; to unite or make continuous. The post-structuralist can accept the joint Booth has fashioned (as Hillis Miller is strategically present to do in "The Limits of Pluralism"); he can refuse the role of the parasite and attend to the objects that have traditionally populated the field of literary criticism, rather than to the processes by which that field is determined and its limits produced and reproduced. The problematic of general persuasion requires only this contending; this *is* our life together.

The alternative is sketched by Williams: one can refuse the place set for the unruly guest. Booth, in a sense, is less anxious about this prospect than Hirsch. The latter closes his essay with a warning: "To be useful, humanistic study . . . needs to be believed" which has the unmistakable overtones of a plea. Hirsch demands that his readers be persuaded to a particular logic; Booth's discourse clarifies that we need only to cling to the ethics of persuasion. But Booth projects the reassuring image of a stable community that will deal harshly with those who decline to honor its rules; the commandments are handed down with an equally unmistakable tone of authority. Booth is as conscious as Hirsch of the crucial role played by the community. Those called "post-structuralists," as diverse and contradictory as their practices are, will either accept the place offered within the pluralist paradigm or move the critique of the problematic of general persuasion forward. We shall now consider one post-structuralist response, a response that has the form of an argument for persuasion and yet takes pluralism as the object of its own polemic.

4 "NOT TO WORRY": THE THERAPEUTIC RHETORIC OF STANLEY FISH

> Everyone is obliged to practice the art of persuasion.
> This includes me, and persuasion is the art that I have
> been trying to practice here.
> —STANLEY FISH, *Is There A Text In This Class?*

Stanley Fish's *Is There a Text in This Class?* takes as its subject the anxiety and resistance characteristic of Anglo-American pluralism as it confronts an intruder variously named deconstruction, relativism, and post-structuralism. This anxiety is quintessentially expressed by the problem of the text; the pluralist's tenacious pursuit of a determinate text that "'always remains the same from one moment to the next'" (F vii) is its most prominent symptom. By tracing the practical and theoretical process whereby he "stopped worrying and learned to love interpretation," Fish hopes to calm the "fears" that he believes provoke Abrams and Booth into periodic assaults on the "new readings" of post-structuralism.

In the process, *Is There a Text* explicitly addresses the problem of persuasion with the aim of reconciling pluralist and (allegedly anti-pluralist) post-structuralist positions. But in the pluralist context as I have thus far defined it, Fish's treatment of persuasion is atypical. The particular silences that generally characterize pluralist polemics, which strain Hirsch's commentary and shade Booth's analysis into circumlocutions, are completely abandoned in this therapeutic reading. Fish attacks the "demonstration" model of criticism, with its free-standing objects and its neutral perceptions, to argue that all of critical activity is "a matter (endlessly negotiated) of persuasion" (F 17).

Yet though his treatment of persuasion departs from the work of such pluralists as Hirsch and Booth, it is not possible to locate Fish in a simple opposition to pluralism, or beyond it. *Is There a Text* is also a response to Booth's offer to reconstruct a critical commonwealth embracing post-structuralists and cognitivists, mysreaders and intentionalists. Booth's price of admission is a monistic pluralist practice: post-structuralists must render their practice(s) compatible with the problematic of general persuasion, offering up a *lisible* post-structuralism and censoring the anti-pluralist elements inhering in the theory of differance.

I

Fish defines his project as a persuasive assault on a series of "anticipated objections," by which he means anticipated pluralist objections. He observes:

> in general, people resist what you have to say when it seems to them to have undesirable or even disastrous consequences. With respect to what I have been saying, those consequences include the absence of any standards by which one could determine error, the impossibility of preferring one interpretation to another, an inability to explain the mechanisms by which interpretations are accepted and rejected, or the source of the feeling we all have of progressing, and so on. It has been my strategy to speak to these fears, one by one, and to remove them by showing that dire consequences do not follow from the position I espouse and that in fact it is only within that position that one can account for the phenomena my opponents wish to preserve. . . . I have been trying to persuade you to believe what I believe because it is in your own best interests as you understand them. [F 369]

In this passage, Fish appears—despite the reservations some traditional pluralists may voice—to be working within the problematic of general persuasion. Yet there is a difficulty here; it lies in Fish's account of pluralism's best interests as pluralists understand them.

To begin, Fish seems unaware of the radical violence that this appealing passage does to the very notions of scholarship and knowledge to which his audience clings most tenaciously. It is precisely the desire to achieve disinterested judgment, to pursue truth or the facts even into disasters, if that is where they lead, that determines the pluralist resistance to post-structuralist claims. (Hence the extreme privilege a critic can claim, within the pluralist problematic, for a study that begins with one set of assumptions and ends with contrary conclusions.) To offer, as the quintessential value of one's analysis, the advantage of furthering the best interests of a pluralist audience is less than tempting; to pluralists, this is a form of intellectual bribe. In the pluralist problematic, when one's interests are involved, the only honorable alternative is to disqualify oneself. Judgment is only clouded by interests and can never be furthered or enabled by them. Fish's account of the actual operation of interpretation seems to me to be correct in many respects; the point here is that he has chosen a rather peculiar—and not at all promising—way of attempting to persuade his pluralist readers. And this in a passage that represents an unqualified attempt to address pluralists persuasively.

Fish wishes to deliver over to pluralism a post-structuralism that is pluralist in character. *Is There a Text* is a strategy, seeking not simply to describe or explain but to contain the significance of post-structuralist theory within a reading that bears as its most telling ideological mark the fact that it is "consoling" (321). Toward this end, Fish radically revises Booth's pluralist understanding of post-structuralism. He refuses the figure of misunderstanding, identifying it as a "caricature" of the post-structuralist position (268). Consequently, Fish's rereading produces a post-structuralism that is fundamentally different from Booth's. This is our first clue to a doubleness in Fish's argument that will eventually reverberate through all its levels. He rejects the standard pluralist line on post-structuralism because *Is There a Text* addresses two audiences. The first is obviously composed of anxious pluralists. But the second is composed of the post-structuralists whose work is the source of that anxiety. Fish sets himself the impossible task of satisfying both audiences. In other words, he refuses to acknowledge the exclusions that constitute audiences. As a "representative" of one form of post-structuralism, he seems to offer an uncompromising account of his theory. Nevertheless, he himself argues that it falls within the boundaries of pluralist discourse as critics such as Booth and Hirsch have established them, indeed, that "it is only within [his] position that one can account for the phenomena [his] opponents wish to preserve."

Fish's Anglo-American pluralist audience is disturbed by the impact his theoretical position (identified, by them and by him, with post-structuralism) might have on their practice as literary critics. His response is soothing: "One wonders what implications [this argument] has for the practice of literary criticism. The answer is, none whatsoever" (370). Consolation consists of severing the tie that binds the *theoretical* content of post-structuralism to any challenge it might present to the *practice* of Anglo-American pluralism. Fish offers pluralism a post-structuralist theory that paradoxically claims as its practice a continuation of Anglo-American literary criticism as it has developed over the last forty-odd years.

The divorce between theoretical speculation and practical consequences recalls Hirsch's tactics (as well as Booth's), but Fish is explicit where Hirsch is circumspect. Fish anticipates the common-sense objection that an argument with no consequences can make no claim to our attention: "Why should I be interested in it? What does it matter?" (370), and he counters it on two levels. He suggests that an argument may be interesting without "directly affect[ing] our everyday experience of poetry" and then adds that to think otherwise—to demand some transformation in the work of practical criticism as an index of the "interest" of his argument—is to participate in a "certain anti-theoretical bias built into the ideology of New Criticism" (371). What is startling is the ease with which Fish adapts the New Criticism's stance to his own purposes. To speak very generally, the New

Critics viewed the aesthetic (Literature) as a privileged realm and the poem as an autonomous verbal structure to be contemplated and understood in itself; the autonomy of the artifact, the lack of instrumentality that kept it aloof from social or political concerns, was essential to its function as a locus of value. The paradox of elevating to a privileged status a discourse defined by its irrelevance to social and political life was hardly an insurmountable problem; Literature—like Fish's theory—was interesting without directly affecting everyday experience.

Fish proceeds to point out that his argument goes to the heart of *institutional* concerns: "the status of the text, the source of interpretive authority, the relationship between subjectivity and objectivity, the limits of interpretation" are "basic topics, and anyone who is able to advance the discussion of them will automatically be accorded a hearing and be a candidate for the profession's highest rewards" (371). The question immediately arises: Is the theoretical discourse of our discipline obsessed with topics that are essentially or inherently irrelevant for the practice of interpretative criticism? Or is it rather Fish's particular solution to these basic problems that has no practical consequence? In either case, one is forced to concede that such speculations are well rewarded in the current climate, and Fish ends his own investigation precisely by thanking his audience for rewarding him with their attention. He repays them in turn by reassuring them that nothing in their classrooms or their essays need change as a response to his theorizing.

This embrace of a paradoxically central irrelevance appears at the very close of *Is There a Text*, and it recalls Hirsch's sudden turn toward persuasion and the problem of the community in the "Afterword" of *The Aims of Interpretation*. In a curious sense, Fish's strategy seems to reverse Hirsch's. The latter moves from a rigorously theoretical argument into a pluralist polemic, but he concludes with an invocation of the "logic of inquiry" in an effort to bind his community together; the "logic of inquiry" functions as a kind of theoretical trump card, fixing the methodological horizon for all inquiry within any discipline whatsoever. Fish pursues an equally theoretical argument in the body of his essay, but he concludes with an almost bizarrely modest or unassuming claim: his discourse will leave no mark; it seeks only to "interest" us. The community will remain intact because theory has˙ no connection to practice. In the place of Hirsch's ultimatums and threats, we find the assurance that nothing will change—nothing essential *can* change.

Fish achieves his peculiar reconciliation of post-structuralism and pluralism through a systematic interrogation and debunking of pluralist anxieties. He argues that many of those attributes of pluralist discourse that pluralists themselves imagine to be essential to it are in fact contingent or misinterpreted; simultaneously, he claims that post-structuralism does not harbor the demons that pluralists so often spy lurking in its theoretical pronouncements. Ultimately, Fish's critique contends that pluralism's fears about post-structuralism, fears of relativism and solipsism, indeterminacy and the loss of authority, are incoherent, inexplicably misconceived.

Fish's analysis comes very close to the claim that the pluralist polemic is a contradiction embodying the ideological crisis of pluralist discourse. But his own view of this "contradiction" is radically different from my own. To posit a general reader embodying universal human qualities (which leave him vulnerable to persuasion from any direction) and then to undertake a polemical catechism of pluralist values in order to cleanse discourse (and the reader) of solipsism and relativism is manifestly incoherent. I take this incoherence as a symptom of the mounting pressure on the pluralist paradigm, a symptom that offers an entryway into pluralist discourse, an opportunity to reveal the functions and the limits of the problematic of general persuasion and to trace the outlines of the anti-pluralist challenges multiplying at its margins. Fish concentrates his analysis neither on the contradiction as such, nor on the problem of its production, but on one element of it: pluralism's curiously misplaced fear of the outsider, the critic as renegade. He observes, parenthetically, "There is something of the police state in Abrams's vision, complete with posted rules and boundaries, watchdogs to enforce them, procedures for identifying their violators as criminals" (337). For Fish, this state is also symptomatic. But it is not a symptom to be exploited, that is, read. Rather, Fish attempts to "cure" pluralism, dissolving its symptoms in a concept of interpretation that covers the field and cannot be dislodged. His analysis works to make the outsider disappear; there is no renegade critic stalking the interpretive community.

In "'Demonstration' versus 'Persuasion,'" Fish describes a model of critical activity generally preferred by pluralists. In this "demonstration" model, "evidence available apart from any particular belief is brought in to judge between competing beliefs," and "interpretations are either confirmed or disconfirmed by facts that are independently specified" (F 365). He identifies this demonstration model as "the more familiar model of critical activity (codified in the dogma and practices of New Criticism)" (365), and he contrasts it with his own persuasion model, as elaborated and put into play in *Is There a Text*. But Fish does not propose to replace the traditional practices derived from the familiar model with innovative practices derived from the persuasion model he constructs. Instead, he suggests that the "practices" that are "codified" in the New Criticism are essentially formulaic justifications for the interpretative act, comprising a rhetoric of "getting-back-to-the-text." In this instance, the phrase "mere rhetoric" is actually more accurate. *Is There a Text* devastatingly reveals that no such demonstration practice is or ever was possible. The demonstration model is an ideological mystification of a persuasive practice. Fish advocates only that we abandon the fiction of the demonstration model that so many have come to accept as fact and acknowledge, theoretically, that our practices actually conform to the persuasion model. And this gesture, of course, is no threat to pluralism.

Obviously, Fish's account of persuasion as it operates in pluralist practice does not simply conform to the model I have elaborated thus far of the problematic of general persuasion. The weakest aspect of his reading is its refusal to consider fully the possibility that the pervasive adoption of the inadequate demonstration model was determined by pressing and specific historical and ideological considerations, considerations that persist. Instead, Fish leaves us to assume that an apparently whimsical or perverse or possibly accidental historical process was responsible for pluralism's choice of a (distorted) analogy to scientific inquiry as the justification for its practice.

As Fish recalls the work that finally led him to abandon the demonstration model, he observes that his opponents often charged him with not *simply* reading, but rather with attempting to *persuade* his audience to a new way of reading. His critical paradigm shifts dramatically once this objection is "no longer heard as an accusation." He recognizes that "what I was trying to persuade them *from* was not a fundamental or natural way [of reading] but a way no less conventional than mine and one to which they had similarly been persuaded, if not by open polemics then by the pervasiveness of the assumptions within which they had learned how to read in the first place" (16). This is a demystifing gesture: the seemingly "fundamental" or "natural" ways of reading are, in truth, "conventional," "learned," produced by persuasion, "if not by open polemic." But in a disturbing parallel to Fish's account of the demonstration model, this passage leaves the relationships between persuasion and the "pervasiveness" of (pluralist) assumptions about the "natural" way to read unspecified. If the pervasiveness is neither due to some overwhelmingly persuasive correspondence to natural facts nor achieved by "open polemic," is it achieved by covert polemic? Or, perhaps, by administrative procedures that necessarily violate the principles in whose service they are carried out? Or by some other means? Perhaps pervasiveness is never the product of polemic as such, but specific to the oxymoronic operation of covert polemic.

What is elided when this distinction is not addressed is the *difference* between a discourse that is consciously persuasive, elaborating its conventions without recourse to naturalizing gestures (without the alibi of the demonstration model) and a discourse that, although it is equally unnatural, is nevertheless unconscious of its conventional and limited scope and pervasively elaborates its interpretations not by open polemic, but by another process which lends to its arguments the force and appearance of nature. The difference is what Barthes identifies with the term "myth."[1] Covert polemics must invoke the categories of nature and objectivity. In Fish's analysis, the history of the pervasiveness of certain assumptions about reading—foremost among them the presumption of a natural reading—is lost.

Fish records the refusal of open polemic—the attacks made on his efforts to persuade readers—but he does not specify its function or "origin." Rather, he construes the replacement of a demonstration model by a persuasion model (covert polemic by overt polemic) as an inessential development that will have no consequences for pluralist practice. Pluralism's historical and ideological commitment to a demonstration model is explained as an unnecessary encumbrance generated by a misunderstanding as to what would be sacrificed if it were abandoned.

This process of strategic reevaluation, separating the essential from the inessential, always to the end of reassuring pluralists that no fundamental violence is being done to their practice, is the characteristic gesture of *Is There a Text*. As I have pointed out, it produces an opposition between theory and practice that allows for the adoption of post-structuralist theoretical postures and the maintenance of pluralist practices—and pluralist ideology. Obviously, this result is consoling to pluralists. It may, however, prove provoking to other post-structuralists. In my reading, the theoretical claims of post-structuralism imply a methodology that could transform the practice of literary criticism; the object of knowledge (and the knowing or knowledgeable subject) is being radically redefined. Consolation seems to be possible only via the weakest rendering of this theory. But the words "possible" and "could" must be heavily qualified. I will not counter Fish's analysis with a reading that predicts only "dire consequences" for pluralism should a post-structuralist idiom thoroughly permeate literary critical discourse. (Many would argue that this has in fact already happened.) Rather, I assume that Fish's reading of post-structuralism as pluralism

---

[1] Roland Barthes, *Mythologies*, tr. Annette Lavers (New York: Hill & Wang, 1972), pp. 109–59 and passim.

could take hold. It isn't simply unbelievable. It could be believed and, consequently, become an effective truth and an extremely useful one for pluralists like Booth. (Thus, the term "weakest," which I use above, is perhaps a premature label.)

Fish anticipates this formulation of the process by which an interpretation acquires force or credence. At the conclusion of "Interpreting 'Interpreting the Variorum,'" he summarizes his position: "Rather than restoring or recovering texts, I am in the business of making texts and of teaching others to make them by adding to their repertoire of strategies. I was once asked whether there are really such things as self-consuming artifacts, and I replied: 'There are now.' In that answer you will find both the arrogance and the modesty of my claims" (180). What is now really true of self-consuming artifacts could become true of the consoling analysis of *Is There a Text*, though one should mark the irony of the qualification embodied in the word "now"—one can answer such questions only in the short term. Much as Booth's strategy waits upon the recognition post-structuralists are able to give to the image he offers of their discourse as a form of pluralism, Fish's analysis depends on the ability of pluralists to adopt his readings of an ineffectual post-structuralist theory and an invincible pluralist practice.

Certain questions remain: How adequately does Fish's post-structuralist text answer pluralism's requirements? Is Fish's persuasive practice contained by the problematic of general persuasion? I have already suggested that by dismissing the difference between a consciously (overtly) polemical discourse and an unconsciously (covertly) polemical discourse, Fish misreads the "demonstration" model, dismissing as inessential the very element that produced its pervasive domination. But this strategic point is a conclusion that rests in turn upon a series of similar, though local readings, each of which claims to separate the essential from the inessential within pluralist ideology. In order to specify and evaluate the interpretative strategy at work in *Is There a Text*, we must begin with these enabling steps. *Is There a Text* is a strategic reading. I suggest that it depends upon a misreading of Fish's pluralist colleagues, their fears, their motives, their politics, a misreading which, despite his intentions and his protests, undermines Fish's benevolent interpretation of post-structuralist theory. Though the consolation encapsulated in the words "none whatsoever" could be extremely useful to the distressed pluralist audience Fish addresses, the rigor of his own post-structuralist practice ultimately forces his reading outside the problematic of general persuasion; consolation lies beyond the limits of pluralism.

II

The title of this chapter alludes to the concluding paragraph of the title essay of *Is There a Text:*

> Of course, solipsism and relativism are what Abrams and Hirsch fear and what lead them to argue for the necessity of determinate meaning. But if, rather than acting on their own, interpreters act as extensions of an institutional community, solipsism and relativism are removed as fears because they are not possible modes of being. That is to say, the condition required for someone to be a solipsist or relativist, the condition of being independent of institutional assumptions and free to originate one's own purposes and goals, could never be realized, and therefore there is no point in trying to guard against it. Abrams, Hirsch, and company spend a great deal of time in a search for the ways to limit and constrain interpretation, but if the example of my colleague and his student can be generalized (and obviously I think it can be), what they are searching for is never not already found. In short, my message to them is finally not challenging, but consoling—not to worry. [F 321]

This passage is a brief for the argument elaborated in *Is There a Text:* a diagnosis of Professors Abrams's and Hirsch's fears, a succinct reprise of the analysis—centered on determinate meaning, solipsism/relativism, and the issue of authority or constraint—which dissolves those fears, and the consoling message, "not to worry." The passage is openly and self-consciously reassuring and addresses a very specific pluralist audience. The issue of persuasion is raised in the closing words, which point toward a reconciliation between pluralism and the post-structuralist theory that powers *Is There a Text*. "Not challenging, but consoling," Fish means to persuade his opponents.

He opens with the problem of determinate meaning. Determinate meaning is at the center of the pluralists' concept of the stable text, and Booth, Abrams, and Hirsch are united by their commitment to a core of determinate, literal meaning which limits or constrains the interpretations a text will—or should—bear. Pluralists recoil at the prospect of a textual universe of free play where all significance is indeterminate and " 'no text can mean anything in particular' " (305). Fish agrees to the extent that he too believes "it would be disturbing indeed if the norm were free-floating and indeterminate" (307). The unremarked shift from literal meaning to "norm" is crucial. Fish proceeds to argue that the necessarily acontextual state in which the *norm* could be indeterminate can never be realized, and he introduces the central concept of the interpretative community to provide a contextual constraint that continually interrupts free play to fix determinate norms.

Fish denies that this normative power is located in language itself, systematically discrediting the essentialist position on literal meaning wherever he discerns it in any form. There is no literal or determinate core of meaning in words (texts) themselves, independent and context-free. But Fish quickly moves to reassure his readers: "There is a text in this and every class if one means by text the structure of meanings that is obvious and inescapable from the perspective of whatever interpretive assumptions happen to be in force" (vii). The pursuers of the transcendental signified may seek out the simplest component of meaning, even unto the molecular level (331), and never discover a literal core of determinate meaning. But they will always find an interpretation—and an interpretative community—awaiting them.

Thus, while literal meaning remains eternally elusive, the text always has *a* determinate meaning, a norm, ensured by the power of interpretative communities. But can this norm satisfy the pluralist bent on unearthing a *literal* meaning? Interpretative communities guard against the kind of paralysis or chaos pluralists seem to fear; in Fish's argument, the existence of the interpretative community means that indeterminacy, in the sense of confused undecidability, or "unintelligibility, in the strict or pure sense, is an impossibility" (307). Fish characterizes his position as congruent with pluralism's essential requirements: "I want to argue for, not against, the normal, the ordinary, the literal, the straightforward, and so on, but I want to argue for them as the products of contextual or interpretive circumstances and not as the property of an acontextual language or an independent world. . . . language does not have a shape independent of context, but since language is only encountered in contexts and never in the abstract, it always has a shape, although it is not always the same one" (268). "Determinate meaning" is always already available; more, it is unavoidable, coextensive with the deceptively simple act of perception. But in Fish's vocabulary, "determinate meaning" signifies "shape." This shape must change over time, dependent as it is on the presently recognized strategy of interpretation that produces it, but there can be no escape from some form of intelligibility, some determinate shape.

The most urgent question at this point should be "intelligible to whom?" But I shall put that matter aside for a moment in order to consider Fish's remarks from a conventionally pluralist perspective. This notion of determinate meaning as a shape that changes over time departs significantly from the common pluralist conception. For the pluralist, determinate meaning is precisely that which does *not* change. Fish is very conscious of this distinction. He observes that "for many people determinacy is inseparable from stability: the reason we can specify the meaning of a text is because a text and its meanings never change" (268). He represents this connection "many people" have forged between determinacy and stability as an instrumental one. Stability *makes* determinacy; the fact of stability over time, from context to context, creates and ensures determinacy. But once this causal chain is established, Fish's analysis exposes the link-

age as an error. In practice, "change is continually occuring but
. . . its consequence is *never* the absence of the norms, standards
and certainties we desire, because they will be features of any
situation we happen to be in" (268–69). Readers can always
specify meaning, or rather, they cannot avoid specifying meaning, because contexts—situations—are omnipresent; "interpretation cannot be withheld" (173). Pluralism can thus dispense
with stability of meaning. Determinacy requires no prop. If our
intention is to preserve the interpretative process and the possibility of knowledge and authority within our scholarly institutions, determinacy alone is quite adequate to our needs.

As an argument for the inevitability of interpretation, this
formulation is quite elegant. But the accuracy of the model as a
general account of interpretation is precisely *not* the issue. We
are concerned with the consolation this reading of determinate
meaning offers to those pluralist readers who have long associated determinacy with stability. Considered in this light, Fish's
analysis falls short of consolation; to the degree that it dismisses
pluralist anxiety about the *stability* of meaning, it feeds rather
than calms pluralist fears.

The urgency that infuses pluralist arguments for determinate
meaning is not merely a symptom of pluralist anxiety, born,
in turn, of a misunderstanding of post-structuralist theory.
Abrams, Hirsch, and Booth rest relatively secure in the knowledge that they will not awaken one morning in a critical universe where they can neither understand nor be understood,
decide or determine. Pluralists have seized upon the issue of
indeterminacy or undecidability because they judge it to be the
weakest link in the post-structuralist argument. The issue of
indeterminacy provides the ground for a strategic pluralist
(mis)reading of post-structuralism; this "caricature" is an *enabling* misunderstanding that produces a pluralist post-structuralism by invoking and then discrediting the specter of that
limit to community which the problematic of general persuasion
cannot admit. In fact, pluralist arguments for determinate meaning are offered in order to defend the *stability* of meaning and of
the reading community; the instability of meaning reintroduces

the nightmare of a limit to understanding and persuasion, a determinate misunderstanding. For Hirsch and Booth, determinacy makes stability, and this stability must be preserved.

Pluralists demand stability of meaning for a complex set of reasons, combining ideological, political, and professional concerns. They consistently celebrate (or betray) their longing for continuity with the body of texts that constitute the Tradition. Hirsch invokes a critical practice modeled after Arnold's example; Abrams avows his preference for Milton's original meanings over those of more ingenious contemporary rereaders; Booth insists upon humility before the canonized genius he would have contemporary critical practice honor. None of these critics defends an abstract or purely theoretical stability. The engine propelling Hirsch and Booth through their polemics is not determinacy of just *any* meaning, guaranteeing the stability of just *any* meaning. The question then becomes why is this segment of the critical community so radically committed to the stability of particular meanings, despite Fish's proof that literary criticism, interpretative authority, and knowledge can be sustained in some form without recourse to an epistemologically flawed theory of determinate meaning as a timeless essence.

One answer to this question lies wholly in the realm of the content of those significances that the traditional pluralist critic wishes to stabilize. Tradition—or the canon—is not a formal category here; it is not an empty set that holds a place in the theoretical model pluralism defends. In a historical and critical sense, these scholars occupy the canonical texts and the canonical readings they seek to preserve. Indeed, one might say they occupy the concept of the canon as the repository of traditional western values and these values are identified as human values—universal and timeless. Any critical voice—such as Macherey's or that of contemporary feminist theory—which threatens the celebratory and confirmatory mode of accounting for that canon, on any level, is a serious threat to the pluralist problematic. A new reading is a challenge because it might displace these critics even as it establishes its difference.

Of course, it is not only possible, but easy and politic and, hence, very common, to offer new readings that do *not* seek to displace the dominant pluralist readers, new readings precisely addressed to these readers, that is to say, "pluralist" new readings. Fish turns to this kind of local, fundamentally conservative new reading when he argues that the process by which a new interpretation must place itself in relation to previous readings makes continuity inevitable and the fear of discontinuity incoherent. Ultimately, he argues that the kind of radical discontinuity or displacement that I suggest as one source of Anglo-American criticism's interest in defending the stability of meaning is not possible. But he cites curiously oblique examples of radical criticism in order to support this claim. We shall examine them in detail when we consider the problem of authority or constraint, but for now it is sufficient to observe that Fish sees an implacable continuity in the history of criticism, and he views this continuity as one way to reassure pluralists. He offers his own work in reader-response criticism as a striking example: "the position I proceeded to take was dictated by the position that had already been taken. . . . To the degree that this argument [for the affective and intentional fallacies] was influential, . . . it constrained in advance the form any counterargument might take" (F 2).   Fish's formulation here seems to parallel the mainstream pluralist's account of the text as an entity that somehow prefigures, constrains, and contains the readings that are produced of it. In textual criticism, this model proposes a criticism that reproduces a pre-established meaning. As Macherey observes, such criticism is a "simulacrum. Analysis is a repetition, another way of saying what has already been said; reading complements writing. This repetition ensures a certain fidelity. . . . we are told that this is not entirely futile because it produces a new meaning: this is obviously a contradiction" (M 143, 152). In Fish's account of the prefigurative power of a prior interpretative strategy, analysis becomes merely the means to articulate a silent presence already in the text. The new strategy fulfills the promise of the original, completes it, providing the rational conclusion to the "position that had already been taken" in a purely logical development. Here, too, there is a certain continuity in Fish's argument; this notion of the "development" of critical discourse is ahistorical. History transforms every argument in a manner that *cannot* be anticipated or "contained in advance"; in fact, it is precisely those developments that cannot be predicted that work transformations. Paradoxically, Fish's theory of interpretative communities (like Hirsch's account of Literature) aspires to a kind of historicism, a defense against the charge of ahistoricism. His rhetoric gives no quarter to essentialism, though he does offer a caveat in the words "to the degree that this argument was influential." Influence, of course, is the prerogative of interpretative communities, not arguments, and there is a historical question wherever there is a question of influence. But this influence cannot be contained in advance; like the continuity of the trajectory of a critical career, it can be produced only in retrospect.

Fish argues that the continuity he sees between his own work and that of his theoretical precursors is characteristic of the practice of interpretation in general. Even the "off-the-wall interpretation" that would challenge a dominant interpretation dictates the forms of counterargument that will be addressed to it.

> It is, in short, no easier to disrupt the game (by throwing a monkey wrench into it) than it is to get away from it (by performing independently of it), and for the same reasons. One cannot disrupt the game because any interpretation one puts forward, no matter how "absurd," will already be *in* the game (otherwise one could not even conceive of it as an interpretation); and one cannot get away from the game because anything one does (any account of a text one offers) will be possible and recognizable only within the conditions the game has established. [F 357–58]

Thus it appears that pluralists like Hirsch and Booth need not fear the constant transformation of determinate meaning. The instability of meaning is of no consequence to pluralism; it cannot endanger critical discourse. In fact, this instability—and our attempts to negotiate it—*are* critical practice and have been historically. As Fish notes, "There are disagreements and . . . they can be debated in a principled way: not because of a stability in texts, but because of a stability in the makeup of interpretive communities" (171). We have seen how volatile these communities have become. But Fish argues that even instability is no cause for pluralist anxiety.

> Of course this stability is always temporary (unlike the longed for and timeless stability of the text). Interpretive communities grow larger and decline, and individuals move from one to another; thus, while the alignments are not permanent, they are always there, providing just enough stability for the interpretive battles to go on, and just enough shift and slippage to assure that they will never be settled. . . . the fragile but real consolidation of interpretive communities . . . *allows us to talk to one another, but with no hope or fear of ever being able to stop.* [F 171–72, my emphases]

The remarkable and, for the pluralist, critical thing about this passage is how calmly it contemplates the decline of specific interpretative communities. There is no trace of concern as to which community will dominate, which fade from the field. This serenity is partially explained by Fish's claim that "individuals move from one [community] to another." Given a high degree of flexibility in individual critics and a low correlation between literary critical orientation and other ideological commitments (the commitments that structure the "self"), one can posit a perpetual critical dance in which individuals regularly change partners. One can always hope to align oneself with a growth industry. Booth seemed to concur with this view: "If you can't beat 'em, join 'em." But his willingness to innovate was highly circumscribed and, finally, a strategic gesture.

  This critical mutability can serve as a counter to the claim that traditional pluralist critics cling to the stability of canonical readings (texts) because they occupy them, or establish their identities in them, as I have suggested. If new readers drive the traditionalists out, the latter have only to become new readers in turn to find themselves reoccupying their old (if strangely unfamiliar) haunts. Unfortunately, perhaps, this kind of critical flexibility is extremely rare. Abrams presents a more familiar spectacle when he cries, "Stop, you're killing me." Of course, as Foucault observes, it is not history itself that is murdered by the discourses of discontinuity and difference but rather that "ideological use of history by which one tries to restore to man everything that has unceasingly eluded him for over a hundred years." But for Abrams and for pluralists like him, this distinction is a (metaphysical) irrelevance. The point is that this murdered history is Abrams's history, is history for Abrams, with the proper name Abrams standing here as a synecdoche for the pluralist literary critic. This is as much a professional and finally a personal matter as a theoretical one; this murdered history is pluralism, its practice, its histories. Pluralists may find it impossible, that is, unthinkable, to desert the interpretations built upon this notion of history, to abandon the old interpretative community and move in with the new readers.[2]

C. S. Lewis, in his debate with the anti-Miltonists, themselves critics who could not adapt to a clearly overwhelming critical tide, remarked of his opponents in the dispute: "I hardly expect to convert many of those who take such a view; but it would be a mistake not to make clear that the difference between us is *essential*. If these are my errors they are not errors into which I have fallen inadvertently, but the very lie in the soul. If these are my truths, then they are basic truths the loss of which means imaginative death."[3] Lewis names one absolute limit to his discourse. That he could do this makes him an anomaly both among the participants in the Milton controversy and among pluralists in general.[4] Lewis was never trapped in the purely formal debates that largely constituted the Milton controversy because his perspective was essentially ideological and historical. This is not to

[2]See Hayden White, "Historical Pluralism," *Critical Inquiry* 12:3 (1986), 480–93, for a critical account of pluralist invocations of history as an "effectively secured" discipline that can ground literary critical claims (484).

[3]C. S. Lewis, *A Preface to "Paradise Lost"* (London: Oxford University Press, 1942), p. 52.

[4]Lewis's "authoritarian Christianity" is not pluralist, as Milton's Christianity was not. Both men would most likely have run afoul of Booth's distaste for critics who accuse other authors of being "less generous, less devoted to truth, justice and the enhancement of life" or "less politically aware" than they.

suggest that Lewis was a historical or theoretical critic in the contemporary senses of those terms. On the contrary, he was a conscious anachronism; his Christian humanism and his Miltonism were unproblematically one for him. As he remarks elsewhere in the *Preface*, Dr. Leavis "sees and hates the very same that I see and love. Hence the disagreement between us tends to escape the realm of literary criticism. We differ not about the nature of Milton's poetry, but about the nature of man, or even the nature of joy itself" (134). Lewis acknowledges the limit that pluralists cannot admit, and he does it by means of the eloquent assertion that his critical truth and his imagination are coextensive. Ironically, with his image of imaginative death, he suggests the fate of those critics who cannot take up a new practice, critics who continue to read according to some method of which the critical community at large remarks, " 'no one reads that way anymore' " (F 172).

When a critic cannot shift his interpretative allegiances, the decline of his interpretative community ceases to be a neutral event. The evolution Fish describes with such equanimity becomes the "loss . . . which means imaginative death." Alignments that are not permanent may shift and change so radically that, contrary to Fish's assurances, the "fear of ever being able to stop" talking to one another becomes a nightmarish reality.

Fish seems to dismiss this possibility. It is a delicate matter, to be sure, for to pursue the question of fading communities in any practical detail could lead to indiscreet (even unkind) remarks about the steadily declining relevance of certain critical perspectives; such blunt discussion of a colleague's professional future—or lack of professional future—is outside the conventions of literary discourse. (It is gossip, perhaps.) Fish evades the matter by the use of the abstract and general term "us." One or another of "us" is sure to survive and to be able to talk to another survivor; the touchy issue of *who* will survive is made to seem irrelevant. But Fish's reticence is not simply a tactful reflex. Nor does he harbor an overly optimistic view of the capacity of individual critics to leap from one interpretative community to another in pursuit of a rising star.

The calm that settles over Fish's discussion of the rise and fall of interpretative communities is fatalistic. It is possible to assess shifts in critical loyalties, to discern why one critic can move from one interpretative community to another, and more important, why another critic cannot make the same move. It is even possible to analyze how this is done if, by how, we mean by what particular series of transformations, compromises, and exchanges. This kind of analysis occupies a large portion of Fish's book in the form of the history of the development that led him from the question "Is the reader or the text the source of meaning?" to his theory of interpretative communities, from "Literature in the Reader" to "Is There a Text in This Class?" But when Fish projects the growth and decline of interpretative communities in the future, he does not examine the possibility of strategic shifts in critical allegiance and the threat of imaginative death with any urgency, because these events cannot be controlled. A critic does not *choose* her interpretative community; rather, it chooses her. To choose another is not an easy matter. On the contrary, to choose another is unthinkable.

Fish develops this point as he begins to shift the focus of his argument from determinate meaning to the problems of relativism and solipsism. Pluralists project the problem of the individual reader through this double optic. Both pejoratives find their way onto Booth's list of discourses that "pluralism is not" (B 407), and Hirsch's harshest denunciations are aimed at the "antirationalism" of "cognitive atheists" (H 13). Fish's notion of the reader-subject as an extension of the interpretative community responds to these attacks and to the anxieties that fuel them, but it first surfaces in the "Introduction," where he sketches his own critical autobiography. At several points in the narrative, he remarks: "what I didn't see" or "though I didn't know it at the time" (F 7, 10). The historical process by which Stanley Fish became the critic who wrote *Is There a Text* is presented as a series of transformations over which he did not preside. He could neither speed nor slow the process significantly; indeed, he comprehends it only now, retrospectively. As for future shifts in his critical perspective, Fish attempts no augury: "if the rehearsing of this personal history has taught me anything, it is that the prosecution of that [critical] task will also be, *in ways that I cannot now see,* its transformation" (17, my emphases). There is no room in this economy for sympathy or anxiety directed toward those who remain behind as interpretative communities grow and decline; one must "believe what one believes," whatever the professional cost, and "one *teaches* what one believes even if it would be easier and safer and more immediately satisfying to teach something else" (364). There is no escape from the "firmness with which we hold our beliefs, or, to be more precise, [from] the firmness with which our beliefs hold us" (362).[5]

For the pluralist committed and confined to a paradigm steadily losing its hold on domination, this is hardly a reassuring prospect. Lewis admits that his beliefs hold him—simultaneously constitute his imagination and constrain him—in just the way Fish suggests. But the problematic of general persuasion does not allow for any such determinate limit upon the capacities of the human reader. Booth calls the infinitely malleable flexibility that pluralism mandates by the modest name of understanding, "molding our minds in shapes established by others" (B 422); Hirsch, more explicitly addressing the matter of cultural and social difference, insists that "it is within the capacity of every individual to imagine himself other than he is, to

[5]The notion of teaching what one believes despite the threat such teaching may present to satisfaction, ease, and safety has a political referent Fish doesn't choose to invoke. His examples include a linguist who can no longer teach Chomsky as she once did ("No matter how convenient it would be if she still believed in the *Aspects* model—convenient for her teaching, for her research, for her confidence in the very future of her discipline" [363]) and a literary critic (Stanley Fish) whose changing sense of pastoral makes it impossible for him to teach Spenser's *Shepheardes Calender* as he was wont ("when I now look at the *Calender* I no longer see what I used to see " [364]). The examples Fish neglects are those in which threats to safety and ease have to do with the politics of teaching what one believes and with the very concrete threat of being denied the right to teach at all because one's teaching challenges some aspect of the political status quo. Such examples exist in every discipline and field, and pluralism is frequently invoked to justify dismissals. For a discussion of the explicitly political purging of the United States academy in the 1950s, see Ellen W. Schrecker, *No Ivory Tower: McCarthyism and the Universities* (New York: Oxford University Press, 1986).

realize in himself another human or cultural possibility" (H 47). Neither critic would accept the anti-humanism implicit in Fish's position, or the dogmatism of Lewis.

Thus, with this account of the subject as an effect of discourse or belief, Fish seems to take a crucial step away from pluralist ideology. The anti-humanism of post-structuralism is perhaps most notoriously enacted in its attack on the classical conception of the unified and originating subject. (This conceit has become so pervasive, at least on the verbal level, that *Newsweek* can entitle an essay on video arcades: "Games That Play People.") Any theoretical account of the subject as an effect of language, a matrix of discontinuous codes that speak the "individual," discredits everything pluralism seeks to preserve. Fish flirts with such an anti-pluralist position when he argues that the reader can never act as an independent agent, that she is always a social product, an extension of her interpretative community, and thus constrained by its limits. He concludes: "If the self is conceived of not as an independent entity but as a social construct whose operations are delimited by the systems of intelligibility that inform it, then the meanings it confers on texts are not its own but have their source in the interpretive community (or communities) of which it is a function" (F 335). Yet despite this clear identification of the self as "a social construct," Fish backs away from the abyss of the deconstructed subject: the Fishian self is an effect of discourse, a function, but in a crucial move, Fish declines to notice the discontinuity of its processes. One looks in vain for the rhetoric of the fragmented or deconstructed self in Fish's work. Perhaps the choice of the word "function," rather than "effect," is symptomatic. In Fish's model, "systems of intelligibility" are always functional, and the self is a continuous, functioning, intelligible unit.

Nevertheless, there is a real sense in which Fish's reader is not an individual at all. And consequently, radical individualism, the absolute otherness that is solipsism, is impossible. "An individual's assumptions and opinions are not 'his own' in any sense that would give body to the fear of solipsism. That is, *he* is not their origin (in fact it might be more accurate to say that they are his)" (F 320). In this model, every interpreter must speak the social codes that structure his subjectivity and produce the effect of individuality; no interpreter can achieve real—threatening—idiosyncracy. "The shared basis of agreement sought by Abrams and others is never not already found, although it is not always the same one" (F 318). This line of argument is clearly consoling to pluralists. But pluralism's "Arnoldian fear" is not the sum of its relationship to subjectivity. Although it is true that pluralism regards radical subjectivity or solipsism as an ever-present danger, the unified and independent self, the individual, is essential to its subject-centered, humanistic discourse. Fish can banish the troublesome specter of solipsism, but apparently only at the cost of the humanist's concept of the self.

Pluralists generally seem to prefer to treat post-structuralism's anti-humanism indirectly, countering it with their own humanist ethic, but rarely naming the enemy. For example, Abrams protests that, although he is not a deconstructionist, neither does he subscribe to the mimetic view of language that Derrida and Miller would seem to ascribe to him. He insists his view of language is Wittgensteinian, based on concepts such as tact and community.[6] What Abrams elides is that the subject as a coherent, stable, and general phenomenon lies at the core of all pluralist views of language, including his own. This unified subject is the *reader* of a "determinably meaningful text, by ,for, and about human beings" (*PR* 587); he is "a man speaking to men" [sic], the *author* as originary consciousness, the authority that guarantees the stability of meaning and the homogeneity of human experience prior to its "representation" in language. This constellation—the author, the reader, and their shared, determinable meaning—constitutes the theoretical imperative for the stability of meaning. If the reading subject is to be preserved in his unified, general, and universal character—which is absolutely essential to general persuasion—the author must be projected as his mirror image, the original site of subjectivity. Au-

---

[6]See Abrams, "How to Do Things with Texts," and Ann Wordsworth, "Derrida and Criticism," *Oxford Literary Review* 3:2 (1978), 47–52.

thorial intention is the talisman of this subject-author, and the reader pursues intention as stable and original meaning. The self-identical totality is reproduced in the form of the reader himself, the author himself, and the reading (text) itself. Poststructuralism may threaten this subject, in all his avatars: the reader, the author, the stable text. When Fish offers a shelter from solipsism in the notion that "the self does not exist apart from the communal or conventional *categories of thought* that enable its operations" (F 335, my emphases), he seems to break with the problematic of general persuasion.

But Fish responds to the contradiction in pluralist discourse, a subject-centered discourse obsessed with the fear of subjectivity, by producing its mirror image at another level of his argument.[7] Whereas he dissolves the problem of solipsism with an anti-humanist account of the reader as the extension of the interpretative community, he replies to the charges of relativism entirely in terms of consciousness and the status of the reader as constituent subject. Fish anticipates that pluralists, robbed of the *stability* of determinate meaning and faced with a plurality of interpretative communities, will respond suspiciously. Confronted with an apparently relativistic universe composed of an infinite *historical* regress of equally valid, determinate meanings, his audience may panic and refuse consolation: "It will do no good, they say, to speak of norms and standards that are context specific, because this is merely to authorize an infinite plurality of norms and standards[:] . . . to have many standards is to have no standard at all" (F 318–19). Fish grants that this objection is "unassailable as a general and theoretical conclusion" (319). He then argues that it is not only general and theoretical, but essentially irrelevant to *practice*. The subject who was caught up and dissolved in a social process reappears now placed at the center of an existential stage. Where the interpretative community, discourse itself, had once been the object of Fish's analysis, now we find that the personal biography of the individual critic

---

[7]De Man makes a similar move. In "The Resistance to Theory," for example, he stresses that he does not anticipate an end to the resistance to theory; his theoretical intervention will not change this aspect of our practice.

sets the terms of the argument, and the problematic of general persuasion is reasserted.

General, theoretical conclusions are "beside the point for *any particular individual*" (319, my emphases). The whole weight of Fish's analysis swings from the deformations that an infinite plurality of norms and standards might produce, to the conscious anxieties of particular, individual critics as they try to write or teach. Such an individual may fear "that his performance or his confidence in his ability to perform would be impaired" (319). He may suspect that he will be "unable to do practical criticism" (370) in the face of proliferating interpretative communities and the absence of any asituational norm by which to distinguish among them. But Fish is reassuring.

> While it is generally true that to have many standards is to have none at all, it is not true for *anyone* in particular (for there is *no one* in a position to speak "generally"), and therefore it is a truth of which one can say "it doesn't matter."
>
> In other words, while relativism is a position *one* can entertain, it is not a position *one* can occupy. *No one* can *be* [Fish's emphasis] a relativist, because *no one* can achieve the distance from *his own* beliefs and assumptions which would result in their being no more authoritative *for him* [Fish's emphasis] than the beliefs and assumptions held by others, or, for that matter, the beliefs and assumptions *he himself* used to hold. [F 319, my emphases]

This consolatory move is remarkably similar to Fish's earlier treatment of determinate meaning. Now, as before, he offers an account of critical practice built on a key insight into the nature of pluralism's resistance to post-structuralism. In fact, for those pluralists who resisted post-structuralist innovation because of a conviction or fear that relativism would lead to critical paralysis, this is a consoling passage. The passage does not, however, respond to the true character of pluralist anxiety (and indignation, in Hirsch's case) about relativism.

Fish locates pluralism's fears about relativism in the personal history of an individual critic because he reads them as a form of apprehension about the corrosive power of unchecked subjectivity operating over a period of *time*, in the time of particular critics' individual practices. In this model, the movement—which "feels like" progress but, in fact, can never be truly progressive—of one critic from interpretative community to interpretative community appears as the relativism pluralists find so objectionable. We can see one sense in which this movement does threaten pluralism; it suggests the dispersion of the subject in discourse, undermining the figure of the sovereign subject manipulating discourses from some high vantage. But this is not a point Fish stops to mention. He seems to view such fragmentation as relatively insignificant, if not utterly irrelevant. He can take such a complacent view because, as he repeats again and again, no one will "feel" the discomfort of fragmentation in practice. By privileging here the feelings of the very subject he previously threw into question, Fish closes the gap between poststructuralist claims and pluralist desires. Although the subject and his feelings have been defined as effects of discourse, they remain the center of the analysis.

A more significant lapse in Fish's effort to solve the problem of relativism for pluralists is his failure to recognize that they are not primarily concerned with relativism as a private experience culminating in self-doubt. Fish consoles *one* pluralist at a time, assuring each that his practice will continue undisturbed, indeed, that the reader must proceed with confidence, for one believes what one believes. But in the pluralist polemic, relativism does not refer to relativism in time, in the personal history of the scholar-critic. Pluralists fear relativism not in the history of a single career, but in the present of the collectivity, the community. Pluralism rejects the relativism that justifies—theorizes—ideological schisms in the *space* of contemporary criticism, the social and political relativism that acknowledges the community's division into hostile camps.

Pluralists tend to label any position that critiques the "logic of inquiry" relativistic. Booth, for example, makes this charge in *Critical Understanding*. Hirsch, taking this line of argument, finds himself opposing relativists who span critical eons, from Marx to Kuhn to Foucault. What unites these disparate figures is their willingness to posit limits—ideological, theoretical, epistemo-

logical, political—that divide the community along lines of conflicting interests. Pluralism insists on an undivided critical community, a community that shares the logic of inquiry, or the
ethics of the communal, a community with no barriers to persuasion. The true name of the "relativism" of Marx or Foucault,
then, is "anti-pluralism." Interpretative communities with determinate boundaries, communities that do not recognize a
higher and general standard of interpretation—indeed, communities that reject the very prospect of such general and neutral
norms—are what Hirsch and Booth condemn. Relativism, then,
lies not in the distance one takes from one's own beliefs over the
span of one's career, but in the distance communities of anti-
pluralists (communities of relativists) *produce* between their beliefs and the problematic of general persuasion. This distance
neutralizes pluralist objections, denying pluralism the authority
(or jurisdiction) to criticize even before it has formulated an
attack. The very rules of discourse are shifted.

The interpretative community founded upon uniform acceptance of the logic of inquiry flounders when that logic is with-
drawn. The power to generalize meaningfully or concretely
about the community-at-large fades. As Hirsch argues, "to the
extent that this sense of the communal enterprise collapses, so
does the discipline itself collapse as discipline. . . . The health of
a discipline as a discipline depends upon the devoted allegiance
of its members to the logic of inquiry" (H 152, 154). The problematic of general persuasion demands that the reading community operate as the general subject of interpretation. Theoretical
schismatics who reject that subject and refuse to address their
criticism to the entire community denature and confound pluralism.

Fish represents his defense against the charge of relativism as
continuous with his defense against the charge of solipsism.
Because the reader's mind is constituted by social categories,
because the reader is these categories, there is no gap for relativism to occupy between the self and the beliefs of the self. But
this view places Fish in contradiction with pluralism's humanism. He insists that "the mental operations we can perform are

limited by the institutions in which we are *already* embedded. These institutions precede us, and it is only by inhabiting them, or being inhabited by them, that we have access to the public and conventional senses they make" (331–32). This "limit" is ominous for pluralism, and for Fish's consolatory project.

III

Despite his reference to the police state, Fish seems to underestimate the will to authority (and knowledge) that lurks beneath all of pluralism's calls for stable and determinate meaning and an end to solipsism and relativism. His theory of interpretative communities is offered as a balm to pluralist fears, yet it begins to resemble an incitement, the very challenge Fish vows not to make. Of course, if pluralists have been misled by their own "caricature" of post-structuralism, genuine consolation will inevitably resemble (at least briefly) the very thing they have most feared. Once it is clear "how little we lose" (367) by embracing post-structuralist theory, this difficulty should fade. Fish comes closest to achieving the reconciliation he seeks when he addresses the problem of authority by way of the concept of continuity.

Initially, it seems that the kind of authority Fish offers to pluralists, authority confined *within* interpretative communities, authority entirely dependent upon contexts or situations and, finally, recognizing differences, would simply not satisfy the requirements of the problematic of general persuasion. At the same time, he makes very strong claims for the authority of the individual interpreter—often figured as a teacher—within the persuasion model. The text persists as an *"obvious* and *inescapable"* structure of meanings; "the shared basis of agreement sought by Abrams and others is *never* not already found": "students *always* know what they are expected to believe." Such statements seem to contradict other remarks that stress that interpretative communities are determinate and limited. The possibility that immediately comes to mind from the title story of *Is*

There a Text in This Class?, that is, the possibility that there might be *two* texts in one class, is never seriously addressed. And its theoretical consequences are ignored. The concept that resolves these apparent contradictions is continuity; continuity governs all relationships *among* interpretative communities in a pluralist commonwealth.

I have pointed out that Fish sees an inevitable continuity in the practice of literary criticism. Whereas Raymond Williams argues that certain forms of radical semiotics fall outside the dominant paradigm of literary studies altogether, Fish argues that even the most radical form of interpretation must have *some* relation to the center of the interpretative community, even if that relation comes under the title of "off-the-wall" interpretation. An outside is defined, first of all, by its relation to an inside. "There is never a rupture in the practice of literary criticism" (358). Furthermore, no matter how exotic or marginal the reading, simply in order to be conceived of as an interpretation, it must fall within the parameters of the game of interpretation. Hirsch says, play by the rules of the logic of inquiry or the discipline will cease to exist as a discipline, and then where will we be? Fish recognizes that if disciplines cease to exist as a disciplines, they will reappear elsewhere as something else, or rather, as more of the same: "interpretation is the only game in town" (355).

Several things are in play here. On one level, Fish has essentialized interpretation, *naturalized* it. Where the bourgeois critic argues for the unmediated perception of a "natural" world, Fish argues for the "naturally" mediated perception of a conventional world, or as the Barthes of *Mythologies* might put it, he naturalizes the mediation of perception. The forming of interpretative communities (the making of conventions) is presented as a general and universal practice. As such, interpretation functions as an unproblematic unity. The absence of distinctions we observe when Fish discusses the growth and decline of interpretative communities reappears. (If Hirsch's discipline is transformed into some other form of interpretation, will Hirsch be one of its practitioners? When a community declines, what happens to its workforce?) The interpretative community emerges as the ahistorical subject of the history of interpretation, and interpretation itself is self-identical. The force of the claim that there is never a rupture in the practice of literary criticism is sharply reduced to the circular claim that "interpretation" is continuous with "interpretation." And interpretation is still the only game in town.

Fish produces a metatheory of interpretation that seeks to encompass both pluralism and post-structuralism. But the apparent absence of distinctions—the appearance of even-handedness—is misleading. His theory ultimately respects the limits of general persuasion; he is a kind of super-pluralist, and his position is a new articulation of the problematic of general persuasion: "in literary criticism, . . . everyone's claim is that his interpretation more perfectly accords with the facts, but . . . everyone's purpose is to persuade the rest of us to the version of the facts he espouses by persuading us to the interpretive principles in the light of which those facts will seem indisputable" (339). Fish eschews the Hirschian posture of prophet of chaos and dissolution. Nor does he merely suggest, as Booth does, that "our life together" will be best served if we all read and write within the ethical terms of the problematic of general persuasion. Fish argues that it is impossible for any other situation to arise. In a sense, history stops here. It is impossible to fall out of the pluralist game, or to escape it. "There are no moves that are not moves in the game, and this includes even the move by which one claims no longer to be a player" (355).

I began by observing that Fish takes pluralism's anxiety about the outsider as his object and attempts to cure it. By the conclusion of *Is There a Text*, the outsider is obliterated, lost, in a cognitive sense indistinguishable from the insider. Fish argues that "the production and perception of off-the-wall interpretations is no less a learned and conventional activity than the production and perception of interpretations that are judged to be acceptable. They are, in fact, the *same* activities enabled by the *same* set of in-force assumptions about what one can say and not say" (357, my emphases). The outsider was really an insider all along. The powers of the police state would be redundant here.

But the character of the examples Fish brings forth to support this image of the continuous discourse of interpretation weakens his extremely consoling claim. The examples "challenge" the dominant paradigm at a variety of levels. What is most remarkable about the Eskimo reading of "A Rose for Emily" is that it in no way constitutes a new strategy for interpretation; instead, it represents a very old (and in some circles outdated) strategy— the use of the author's biography as revealed in his letters. The discovery of a Faulkner letter and the subsequent introduction of that letter as evidence for new readings of Faulkner's *oeuvre* do not constitute a new "Eskimo strategy" of literary analysis. The Faulkner letter is a new *object* to be examined, but one that is perfectly congruent with other objects already established in the domains of literary criticism and Faulkner studies. In the context of pluralism's essentially positivist practice (the demonstration model), the challenge presented by the discovery of a heretofore missing object is qualitatively different from the production of a new theory. The very least one expects from a new theory is that it produce new, that is to say, heterogeneous objects for analysis. The discovery of a new (in the sense of another) object functions precisely as an empirical advance in pure, non-theoretical knowledge and never as a repudiation of past theory. Indeed, it is an application and thus a reinforcement of the theoretical problematic that characterizes the status quo. This is certainly not an instance of a theoretical challenge to pluralist hegemony.

According to their own testimony, it is precisely a new theory that so disturbs such pluralists as Hirsch, Booth, and Abrams, post-structuralist theory. Fish's choice of Stephen Booth's *Essay on Shakespeare's Sonnets* as an exemplar of a challenging reading is again rather disappointing. Booth is chosen because he "self-consciously locates and defines his position in a differential op-position to the positions he would dislodge" (F 352). "Position" is an unfortunately vague term. Fish points out that despite his oppositional rhetoric, Booth "manages to claim for his interpretation everything that certifies it as acceptable within the conventions of literary criticism," foremost among these, its superiority to earlier criticism, which is insufficiently literary, and its commitment to get "back-to-the-text." Fish observes that both these moves are attempts to "disavow interpretation in favor of simply presenting the text" (353), and he points out several other basically conservative literary assumptions that go unchallenged in Booth's essay.

Fish's analysis reveals that despite his subsequent "revisionary" claim that the Sonnets should be examined not as spatial objects but as temporal experiences, Booth relies heavily on traditional literary assumptions that in turn undermine his claim to radicalism. But Fish softens his apparent criticism of Booth by confessing that it is "beside the point." (This passage recalls the peculiar "modesty" we observed earlier.) Though Booth is not "truly radical," Fish's point is that "he *couldn't* be. Nor could anyone else" (F 354). This is because the very intelligibility of Booth's essay depends on the availability of the shared conventions of literary analysis. "A wholesale challenge would be impossible because there would be no terms in which it could be made; that is, in order to be wholesale, it would have to be made in terms wholly outside the institution; but if that were the case, it would be unintelligible because it is only within the institution that the facts of literary study . . . become available. In short, the price intelligibility exacts . . . is implication in the very structure of assumptions and goals from which one desires to be free" (354–55). These conclusions are in one sense inescapable, although they depend on a common-sense gloss of the term "intelligible," which I have been at some pains throughout this book to problematize. At the same time, there are interpretative positions—contemporary marxism, radical feminism, Lacanian psychoanalysis—that present challenges considerably more "radical" than Booth's. As a proof text, an interpretation that declined the critical posture of innocence, that openly theorized the literary work as an object that cannot "know" itself, that rejected the category of "Literature," would offer more resistance to Fish's effort to assimilate it to the institutional paradigm.

By focusing on Booth's "aggressive humility" (F 355), Fish avoids several difficult questions. Having abandoned the mission of demonstrating the enduring value of the text and the universal insight of its author; having embraced an interested criticism, perhaps even a programmatic, prescriptive criticism; having made the ideological complicity between the canon and its critics a matter of political significance; a "radical" critic (in this broader sense) presents a challenge to pluralism which, though still not wholesale, is entirely different from the one Booth's argument for the temporal experience of the poem offers. The critical point is that Booth accepts pluralism's general reader and attempts to persuade him. The radical new reader refuses the general reader, both in the critical texts he critiques and as the ground of his own reading. In his place, he posits a fundamentally divided "community" composed of irreducibly differentiated readers. At the present time, within the institution of Anglo-American pluralism, radical criticism is necessarily anti-pluralist criticism.

We have seen the panic with which Hirsch and Booth regard the advent of this sort of anti-pluralist reading. *The Aims of Interpretation* is bent upon containing the significance of transformations in the composition of the critical community, assimilating new strategies of reading to Arnold's critical model, fixing their (implicit) critique of aestheticism within the narrative of the classical mean. Booth gestures disapprovingly toward these critics when he chastises those who would accuse others of being less generous or less politically aware. But Fish sees no danger here. He reads the challenge presented by an anti-pluralist or radical reader in the same terms as the Eskimo reading and Booth's reading of the Sonnets. Different in scale, perhaps, but all of the same *kind*. On every level, the pattern of revisionism and complicity repeats itself, and this necessary historical relation ensures against ruptures and discontinuities, preserving the pluralist's tie to the future.

Fish's concepts of continuity and discontinuity parallel the pluralist's "caricature" of indeterminacy. By construing discontinuity as a necessarily "wholesale" challenge, Fish misreads the concept and in the same direction that Abrams (according to Fish) misreads Derrida's account of indeterminacy. The "epistemological break," "discontinuity," "rupture," as they appear in the works of Althusser, Foucault, Williams, are never presented as total or pure fractures in history. On the contrary, Williams stresses that common "works" are at the center of radical semiotics and literary criticism, though these works appear as different "objects"; Foucault insists on the uneven, strategically dispersed process that only through theoretical *work* can be realized as "discontinuity"; Althusser, also, emphasizes the overdetermined historical conjuncture and the theoretical struggle that finally produces a "break" in the form of new problems and a new practice. All these theorists of discontinuity insist that it is a product rather than a natural phenomenon *in* history. Discontinuity is a theoretical object in each of their discourses. "The notion of discontinuity," Foucault argues, "is a paradoxical one: because it is both an instrument and an object of research."[8] Fish's continuities are similarly products of his theoretical model. By defining discontinuity as a pure state and then concentrating his examples illustrating the continuity of literary discourse on those kinds of interventions that are not particularly frightening to pluralists, Fish can establish a kind of safety net for pluralists like Booth and Abrams. Continuity appears as the natural and inevitable condition of all interpretations that are recognized as such. But anti-pluralist discourses tend to resemble Althusser's and Foucault's practices; they *produce* discontinuity, in part so as to take pluralism as an object of inquiry. The gaps they establish are enabling and disabling, not wholesale, but strategically. One sign of the presence of this discontinuity is a tendency to acknowledge pluralists only as those who fall outside of one's potential audience. Although this gesture is essential if one wishes to break with the problematic of

[8]Michel Foucault, *The Archaeology of Knowledge*, tr. A. M. Sheridan Smith (New York: Harper & Row, 1972), p. 9.

general persuasion, it is not without risks. It could be suicidal, given that pluralism may retain its position at the center of interpretative power, a position which, Fish suggests, gives it a peculiar capacity to anticipate all the developments that may rise up against it. As Booth observes at the close of "'Preserving the Exemplar,'" we cannot yet predict who will survive the current conflict. I have tried to suggest the opposite of Fish's view: pluralism is uniquely disabled in that it can never explicitly name the character of its anti-pluralist opponent.

Fish, however, does name it, and in that moment his discourse transgresses the boundaries of the pluralist problematic. Although he argues throughout *Is There a Text* for the continuity of interpretations and for the normative power of interpretative communities, Fish also consistently invokes the *limits* of those communities. In this notion of the limit, we can locate the anti-pluralism of his text. There are hints of Fish's willingness to name the limits of persuasion throughout his argument. Thus, he briefly addresses the problem of the class with not one but two texts when he relates that he has told the anecdote "Is there a text in this class?" "to several competent speakers of the language who simply didn't get it" (312). He also emphasizes that there is no way to be certain that anyone who listens to the story will be able to understand it. One wonders, for example, what the consequences are when the teacher is the competent speaker who doesn't get it. Fish's programmatic statement of this view bluntly admits that "what was normative for the members of one community would be seen as strange *(if it could be seen at all)* by the members of another" (15–16, my emphases). This is precisely the limit—the limit of persuasion and understanding— pluralism can never admit.

In his own discourse, Fish dramatically enacts an anti-pluralism far more radical than his theory suggests. The essay "A Reply to John Reichert" is a short piece in relation to the other essays in the collection. Sandwiched between the *tour de force* of "Normal Circumstances, Literal Language, Direct Speech Acts, the Ordinary, the Everyday, the Obvious, What Goes Without Saying, and Other Special Cases" and the four essays on "Interpretive Authority" (including the title essay) that close the book, the Reichert piece is perhaps easy to overlook. This impulse is reinforced by the fact that it is the only reprinted essay in the book lacking a short introduction to place it in relation to Fish's work or to indicate its importance. In his "Reply," Fish responds to some of the criticisms Reichert offers to "Normal Circumstances . . . and Other Special Cases," but his counterargument stops well short of a full defense of his views. He concludes with something like a theoretical shrug. "I am not, however, optimistic that Reichert will ever become a convert because the fears that impel his argument are so basic to his beliefs. . . . Reichert's commitment to what he would like to be able to do and his conviction that if what I say is true he will be *unable* to do it make it impossible for him to regard my position as anything but perverse and dangerous" (298–99, my emphasis). The pessimism of these lines is more significant than the rehearsal of earlier arguments that makes up the bulk of Fish's reply. This resignation represents what Booth wants to exclude: the naming of a limit to persuasion in the form of a reader who can neither be persuaded *nor made to understand*, not because meaning is indeterminate, but precisely because meaning is determinate, because of the limits of discourse, and because the community is split. Fish continues: "Any argument I might make would be received within the belief that it *had* [Fish's emphasis] to be wrong, and within that belief [Reichert] *could* only hear it *as wrong*" (299, my emphases). With this statement, the distinction between persuasion and understanding dissolves; right and wrong are functions of the capacity to believe. The statement "I understand but am not persuaded" (with its equivalent epithet: "eloquent persuasive nonsense") takes on the character of a statement of allegiance rather than a judgment of truth-value. In his reply to Reichert, Fish employs the notion of the unthinkable that pluralists avoid: "unless someone is willing to entertain the possibility that his beliefs are wrong, he will be *unable even to hear* an argument that constitutes a challenge to them" (299, my emphases). There is some trace of voluntarism and the pluralist value of openmindedness in this remark. But when Fish offers himself as an example of such deafness, the implication that Reichert is perhaps merely stubborn fades: "When Reichert, or anyone else identifies something—an object, a text, an intention—as being available independently of interpretation, I know in advance that it could not be so and I look immediately for ways to demystify or deconstruct it. I always succeed" (299). These are the words of pluralism's "bad reader," the reader who does not read to be persuaded. "A Reply to John Reichert" appears as an instance of the bad reader's writing: although Fish insists on areas of agreement that lead him to take Reichert's point seriously and to reply to it (thus preserving his notion of continuity), the piece is really a proleptic defense of its own failure to "reply" in a way that could convince Reichert or make him understand. It is finally only an articulation of its own principle of exclusion.

Is There a Text seeks to persuade pluralism that it can be reconciled with post-structuralist theory, and this attempt hinges on the rhetoric of persuasion itself, on the claim that "everyone is obliged to practice the art of persuasion." Despite this promising remark, Fish does not escape the problematic of general persuasion. Even as he appeals to pluralists in particular and acknowledges the interests of readers, he continues to address the general audience pluralist ideology posits and to assume a pluralist concept of persuasion as such. In his analysis, persuasion is a radically empirical matter of assembling the facts most convincing to a reader, not the object of theoretical interrogation. At the level of practice, Fish ignores the possibility that to speak consolingly to the pluralist is to exclude the anti-pluralist. Indeed, had he conceded this point, he would not necessarily have been forced to abandon the problematic of general persuasion; as I have argued, practical failures alone are not sufficient to disrupt pluralist ideology. More important, Fish celebrates rather than questions the very object of pluralism when he argues that the imperative to persuade guarantees pluralism's recuperative powers; persuasion thus remains the answer to an unposed question. Yet the final effect of Fish's argument and his foregrounding of the rhetoric of persuasion is to make explicit those conditions under which one *must* fail to understand and fail to be persuaded, the conditions under which one must abandon the problematic of general persuasion. His elaboration of his ideal reader produces, in relief, the image of the reader for whom *Is There a Text* is not consoling: the anti-pluralist.

Fish's text demonstrates the dangers—for pluralism—of explicitly addressing the rhetoric of persuasion. From this vantage point, Hirsch's circumspection, his evasion of the problem of persuasion until the closing pages of his text, takes on the stature of a cautious but farsighted policy. Fish takes the defense of general persuasion into uncertain terrain and slips, at least momentarily, over the border of the pluralist problematic. The very discontinuity Fish's theory strains to exclude suddenly emerges, in the figure of Reichert, as an intractable reality; Fish and Reichert enact the pluralist nightmare of not being able to talk to one another.

But the transgression is hardy a fatal one. Fish's representation of the figure who can neither understand nor be persuaded as an individual, one John Reichert, rather than as part of a class or group, is symptomatic. (This move anticipates the existential argument, centered on the individual teacher-critic, that Fish wields to banish pluralist anxieties about solipsism.) He thus names the limits of pluralism in the narrowest possible terms, quite literally as the problem of one man, a person(al) problem, really. This makes it easier to fold the anti-pluralist figure back into the pluralist problematic. He remains the answer to a question the pluralist cannot ask. And so, we must read *Is There a Text* in general and "A Reply to John Reichert" in particular as revealing the limits of any pluralist discourse that attempts to confront the rhetoric of persuasion directly. A strategic retreat becomes essential.

IV

Toward the close of the introduction to *Is There A Text In This Class?* Fish summarizes his theoretical efforts to calm the fears of the pluralist audience. He describes his own conclusion as a reading of the relationship between rhetoric and literary theory. We might say he conceives his practical task as a work of rhetoric even as he conceptualizes his current position as the theoretical recognition of the essentially rhetorical nature of all literary critical discourse. Fish confesses that at a certain juncture in his career he resisted his opponents' efforts to characterize his work as an attempt "to persuade [others] to a new way of reading"; but, as we have seen, he eventually discovers that "what I was trying to persuade them *from* was not a fundamental or natural way [of reading] but a way no less conventional than mine and one to which they had similarly been persuaded, if not by open polemics then by the pervasiveness of the assumptions within which they had learned how to read in the first place" (16). Fish's deconstruction aims at the opposition between "open polemics" for a new way of reading and "fundamental" reading conceived as merely doing what comes naturally. In his model, all discourse emerges as a form of polemic—either operating openly or as a function of "the pervasiveness of the assumptions within which" we learn, work, read, write. To the extent that he insists that interpretation is "the only game in town," Fish must argue that polemic, in turn, is the only way to play, with the qualification that strategies will differ: overt moves or covert moves may predominate in any given situation.

Fish assimilates the term "rhetoric" to the notion of persuasion, that is, to the polemical. The introductory narrative of his critical autobiography concludes: "In the end I both gave up generality and reclaimed it: I gave it up because I gave up the project of trying to identify the one true way of reading, but I reclaimed it because I claimed the right, along with everyone else, to argue for a way of reading, which, if it became accepted, would be, for a time at least, the true one. In short, *I preserved generality by rhetoricizing it*" (16, my emphases). In Fish's analysis, pluralists fear that a loss of generality is the necessary corollary to any deconstruction of literal meaning; from their perspective, to give up the core of determinate meaning is to abandon the critical community to skepticism, relativism, and subjectivism. In order to calm those fears Fish wants to preserve pluralism's generality, but without compromising on the question of the text itself. In *Is There a Text*, to "rhetoricize" generality is to disclose the omnipresent rhetorical process that produces a "true" (general) reading. Generality is the product of persuasive rhetoric, a rhetorical effect (or a trope), and not the result of the discovery of a pre-existing determinate meaning, but this rhetorical process itself is general, that is, universal. Although Fish gives up determinate meaning, he relocates the possibility of generality elsewhere, in the unavoidable procedures by which the community of readers produces meaning. I have argued that in Fish's work the generalization of rhetoric constitutes itself precisely as a post-structuralist instance of the problematic of general persuasion. Fish is a super-pluralist, arguing that we must all "practice the art of persuasion" and taking the signs of resistance to his argument as misunderstandings and caricatures, vulnerable to the clarifying force of his own persuasive explanations.

But there are other readings of rhetoric in contemporary American literary theory. In the opening chapter of *Allegories of Reading*, Paul de Man seeks to distinguish rhetoric from what he regards as mere persuasion. He will frequently use rhetoric to designate the study of tropes and figures "and not in the derived sense of comment or of eloquence or persuasion."[9] Yet de Man,

---

[9]Paul de Man, *Allegories of Reading: Figural Language in Rousseau, Nietzsche, Rilke and Proust* (New Haven: Yale University Press, 1979), p. 6. Further references to this volume (*AR*) will appear in parentheses in the text. There is perhaps a certain blurring in de Man's own gloss. In *Allegories*, he frequently opposes the rhetoric of tropes to the rhetoric of eloquence *and* persuasion (104, 105, 130). Tzvetan Todorov is only the most recent historian of rhetoric to argue that the equation of rhetoric with eloquence represents a historical shift from a prior identification of rhetoric and persuasion; it is not to be taken for granted that eloquent means "persuasive." As Todorov observes, "the new eloquence differs from the old in that its ideal is the intrinsic quality of discourse rather than its aptitude for serving an external purpose": *Theories of the Symbol*, tr. Catherine Porter (Ithaca: Cornell University Press, 1982), p. 65. At the moment when persuasion *ceases* to be the work of rhetoric, the latter is identified solely as eloquence or beauty: "If eloquent speech was once defined by its efficacity, now, quite to the contrary, it is useless speech, speech without purpose, that draws praise" (p. 67); "thus useless, inefficacious speech is to become the object of

too, works to "preserve generality by rhetoricizing it," even as he moves decisively away from the polemical arena Fish so relishes. De Man's decision to privilege the rhetoric of tropes over the rhetoric of persuasion is not unambiguous, as we shall see. His claim, in the most frequently cited sentence from the text, that "rhetoric is a disruptive intertwining of trope and persuasion" [*AR* ix] will lead him to the verge of antipluralism—in a gesture remarkably similar to Fish's. But the apparent distaste with which he puts aside the "derived" sense of rhetoric is symptomatic of a critical tendency that cuts across his text. It signals his desire to escape the problem of derivation itself, which always reinscribes itself in his work as the problem of history. This flight from history is profoundly entangled with de Man's rejection of polemic, in theory and in practice, and with the form of his deconstruction of the "rhetoric of persuasion." It is also, as we have seen, a pluralist signature. By pursuing the question of de Man's polemic—or perhaps what we shall have to call his anti-polemic—we can reveal an unsuspected conjuncture of general persuasion and the allegory of reading.

In de Man's rhetoric of tropes, we discover a more cautious pluralism. Subordinating chronology to the logic of pluralism's discursive strategies, I will argue that his contribution to the problematic of general persuasion represents a retreat from the exposed position Fish stakes out at the limits of pluralism. De Man successfully displaces the question of polemic and thus produces a new and less vulnerable inscription of the rhetoric of general persuasion.

---

rhetoric, and rhetoric itself becomes the theory of language admired in and for itself" (p. 68). Any identification of rhetoric as persuasion *and* eloquence over against rhetoric as trope is at the very least premature.

5 NOT TAKING SIDES: READING THE RHETORIC OF PERSUASION

> In short, knowledge, whatever its conquests, its
> audacities, its generosities, cannot escape the relation
> of exclusion, and it cannot help conceiving this
> relation in terms of inclusion, even when it discovers
> this relation in its reciprocity; for the most part, it
> reinforces this relation of exclusion, often just when it
> thinks it is being most generous.
>
> —BARTHES, "Taking Sides"
>
> There seems to be no limit to what tropes can get
> away with.
>
> —DE MAN, *Allegories of Reading*

If, as I have been arguing, the problematic of general persuasion dominates American literary studies as a whole, we can expect to discover it at work even in the discourses of theorists—like Paul de Man—who position themselves at a considerable distance from pluralism and self-described pluralists. In de Man's text we confront a theoretical discourse that aligns itself more dramatically than Fish's does with the discourses of deconstruction, in part by refusing to follow Fish's polemical path. The relationship between pluralism and de Man's work is more oblique and surprising than that of the critics we have considered thus far. But to mistake the rhetoric of deconstruction for an unerring mark of anti-pluralism would be to endorse the (fundamentally pluralist) oppositional logic that installs poststructuralism as pluralism's absolute Other. (This view appeals both to supporters and opponents of deconstruction, as, in fact, there are pluralists in both camps.)

Thus, while de Man's work offers a pluralism quite distinct from Hirsch's commitment to the logic of inquiry or Fish's polemic on the status of persuasion, his text is of central significance precisely because of this difference. The importance of de Man's contribution to pluralist discourse lies in his effort to theorize (the) rhetoric (of general persuasion) in a new way, conceiving rhetoric not primarily as a polemical strategy, but as a tropological system. Despite the complex and tireless movement of his analyses—and despite his often cited indifference to the temptation to engage in polemics, that is, to the practical problem of persuading either his adversaries or his admirers—de Man does not break with the pluralist problematic of general persuasion. In order to trace his specific contribution to that problematic, we must pose his solution as a problem, a question his text answers but never asks: what is the rhetoric of general persuasion?[1]

We have seen that Fish works as a polemicist to demonstrate that the imperative to persuasion is a universal; he argues that polemic or rhetoric in the pursuit of persuasion is essential to literary studies, literally impossible to evade because we are all inside interpretation. Now we shall see that de Man offers an anti-polemic that universalizes figural language, defending the "rigorously unreliable" rhetoric of tropes as essential to all discourse, impossible to evade because we are all inside language; de Man's tropological analysis refuses polemic, seeming to render it not covert, but impotent.[2] Thus, de Man's intricate rhetor-

[1]This chapter was written in 1985–86, prior to the disclosure of de Man's wartime writings in collaborationist journals, and has not been revised to take them into account.

[2]To compare de Man to Fish is, admittedly, not a project that immediately seems likely to be fruitful. But unexpected parallels between their recent concerns repay exploration. Like Fish, de Man investigates metatheoretical issues and questions the status of contemporary theory; he examines "the resistance to theory" and its place in literary studies, and remarks the shrillness of the polemics on both sides. But de Man seems considerably less sanguine than Fish on the matter of reassuring those who are suspicious of the theoretical project in literary studies. One interesting effort to read de Man against Fish is the opening of William Ray's chapter on de Man in his *Literary Meaning* (London: Basil Blackwell, 1984), pp. 186–205, which more or less reverses the terms of my com-

ical strategy is an ironic reversal of Fish's open polemic for open polemic. The impossibility of escaping polemic is replaced by the impossibility of entering polemic. But the pluralist problematic remains undisturbed; the general reader may be constituted in the rhetoric of tropes as effectively as in the rhetoric of persuasion.

I shall argue that for de Man "aporia" or "undecidability" constrains polemic, and that this impossibility of polemic enables him to reassert the generality of (mis)understanding and, with it, the pluralist problematic. The aporia that renders polemic impossible returns de Man to pluralism; in his text, pluralist discourse refuses the possibility of exclusion by refusing to take sides—by appearing to take all sides, or by undecidability. In this chapter, I will consider the status of "polemic," its relation to theory, to history, and to rhetoric in de Man's text; finally, rereading his analysis of Archie Bunker's rhetoric, we shall discover this intricate complex of relations operating to produce the rhetorical reader as the subject of general persuasion.

The paralysis of de Manian polemic has been (mis)recognized, commented upon, bewailed and even attacked, but it has not been theorized. Indeed, critics have frequently been distracted from the question of polemic as a discursive structure to speculate in an *ad hominem* way about "the man" behind the polemical—or, rather, anti-polemical—posture. I am concerned here with neither defending nor criticizing de Man in these terms, but with delineating the textual practices that have produced such readings and disclosing their place within pluralism. Rather than dismissing the problematic of polemic in de Man's text as somehow idiosyncratic or personal, I will argue that it is symptomatic of a major revision of the pluralist problematic, a rewriting that has attracted numerous readers and which may reinvigorate a pluralism that comes dangerously close to displacing itself in Fish's work. The neutralization of polemic is both one of

---

parison. Ray's analysis touches on texts and issues that I consider below, but our conclusions differ considerably. Further references to this book (*LM*) will be given in parentheses in the text.

the theoretical consequences of his argument and a characteristic trope of his form of deconstructive practice, which is a pluralist practice. De Man both argues against any relation between polemic and theory and avoids any obvious polemic in his own exposition; I will argue that this very lack works "polemically" and, together with his account of figuration as such, constitutes his text's peculiar instantiation of general persuasion.

According to *Allegories of Reading*, deconstruction depends upon the exposure of a textual aporia, an impasse, which is never a simple contradiction. In the case of *The Birth of Tragedy*, for example, de Man points out that "the deconstruction does not occur between statements, as in a logical refutation or in a dialectic, but happens instead between, on the one hand, *metalinguistic statements* about the rhetorical nature of language and, on the other hand, a *rhetorical praxis* that puts these statements into question. The outcome of this interplay is not mere negation" (98, my emphases). This juxtaposition, which opposes "metalinguistic statements" to "rhetorical praxis," without lapsing into "mere negation," is pivotal to de Manian analysis. To focus on the binary couple statement/praxis is to privilege *aporia*, that dilemma which emerges for the reader who finds it both necessary and impossible to choose between "two incompatible, mutually self-destructive points of view," "two readings [that] have to engage each other in direct confrontation, for the one reading is precisely the error denounced by the other and has to be undone by it" (131, 12). Aporia reveals the text as an allegory of its own unreadability and forces the (apparently unwilling) reader into a "state of suspended ignorance" (19).

The moment of aporia depends on the identification of a certain kind of couple, an opposition roughly paralleling the opposition between content (statement) and form (rhetoric). De Man explicates this relation in a self-consciously technical vocabulary, with the "impersonal precision" (*AR* 16) characteristic of any taxonomy. This tone marks the moment of general persuasion: in de Man's text it signals a general agreement among technically trained readers that sentence x is a statement, or that a given phrase constitutes a particular rhetorical figure, a metonymy rather than a synecdoche, for example. This assumption of the objectivity or the rigor of the technical must be questioned on two fronts. First, de Man uses it as a rhetorical figure with a complex relation to his own metalinguistic statements. Second, his examples—and we shall consider the Bunkers in particular—obscure their exclusions of some readers and thus project a homogeneous community of readers, that is to say, they assume general persuasion. I should emphasize that in my interpretation de Man's "rhetorical praxis" sustains his "metalinguistic statements" about the rhetorical nature of language. His anti-polemic appears both as a theoretical position and as what he would call a "rhetorical mode," "acted out theatrically" in the text (100). Translating my argument into de Man's terms makes it obvious that my practice here does not conform to his model of deconstruction. But more important, the act of translation itself enables me to isolate the locus of general persuasion in his analysis in the act of reading rhetorical practices as such.

In de Man's analysis, the technical identification of a rhetorical praxis, of *figure as figure*, and, most important, as a *particular* figure, produces a rhetoric of general persuasion. In every case, the analysis turns on a rhetorical discrimination, a crux where the reader identifies a figure as such, literally in its naming: metalepsis, catachresis, anacoluthon, prosopopeia, metaphor, metonymy, even, as we shall see, the rhetorical question. "The seductive powers of identification" (ix) are at work here in the interests of general persuasion.[3] For de Man, the trope, rhetoric as figural language, is rigorously anti-polemical because it operates, and can—really, must—be read technically, with indifference to interests; a trope as such is outside ideology insofar as it is impervious to the constraints and demands of persuasion, history, meaning, reference. Tropes are neutral, general in the

[3]See Jeffrey Barnouw's review of *Allegories of Reading, Comparative Literature Studies* 19 (Winter 1982), 459–63, which makes this point implicitly in the course of objecting to de Man's reading of a passage from Proust, and Jane McLelland's review in *MLN* 96:4 (1981), 888–97, which considers the same passage, and asks the intriguing question: "But what if—by reading Proust very carefully ourselves—we discover that the deconstruction stands, but the passage does not support it?" (891).

sense of universal; they are intralinguistic, formal. In this model, the historicity of rhetoric, that is, of *particular* figures, is repressed. Rhetoric is generalized by reference to its epistemological function (or malfunction) and thus emerges as that in language which resists logical codification and the pressure of interests, which are associated with history, content, contingency. For de Man, rhetoric as trope is persuasive, but its persuasions take the special form of general or universal seductions; they offer logical seductions, seductive reasoning. Thus, while the persuasiveness of tropes is always epistemologically unreliable (always a case of bad persuasion, as I noted in Chapter 2), theoretically, it never fails to persuade any particular reader. This seductive operation is indifferent to the heterogeneity among readers, to their differences, and especially to their limits. As de Man suggests, "there seems to be no limit to what tropes can get away with" (62).

"Seductive" is a word de Man uses frequently, most often to characterize the epistemologically misleading character of figural language: "the most *seductive* of metaphors" (*AR* 11); "Nietzsche, who as a philosopher, has to be concerned with the epistemological consequences of the kind of rhetorical *seductions* exemplified by the Proust passage" (15); "when literature *seduces* us with the freedom of its figural combinations, so much airier and lighter than the labored constructs of concepts, it is not the less deceitful because it asserts its own deceitful properties" (115, my emphases). Seduction undermines epistemological rigor in the service of general persuasion, which is also a false persuasion, and de Man often opposes it to an (im)possible truth, as when he wonders if Rilke's poetry offers "a legitimate promise, whether it is a *truth* or a *seduction*" (24, my emphases). The epithets "seductive metaphor" and "rhetorical seductions" recur so commonly as to argue that reading (reasoning) itself is a seduction. Indeed, in de Man's text, the general impossibility of reading is an effect of the endless and endlessly successful seductions of language itself, that is to say, of rhetoric.

Language is characterized primarily by the unlimited and

therefore treacherous play of substitutions, which lead inevitably to epistemological error.

> From the moment we begin to deal with *substitutive systems*, we are governed by *linguistic* rather than by natural or psychological models: *one can always substitute one word for another* but one cannot, by a mere act of the will, substitute night for day or bliss for gloom. However, the very ease with which the linguistic substitution, or trope, can be carried out, hides the fact that it is epistemologically unreliable. It remains something of a mystery how rhetorical figures have been so minutely described and classified over the centuries with relatively little attention paid to their mischievous powers over the truth and falsehood of statements. [*BI* 274, my emphases][4]

The precise nature (or the limits) of the reader's vulnerability to the seductions of figural language, to the easy but unreliable operation of substitution or trope, is never specified, but the claim that "one can always substitute one word for another" hints at the direction de Man ultimately takes. Such substitutions have more than a relative power; it is impossible to differentiate among tropes in terms of their particular seductive power for particular readers. This question is unthinkable because this vulnerability is identified with the practice of reading or with the operations of figural language as such (which is very nearly the same thing, for de Man). The reader is defined solely by his vulnerability to "what is linguistically motivated in a rhetorically conscious reading."

De Man's particular contribution to the elaboration of the problematic of general persuasion is this view of language. In his text, rhetoric, conceived as trope, becomes the object of gen-

[4]This formulation appears in de Man's review of Harold Bloom's *Anxiety of Influence*, which was first published in *Comparative Literature* 26 (1974), 269–75. For an interesting account of this celebrated review, see Shuli Barzilai, "A Review of Paul de Man's 'Review of Harold Bloom's *Anxiety of Influence*,'" *YFS* 69 (1985), 134–41. See also de Man's discussion of epistemology and persuasion in "Pascal's Allegory of Persuasion," in *Allegory and Representation*, ed. Stephen J. Greenblatt, Selected Papers of the English Institute, 1979–80 [N.S. 5] (Baltimore: Johns Hopkins University Press, 1981), pp. 1–25.

eral persuasion. The disruptive work of rhetoric produces aporia and in this process constitutes both the text and the general reader. The displacement of polemic from the realm of historical struggle into a theory of language constitutes an extremely canny pluralist response to Althusser's question: what is it to read? To accept responsibility or guilt is one of Althusser's answers; every reading is a guilty reading because every reading necessarily takes a position. For de Man's rhetorical reader, every reading is guilty, but every reading is necessarily guilty of the *same* thing, of being seduced into (mis)reading by the work of figural language.[5] Every reader is thus equally guilty. Every crime repeats every other, because the "necessity" that imposes this guilt is linguistic, inescapable and universal. "There seems to be no limit to what tropes can get away with."

De Man offers the "deliberate emphasis on rhetorical terminology," as a solution to certain theoretical problems clustered around reading. The consequence is a powerful reaffirmation of the problematic of general persuasion.

I

De Man's strategy for reading contemporary literary theory offers an inversion of Fish's approach. As we have seen, Fish examines in some detail the objections pluralists have made to recent innovations in literary theory, and he responds to them with a kind of sympathy. De Man proceeds without naming any particular critic as an adversary. The anonymity of his opponents is not an index of academic gentility or a mark of the aloofness critics so often attribute to him; on the contrary, it recalls Booth's distinctively pluralist unwillingness to name his adversaries, and it is similarly essential to de Man's point and to his method. In "The Resistance to Theory," he asks:

> what is it about literary theory that is so threatening that it provokes such strong resistances and attacks? It upsets rooted ide-

[5]See *Allegories of Reading*, pp. 64–65, and chap. 12, "Excuses."

ologies by revealing the mechanics of their workings; it goes against a powerful philosophical tradition of which aesthetics is a prominent part; it upsets the established canon of literary works and blurs the borderlines between literary and non-literary discourse. By implication, it may also reveal the links between ideologies and philosophy. All this is ample enough reason for suspicion, but not a satisfying answer to the question. For it makes the tension between contemporary literary theory and the tradition of literary studies appear as a *mere historical conflict* between two modes of thought that happen to hold the stage at the same time. *If the conflict is merely historical, in the literal sense, it is of limited theoretical interest,* a passing squall in the intellectual weather of the world. As a matter of fact, the arguments in favor of the legitimacy of literary theory are so compelling that it seems useless to concern oneself with the conflict at all. Certainly, none of the objections to theory, presented again and again, always misinformed or based on crude misunderstandings of such terms as mimesis, fiction, reality, ideology, reference and, for that matter, relevance, can be said to be of *genuine rhetorical* interest. [11–12, my emphases]

This passage touches upon many issues crucial to the problematic of general persuasion. The trivialization of the historical as accidental or contingent—"a mere historical conflict between two modes of thought that happen to hold the stage at the same time"—is a gesture native to pluralism. It is also an enabling condition for de Man's allegorizing project and its refusal of polemic. As he observes, *"Allegories of Reading* started out as a historical study and ended up as a theory of reading" (*AR* ix), an "allegory of reading [that] narrates the impossibility of reading" (77). Historical inquiry can only mystify the "problematics of reading" (ix); categories such as meaning and reference are similarly inhibiting. Happily, "the entire question of meaning can be bracketed, thus freeing the critical discourse from the debilitating burden of paraphrase," once we recognize that "the perception of the literary dimensions of language is largely obscured if one submits uncritically to the authority of reference" (5).[6]

[6]De Man does voice a caveat. In his analysis of Rilke's *Duino Elegies*, he observes that "the notion of a language entirely freed of referential constraints is

The assertion that historical conflict cannot have real theoretical interest gives voice to the pluralist's longing to lift theory out of the realm of significant historical conflict into an allegedly more rigorous (more general) space; in de Man's work, this appears as a kind of theoretical ascent, a strategic move above the "weather." But his suggestion that it "seems useless" to concern oneself with the objections to theory is also a striking refusal of polemic, offered when we might expect a polemical assault. Although these remarks employ slightly more heated language than is characteristic of de Man ("misinformed," "crude misunderstandings"), the general lack of polemical energy is nevertheless striking, and his final remark suggests a theoretical explanation. Crude, historical objections have no "genuine rhetorical interest." Rhetorical does not have here "the derived sense of comment or of eloquence or persuasion" (though we might assume misinformed commentaries also lack persuasiveness); rather, it refers to the "study of tropes and of figures" (*AR* 6). In this passage, rhetorical interest takes a place in the argument parallel to theoretical interest. Both are opposed to the historical and to the passing squall of polemic, which throws up a collection of ill-considered objections. Genuine rhetorical interest is allied with genuine theoretical interest, and neither has any "literal" history.

The distinction between history and rhetoric/theory rests uneasily on this notion of the literal. De Man does not claim that the conflict between the tradition of literary studies and contemporary literary theory has no history whatsoever. But its history is of "limited theoretical interest," if we take history "in the literal sense." A puzzling caveat. We can get some idea of what de Man means by literal history if we consider another example of his resistance to historical argument. This instance is doubly

---

properly inconceivable. Any utterance can always be read as semantically motivated, and from the moment understanding is involved the positing of a subject or an object is unavoidable" (*Allegories of Reading*, p. 49). But his interpretative practice strongly suggests that although this possibility exists, it does not represent a rich field of inquiry. A "rhetorically conscious reading" also posits or interpellates a subject; that subject is the reader of general persuasion.

useful from our perspective because the relevant passages are also remarkably unpolemical—or anti-polemical—even for de Man.

Polemic is all but entirely absent, despite the fact that "The Rhetoric of Blindness" criticizes Derrida's reading of Rousseau on fairly serious grounds.[7] De Man's opening passages include a tart criticism of those commentators who read from

> a position of unchallenged authority, like an ethnocentric anthropologist observing a native or a doctor advising a patient. The critical attitude is diagnostic and looks on Rousseau as if he were the one asking for assistance rather than offering his counsel. The critic knows something about Rousseau that Rousseau did not wish to know. One hears this tone of voice even in so sympathetic a critic as Jean Starobinski . . . : "No matter how strong the duties of his sympathy may be, the critic must understand [what the writer can not know about himself] and not share in his ignorance," he writes, and although this claim is legitimate . . . it is perhaps stated with a little too much professional confidence. [*BI* 112]

De Man will have none of this diagnostic tone or professional overconfidence in his approach to Derrida.[8]

He grants that "at first sight, Derrida's attitude to Rousseau seems hardly different" from the diagnostic pose of authority (*BI* 113); but, almost immediately, he insists that this "reading of Rousseau diverges fundamentally from the traditional interpre-

---

[7]See *Blindness and Insight*, p. 118. See also Suzanne Gearhart's very interesting discussion of de Man's and Derrida's different relations to history, "Philosophy *before* Literature: Deconstruction, Historicity, and the Work of Paul de Man," *Diacritics* 13:4 (1983), 63–81.

[8]De Man cites Starobinski's "Jean-Jacques Rousseau et le péril de la réflexion," *L'Oeil vivant* (Gallimard: Paris, 1961), but one cannot help but think of Althusser's well-known explication of "symptomatic" reading and his essay on Rousseau. "Diagnostic" is certainly a close cousin of "symptomatic." The strategy of symptomatic reading structures the whole of my own analysis, but I would resist any effort to reduce that strategy to a "tone of voice," and its own problematic deconstructs the possibility of unchallenged authority from any critical attitude whatsoever. De Man's strictures might apply to his own "insight" into the works of Lukács, Blanchot, and the American New Critics in *Blindness and Insight*.

tation. . . . Derrida takes Rousseau seriously as a thinker and dismisses none of his statements" (114). (De Man's treatment of Derrida's statements is perhaps more ambiguous, although I would suggest that it is the seriousness of his analysis that leads him to dismiss certain effects in the text.) In Derrida's analysis of Rousseau, "the repression of written language by what is . . . called the 'logocentric' fallacy of favoring voice over writing is narrated as a *consecutive, historical* process" (*BI* 137, my emphases). But rather than criticize this dependence on historical contingencies, de Man reads it, that is, he rhetoricizes it. He reminds us that "Derrida's Nietzschean theory of language as 'play' warns us not to take him *literally*, especially when his statements seem to refer to *concrete historical situations* such as the present." He then names this narration a mere story: "we are reading a fiction and not a history" (137, my emphases).

De Man's interpretative principles require that this reading not be (either simply or complexly) his own, something he imposes on Derrida's text, for that would place him in the diagnostician's role, posing as though "he knows something about Derrida that Derrida did not wish to know." Rather, he assures us that "none of this seems to be inconsistent with Derrida's insight, but it might distress some of his more *literal-minded* followers: [Derrida's] historical scheme is merely a narrative convention" (138, my emphasis). Derrida is fully aware of this conventional strategy; he is not "taken in by the theatricality of his gesture or the fiction of his narrative" (137). This is the crux of de Man's reading; "narrative convention" here means trope, and "literal-minded" seems a (polite) way of saying "slow-witted." "Literal-minded followers" are not rhetorically conscious readers; they literally miss Derrida's "insight" (his trope), mistaking theatricality, fiction, and convention for history. The rhetorical reader corrects this error; he recognizes (or reads) history as a figure for language, a narrative inscription of an intrinsically linguistic problem.[9]

[9]Derrida comments on these questions in *Memoires for Paul de Man*, tr. Cecile Lindsay, Jonathan Culler, Eduardo Cadava (New York: Columbia University Press, 1986).

If we look back now to de Man's analysis of the resistance to theory and the problem of literal history, we see that his strategy there vis-à-vis the historical seems to cross with Fish's; in a chiasmic reversal, each critic arrives at the conclusion that we might have predicted for the other. Fish diagnoses his opponents' objections as a prelude to prescribing his therapeutic readings; but he isolates the symptoms of pluralist resistance to post-structuralist theory in order to cure them, to make them disappear, by demonstrating that they are grounded in misconceptions and caricatures. Fish's attentiveness to the specific objections offered by his opponents is an ironic means to his end, which is to eradicate their objections and their position entirely. His final suggestion—that this theoretical mopping up will have no consequences for the practice of literary criticism—underscores the paradoxical dismissiveness underlying a project that treats the many objections raised to contemporary theoretical developments in such detail.

De Man, on the other hand, brushes aside the historical specificity of the resistance to theory; just as a "literal" historicity is excluded from his analysis of Derrida, read as a theatrical narrative convention, so the details of the historical objections offered to contemporary innovations in theory have no (literal) consequence. But de Man interprets the sheer existence of these misunderstandings as an index of a profound and inevitable (transhistorical) resistance to the introduction of any form of linguistic terminology into the discourse of literary studies. "Crude" historical objections "literally" don't matter. (The bizarre abstraction of this reference—who *are* these "misinformed" critics with their "crude misunderstandings"?—mimics de Man's procedure.) But that such objections persist and, indeed, flourish, signals to de Man that they are the superficial effects of a deeper cause, the historical and polemical traces of a genuinely theoretical impasse—or a trope—which can never be eradicated. This is the aporia of literary theory.

De Man is not concerned to end anti-theory polemics; misunderstanding, like the literal-minded, will always be with us. On the contrary, he concludes that such resistance is inherent in literary theory; indeed, it is literary theory: "Nothing can over-come the resistance to theory since theory *is* itself this resis-tance. The loftier the aims and the better the methods of literary theory, the less possible it becomes. Yet literary theory is not in danger of going under; it cannot help but flourish, and the more it is resisted, the more it flourishes, since the language it speaks is the language of self-resistance. What remains impossible to decide is whether this flourishing is a triumph or a fall" (R 20). Theory itself is aporetic, undecidable, a triumph or a fall. It resists and in its resistance, in the language of self-resistance, comes into being and flourishes. Where Fish uncovers an inevi-table, though temporary, triumph ("you believe what you be-lieve" [F 363]), de Man offers a transhistorical moment of "un-decidability," a "necessary" flourishing, "necessarily" deprived of the epistemological confidence that Fish sees as an unavoid-able effect of belief.

This displacement of historical conflict into aporia allows an escape from the critical attitudes of diagnosis and polemic. Only when rhetoric is reconceived as such a figure is it possible to elude the work of polemic, of rhetoric as persuasion, and to offer instead an unpolemical, "rhetorically conscious reading." Fish's epistemological confidence, though set in a context of fatalism about change and the possibility of intellectual prog-ress, is one of the enabling conditions for his commitment to open polemic, to rhetoric as persuasive action. De Man's retreat from history to trope is bound to his refusal of polemic, but the question of "confidence" is an awkward one. What is the rela-tion between undecidability—"what remains impossible to de-cide is whether this flourishing is a triumph or a fall"—and what we commonly call confidence? Why does aporia entail (or en-able) the de Manian rejection of polemic?

II

It would certainly be possible to object to my claim that de Manian analysis precludes polemic. Critics who have ventured observations on this aspect of his text are divided, if not confused.[10] De Man's own remarks concerning polemic are often critical; he has characterized the "polemical response" to contemporary theory as "quarrelsome" and "ill-humor[ed]," the effect of "indignation," "anxiety," and "disturbed moral conscience".[11] He begins his meditation on the resistance to theory with the observation that interpretation "is admittedly an open discipline, which can, however, hope to evolve by rational means, *despite* internal crises, controversies and polemics," and he associates "the polemical opposition" to theory with "systematic non-understanding and misrepresentations," and "unsubstantial but eternally recurrent objections" (R 4, 12, my emphasis). These comments suggest that rationality and polemic are rarely, if ever, aligned. Polemic obscures technical matters and blandly historicizes epistemological issues. For de Man, "reading is an argument (which is not necessarily the same as a polemic),"[12] and an adequate theory of reading can be composed only if one can transcend the polemical. "The ideological shrillness of the polemics that surround the advent of literary theory in our time," he wrote, "cannot entirely conceal that these debates, however ephemeral and *ad hominem* they may be, are the external symptoms of tensions that originate at the furthest remove from the stage of public debate."[13] I would suggest that it is from this great distance, literally from off stage, that de Man seeks to intervene in that debate: there, he establishes a position for the rhetorical reader of general persuasion outside the realm of polemic.

This effort has not been wholly successful. Commentators

[10]Fish's case is naturally quite different; references to his polemic are virtual signatures of discussions of his work. In "Fish vs. Fish," Steven Rendall suggests that sheer delight in controversy finally leads Fish in *Is There a Text in This Class?* to take himself as an opponent: "Fish, like his pugilistic counterpart Muhammed Ali, is at his best as a counterpuncher. The essays reprinted here suggest that he thrives on opposition and that if he had no critics he would have to invent them": *Diacritics* 12:4 (1982), 49.

[11]De Man, "The Return to Philology," p. 1355.

[12]De Man, Foreword to Carol Jacobs, *The Dissimulating Harmony* (Baltimore: The Johns Hopkins University Press, 1978), p. xi. Further references to this volume (*DH*) will be given in parentheses in the text.

[13]De Man, "Sign and Symbol in Hegel's *Aesthetics*," *Critical Inquiry* 8:4 (1982), 761.

display a certain revealing awkwardness when they attempt to characterize de Manian polemic. Edward Said is tempted to identify the polemical moment in de Man's work. He resorts instead to a strangely tentative comment: "I would hesitate to call de Man a polemicist, but insofar as he exhorts critics to do one thing rather than another, I would say that he tells them to avoid talking as if historical scholarship, for example, could ever get beyond and talk seriously about literature."[14] From polemic to exhortation to telling, the confidence of the language declines; Said actually feels constrained to qualify the claim that de Man offers any prescription whatsoever for criticism with the words "insofar as." This is a peculiar reticence. In a more extended analysis, Frank Lentricchia sees de Man's "Olympian stance" as an effect of his "rhetoric of authority."[15] He argues that de Man's texts offer "crafty rhetorical maneuvers" and "prepackaged conclusions, not arguments" (*ANC* 293). But Lentricchia never reads these rhetorical gestures as polemical. Rather, he implies that, thanks to its "rhetoric of authority," "the de Man style at its most intimidating" precludes the necessity of polemic. "De Man has found it necessary to speak only sparingly" and "has not had to speak in anything but a cool and straightforward manner" (284).

Even Jonathan Culler, who shows little sympathy for most of Lentricchia's claims, adopts the rubric of the rhetoric of authority to describe de Man's text. Culler suggests that "de Man's writing is special—and often especially annoying—in its strategy of omitting crucial demonstrations in order to *put readers in a position where they cannot profit from his analyses without according belief to what seems implausible or at least unproven. . . .* His essays often assure the reader that demonstration of these points would not be difficult, only cumbersome, and they do provide much detailed argument and exegesis, but these gaps in argumentation may be quite striking" (*OD* 229, my emphases). It is at the very least unusual to find one theorist assuring us that an-

[14]Edward Said, *The World, the Text and the Critic* (Cambridge: Harvard University Press, 1981), p. 163.
[15]Lentricchia, *After the New Criticism*, pp. 300, 283.

other writes essays that "do provide much detailed argument and exegesis." Argument and exegesis being the ordinary work of a literary critic, such things generally go without saying. Culler prefaces his discussion of de Man with considerations of essays by Walter Benn Michaels and Barbara Johnson. He explains: "an account of deconstructive criticism cannot, of course, neglect de Man's writings, but his 'rhetoric of authority' often makes them less exemplary than those of younger critics who must still try to demonstrate what they wish to assert and who therefore may provide a clearer view of important issues and procedures" (229). Culler's remarks and his expository strategy suggest, as Lentricchia's do, that de Man's text has an oblique and problematic relation to the polemical. Persuasiveness seems, in some sense, to be sacrificed to a certain kind of a rhetoric; but, paradoxically, Culler and Lentricchia characterize this rhetoric primarily by its (too easy) assumption of an always already persuaded audience, by its "authority," and its consequent refusal to try to persuade. Thus, the rhetorical stance seems to block the very end which it has either taken for granted or forsworn. This paradox can be displaced if we recall that for the reader de Man posits, persuasiveness is opposed to polemic, that is, the persuasiveness of an argument increases as the polemical is excluded. The absence of polemic (or of the rhetoric of persuasion) constitutes a persuasive argument; hence the pivotal function of undecidability—of not taking sides—in critical practice.

De Man excludes polemic as he privileges undecidability, but, ironically, the trope of undecidability figures the possibility of persuasion without limits, of general persuasion. In one sense, the de Manian text reads as though it were written before the "crisis" that produced pluralist polemic, or as if this crisis were an event in the distant past, so remote as to have lost all its threatening unpredictability. In fact, de Man's text represents a revision of the problematic of general persuasion that seeks to reestablish its hegemony in more secure terms. For Fish, the continuity essential to pluralism is established by the imperative to persuasion: "everyone is obliged to practice the art of persuasion." Undecidability is de Man's strategy for establishing a similar continuity. No reader is explicitly excluded from de Manian analyses, even as they eschew overtly polemical seductions. The figure of aporia is persuasive precisely insofar as it is an inclusive space, where rhetoric springs its seductive epistemological trap on every reader. There, misunderstanding is generalized by the seductive rhetoric of tropes.

The intricacy and complexity of de Man's analyses are a form of relentless self-questioning, a kind of internalized polemic, de Man versus de Man. For the de Manian reader, polemic has been displaced inward. Undecidability is the internalized trace of "shrill polemics." Rather than confront readers across a potential discontinuity, de Man discovers discontinuities within texts and offers them to every reader. Barbara Johnson has pointed out that "the de-construction of a text does not proceed by random doubt or arbitrary subversion, but by the careful teasing out of warring forces of signification within the text itself."[16] The American Heritage dictionary defines "polemic" as "a controversy or argument, especially one that is a refutation of or an attack upon a specific opinion, doctrine, or the like," and the word derives from the Greek *polemikos*, "of war, hostile." The warring forces that take their historical or literal form in polemics in the rhetoric of persuasion are, in de Man's analyses, located within his/the text. The displacement empties the relationships among readers of their warring, polemical character. The representation of the text as always already "deconstructed," as already the site, the anticipation, of all polemic, returns us to a pluralist discourse that refuses the possibility of exclusion.[17]

[16]Barbara Johnson, *The Critical Difference: Essays in the Rhetoric of Criticism* (Baltimore: Johns Hopkins University Press, 1980), p. 5.

[17]This de Manian articulation of general persuasion shares certain features with those of the other pluralists we have encountered. For example, Fish's insistence that his current positions only play out a role already inscribed in/anticipated by earlier texts similarly effaces the historical contingency of reading. Hirsch's invocation of the Golden Age of Literature, though remote in tone from de Man's valorization of literature as rhetoric, projects a utopian space in which "conflicting appetences . . . are nourished, with none subjected to the tyrannical domination of another" (H 139). Of course, for Hirsch, this aporia is harmonious, but its enabling conditions include the reader of general persuasion. We

This anticipation and internalization of polemic constitutes de Man's rejection of history. William Ray suggests that de Man "never waits for history; he appropriates its privilege by putting his conclusions into question almost before they have been reached. . . . de Man's approach *generates history out of the tension between meaning's warring identities*" (LM 191, 203, my emphases). But history is nothing if not something we must wait for; its privilege cannot be formally appropriated, unless one has already reduced contingency and discontinuity, that is, the disruptive play of historical conflict, to an intralinguistic/intrasubjective figure. The temptation "to anticipate a certain historical process" is, as Luce Irigaray points out, always a "prescription," and as such, a fiction of power.[18] Any such "anticipation," then, is part of a struggle, an effort, not simply to dominate a field, but to constitute it, to set its problematic. De Man's refusal to acknowledge this struggle is symptomatic of his effort to interpellate an anti-polemical and ahistorical reader for the rhetoric of general persuasion. To defend this rhetorically conscious reader he must resist any effort to reassert the polemical.

Stanley Corngold is virtually the only observer to argue that the de Manian essay is a "polemical instrument." In his reading, de Man's is an "incessantly polemical stance," characterized by an "attack attitude"; "the extremity, the provocative display, the rush to the apodictic, the modish polemical tone" of de Man's text are all judged to be plainly evident and "scandalous."[19] Corngold's view is noteworthy if only because he labels de Man polemical with such ease whereas other critics find it impossible. But I cite his remarks mainly because de Man responded to them in a revealing way. "A Letter from Paul de Man" was published in *Critical Inquiry* alongside Corngold's article, and it

---

even find, in de Man's insistence on the centrality of epistemological questions ("no reading is conceivable in which the question of its truth or falsehood is not primarily involved" [*Dissimulating Harmony*, p. xi]), an echo of Booth's emphasis on critical understanding.

[18]Luce Irigaray, *This Sex Which Is Not One*, tr. Catherine Porter (Ithaca: Cornell University Press, 1985), p. 124.

[19]Stanley Corngold, "Error in Paul de Man," *Critical Inquiry* 8:3 (1982), 490. Further references to this essay (C) will be given in parentheses in the text.

opens with expressions of gratitude and the rather modest claim that it will try only to "set the record straight on one specific point." "You generously invited me to reply to Stanley Corngold's essay, a somewhat ambivalent assignment since I can hardly feel to be 'addressed' by a discourse which, as is so often the case, addresses its own rather than my defenses or uncertainties. But since the tone of the essay suggests indictment rather than dialogue. . .the only alternative thus left to me is a plea for mercy."[20] The "Letter" avoids an extended confrontation with Corngold's critique and provides no ammunition for a reading of de Man's work as polemical. But the figure that founds de Man's elusive response is unusual; he insists he can hardly feel "addressed" by "Error in Paul de Man." This remark is momentarily puzzling because Corngold's piece is addressed in an almost idiosyncratic manner to de Man the man. The opening of the essay gives new meaning to the phrase *ad hominem*. It begins with two footnotes that present a series of personal references to de Man's life, his age, one of his relatives, and said relative's politics, and with a less unusual, but equally personal, acknowledgment of Corngold's "indebtedness—and that of many others—to Paul de Man as a teacher" (C 489). To add to its interest, the acknowledgment poses as a disclaimer: "I leave out of this account my indebtedness. . . ."

Had de Man explicitly noticed this remark, he might have observed that it is a paralepsis. The footnote precisely enters into the account the author's indebtedness (perhaps thought to be less obtrusive when coupled with the debts of many other, anonymous, students). But de Man refers to Corngold's personal salutation only to correct the date of his birth. At the same

[20]De Man, "A Letter from Paul de Man," p. 509. Further references to this essay (L) will be given in parentheses in the text. Daniel T. O'Hara points out that "of the several recent critiques of his work offered by liberal humanists, sociologically minded, anti-humanistic historians of the critical institution, deconstructive scholars of the abyss of intertextuality, et al., the late Paul de Man chose to respond to only one of them, Stanley Corngold's." *The Romance of Interpretation: Visionary Criticism from Pater to de Man* (New York: Columbia University Press, 1985), p. 207.

time, his "Letter" comments on the critic's relation to his work, his diction, and his audience (which must be said to include his students—quite literally in this case). De Man's complaint that he "hardly feels addressed" arises from the fact that he has been all too intimately addressed, and that the problems of address and of debt—which are in fact problems of audience—are integral to the theoretical problems at hand.

What is of interest to me here is not any genuinely personal question about this student and this teacher, but the reinscription of a pluralist reader in the rhetoric of general persuasion. Corngold's "personal" address forces de Man to reassert his view of the reader as the subject of a rhetorically conscious discourse. As de Man sees it, Corngold's animus and his preoccupation with his own defenses infect his representation of de Man's text. The "trenchant tone of accusation," is "transposed to my own diction: I am said to *force* crisis, to *devastate* horizons and perceptions, to *demolish* metaphors, and to *hate* genealogies, but all this sound and fury never allows me to move one jot beyond the benign and self-tolerating universe somewhat surprisingly attributed to Kant. I sound, in short, like a bully who also wants to play it safe" (L 510). The phrase "somewhat surprisingly" is a perfect index of the restraint this writing sustains. Even my proleptic gloss—Corngold's animus "infects" his representation—is overheated when compared to de Man's choice of the neutral word "transposed," with none of the darker overtones of my disease metaphor. Only the introduction of the word "bully" jars, with its obvious hint that Corngold must be the bully. De Man emerges only "somewhat surprised" by such behavior.

That he is not anything more than "somewhat" surprised is reiterated as the passage continues:

> The pattern of defense is familiar coming from those who feel threatened by readings that lay claim neither to hostility, nor to tolerance, nor indeed to any easily personifiable mode of relationship. With regard to concepts or to the fellow-critics I write about, I have never felt anything approaching hostility nor, for that

matter, benignity; very different sets of terms would have to be used to designate a rapport that is a great deal less agonistic than that of forensic, familial, or erotic combat. [L 510.]

The comforting assertion of familiarity is quintessentially de Manian.[21] This tone and not a "rhetoric of authority" or an "incessantly polemical stance" is most characteristic of his text, and, it is a symptom of its pluralist character. De Man simultaneously refuses Corngold's address and asserts the model of the general reader by invoking an apparent opposition between the public and the private. In erotic or familial conflict, he suggests, "hostility," "tolerance," and "benignity" are relevant terms; emotion, even as civic an emotion as "tolerance," belongs to this private realm. In the arena where we meet and act as persons, "easily personifiable" modes of relation are appropriate. But "readings," "concepts," and "fellow-critics" occupy the public realm. This public sphere is apparently less agonistic than private spaces, the home, the bedroom, and easily personifiable modes of relationship as well as feeling, in the sense of emotion, are out of place.

The deconstruction of the opposition private/public (or personal/political) has been carried out in numerous discourses across disciplines and within the popular discourse of feminism. And, indeed, de Man's own rhetoric crosses the opposition when he invokes the "forensic" alongside the erotic and the familial. Nevertheless, the burden of de Man's argument in this passage is sustained by the emergence of the trope of personal voice. This voice testifies authoritatively to an inner state which guarantees the very division that produces its authority: "With

[21]When referring to contemporary critics and polemics, de Man frequently asserts the familiarity or predictability of the postures assumed. Writing theoretically about theory generates "predictable difficulties": "Resistance to theory," p. 4. "Deconstruction, as was easily predictable, has been much misrepresented": *Allegories of Reading*, p. x. This is not surprising (to borrow de Man's formula) given his view of history; if literal history is external to the theoretical, theory will predictably return to familiar problems, to the intractable problem of figural language. The effect of this gesture is reassuring, indeed, almost consoling; a familiar problem is probably one we can handle in a traditional way, as we always have.

regard to concepts or to the fellow critics *I* write about, *I* have never *felt* anything approaching hostility nor, for that matter, benignity" (my emphases). What is more, de Man attributes Corngold's "transposition" to *his* feelings: "the pattern of defense is familiar coming from those who *feel* threatened." (my emphasis), even as the distinction between the public and private is muddied again by a second opposition between those critics who "feel threatened" and those who "have never felt anything approaching hostility nor . . . benignity."

Corngold's essay actually says almost nothing about de Man's feelings. His remarks, as de Man quite faithfully represents them, concern the distinction between error and mistake and a translation of Nietzsche. But his argument is framed by his salutation to his teacher, a biographical reflection on de Man's style, and, at the close, by a speculative passage that introduces the possibility that de Man's reading may be determined by his interest in finding "a certain reading of Nietzsche *which he needs*" (507). This concluding introduction of desire and need is linked to the earlier address. It warrants de Man's response not because it undermines his reading of a particular passage in Nietzsche, but because it puts into question the detachment of the de Manian reader, and thus the technical status of rhetoric as well. The eruption of need threatens the very possibility of rhetorically conscious reading within the problematic of general persuasion.

De Man refuses Corngold's "address" and thus his implicit characterization of reading because a pluralist model of rhetorical reading must exclude need, interest, and desire; they place unacceptable limits on the possibility of persuasion. In the act of reading, the de Manian reader is not "subject" to the imperatives of a temporal body in history: the rhetorically conscious reader is subject only to the text. This view allows de Man to articulate and defend his readings—and his concept of literature—by insisting that they are in fact the work of the text itself.

> The reading is not "our" reading, since it uses only the linguistic elements provided by the text itself; the distinction between au-

thor and reader is one of the false distinctions that the reading makes evident. The deconstruction is not something we have added to the text but it constituted the text in the first place. A literary text simultaneously asserts and denies the authority of its own rhetorical mode, and by reading the text as we did we were only trying to come closer to being as rigorous a reader as the author had to be in order to write the sentence in the first place. Poetic writing is the most advanced and refined mode of deconstruction; it may differ from critical or discursive writing in the economy of its articulation, but not in kind. [*AR* 17]

Although de Man says that the reader/author distinction is a false one, the reader alone has vanished from this scene. To assert that a given reading "only" reflects an effort "to come closer to being as rigorous a reader as the author had to be to write the sentence in the first place" is a hollow assertion of authority. The author's rigor is erected as the absolute measure of the reader's rigor—despite the claim that such a distinction is false; the remark recuperates that authoritative rigor solely to naturalize its own reading. It also strangely echoes the response every teacher offers the beginning student who wonders: "Do you really believe all that stuff is *in* there?" De Man invests "the text itself" with his values and veils that investment with the claim that "only the linguistic elements provided by the text itself" have been put into play by the reading. But if nothing is added to the text, there is no reading—only what Macherey calls a "simulacrum," wherein "analysis is a repetition, another way of saying what has already been said" (143).

For de Man, both reader and reading are identified with the pre-existing text. There is only one such reader; every reading subject is this reader, and only this reading can genuinely be said to be reading at all. "Deconstruction is not something we can decide to do or not to do at will. It is co-extensive with any use of language, and this use is compulsive or, as Nietzsche formulates it, imperative" (*AR* 125). Deconstruction has always already been achieved, and its seductive operation is identical for every reader. We might gloss this position by arguing that de Man views subjectivity as a textual or rhetorical effect. Obviously, I have no quarrel with the claim that subjects are discursively constituted. (This is not, by this time, necessarily a radical position, and we have seen, in Fish's case, that it is not per se incompatible with the problematic of general persuasion.) But although de Man observes that "by calling the subject a text, the text calls itself, to some extent, a subject" (*AR* 112), he consistently evades the insight that discursively constituted subjects differ among and within themselves in ways that necessarily impinge on the problematics of reading. Difference and discontinuity trouble every reading subject—even at the level of the trope.

Corngold's "address" introduces the scandal of differences among readers, in the form of debts, needs, and desires, and de Man responds by denying that hostility, tolerance, benignity, or agon have any relation whatsoever to proper reading. These terms are not inscribed as textual effects; they are denied as feelings: "I have never *felt* . . . ." The voice of authenticity (experience) speaks authoritatively in order to deny its own significance to the problematics of reading. By excluding the "easily personifiable," de Man seeks to ground the "rhetorically conscious reader" whose subjectivity/reading is an effect of the generalizing rhetoric of the text at hand, and only of that text. Thus, the subject is *the* text, rather than (just) any (other) text; the reader is undecidable, an aporia beyond the reach of history and polemic. The unpredictable and contingent investments and interests that determine discourses of the familial, the erotic, and the pedagogical are excluded. The reader of general persuasion emerges as an impartial observer of familiar figures.

III

A few pages into the opening chapter of *Allegories of Reading*, de Man makes a remark that we have come to recognize as characteristic of pluralist discourses. He has been considering the relationship between grammar and rhetoric as it is treated in contemporary literary theory. But after a few passages touching on Genette, Todorov, and Peirce, among others, he feels constrained to change the strategy of his exposition, commenting: "These remarks should indicate at least the existence and the difficulty of the question, a difficulty which puts its concise theoretical exposition beyond my powers. I must retreat therefore into a pragmatic discourse and try to illustrate the tension between grammar and rhetoric in a few specific textual examples" (9). By now, this is a familiar pluralist move: the theoretical effort; the exhaustion or failure of that effort; the imposition of an opposition between theory and pragmatism; finally, the so-called retreat into "specific textual examples." Although de Man's relationship to the question of theory cannot be simply assimilated to Fish's or Booth's or Hirsch's, he too feels constrained to claim that theoretical exposition is inadequate and prefers the illustrative power of example. That this gesture of retreat takes place under the rubric of an acknowledgment of his own limitations—a concise theoretical treatment is beyond his powers, though not impossible—only strengthens the affinities between this passage and the pluralist discourse we have examined.

De Man represents his decision to enter a pragmatic discourse as a practical rather than a theoretical decision. A concise theoretical exposition is out of the question, a lengthy one (apparently) impractical; hence, the move to illustrations. But the practical decision (again) has theoretical consequences. When de Man turns toward his examples, he moves immediately out of the polemical arena. This retreat carries a theoretical weight unmatched in the other texts we have considered. The remainder of "Semiology and Rhetoric" is devoid of references to theorists like Todorov and Genette, critics who might appear to be de Man's theoretical and polemical opponents.

The Preface notes that "most of this book was written before 'deconstruction' became a bone of contention, and the term is used here in a technical rather than a polemical sense" (*AR* x). This is not a surprising distinction. As de Man informs us, the "opponents of [his] approach [to reading] have been more eager to attack what they assume to be its ideological motives rather than the technicalities of its procedure. This is particularly true with regard to the term 'deconstruction,' which has rapidly become a label as well as a target" (ix-x). Polemicists attack deconstruction, but only insofar as it is an ideology. De Man is not a defender of deconstruction—that would be a polemical project—but someone who works with it, technically, with indifference to the possibility of polemical response to its opponents. As we've seen, polemical defenses are a waste of time, almost naive. "Deconstruction, as was easily predictable, has been much misrepresented, dismissed as a harmless academic game or denounced as a terrorist weapon, and I have all the fewer illusions about the possibility of countering these aberrations since such an expectation would go against the drift of my own readings" (x). De Man's disdain for polemic has two aspects here. First, polemic tends toward misrepresentations, hyperbolic dismissals, and denunciations, and neglects the technicalities of reading. In addition, polemic is ineffective, a fundamentally illusory project, another historical response to intractable, transhistorical problems. In "Semiology and Rhetoric," theory, as polemic, is displaced by illustrations. Or, more precisely, de Man's theoretical claims are wholly mediated by readings of particular (literary) texts, with all the ideological effects attending this strategy of exposition.

De Man's first and most interesting example is an unusual one. In the rest of his book and in his work in general, he prefers to address major canonical authors, literary and philosophical: Rousseau, Nietzsche, Rilke, and Proust. But as he begins his excursus into pragmatic discourse, his text is a television sitcom. The topic is the "so-called rhetorical question," "perhaps the most commonly known instance of an apparent symbiosis between a grammatical and a rhetorical structure" (9).

> I take the first example from the sub-literature of the mass media: asked by his wife whether he wants to have his bowling shoes laced over or laced under, Archie Bunker answers with a question: "What's the difference?" Being a reader of sublime simplicity, his wife replies by patiently explaining the difference between lacing over and lacing under, whatever this may be, but

provokes only ire. "What's the difference" did not ask for difference but means instead "I don't give a damn what the difference
is." The same grammatical pattern engenders two meanings that
are mutually exclusive: the literal meaning asks for the concept
(difference) whose existence is denied by the figurative meaning.
[*AR* 9].

This is the kind of illustration Fish relishes, fortuitously granted
by popular culture, like a baseball player's homerun record or
the sign on the door of a private club.[22] But the difference between de Man's treatment of his illustration and the reading one
would expect from Fish is striking. The passage engenders a
rare de Manian pun: Derrida and Nietzsche appear in the guise
of "archie De-Bunker[s]." But overall, de Man's treatment of the
passage is brief, amusing but almost subdued, and, to use the
term he most privileges, technical. The polemical exploitation
that such an illustration would certainly have received in Fish's
hands is almost wholly absent. This despite the fact that the
rhetorical question, as de Man notes elsewhere, is characteristic
of polemic.

More important, one misses any particular attention to the
internal polemics in this text, to the warring forces represented
by Archie and Edith, two readers at work figuring this text. In
fact, de Man's reading retreats from the anti-pluralist moment of
Fish's "Reply to John Reichert." De Man generalizes the failure
of understanding that Fish represents in the person of John
Reichert, and he founds a rhetoric of general persuasion on that
failure. In de Man's text, every reader is a Reichert figure;
(mis)understanding is built into the structure of language, and it
excludes no one.

In order to generalize misunderstanding, de Man must ob-

---

[22]Fish also makes illustrative use of a woman's confusion over a question
although it is not a rhetorical question; at least, not when she asks it. When it
reappears as the title of Fish's book, it has perhaps begun to function both
rhetorically and polemically. Mary Jacobus considers Fish's text and the place of
"woman" in theory in "Is There a Woman in This Text?" *New Literary History* 14:1
(1982), 117–141.

scure the particular anti-pluralist figure in his text: Edith. To overlook Edith is simultaneously to overlook the internal polemics of the text, to displace them into language as such. To explore this oversight, we must align ourselves with Edith's "sublime simplicity." We can begin with a question. De Man reports that Archie's "wife replies [to his question] by patiently explaining the difference between lacing over and lacing under." Why does he then add/ask his own unmarked (rhetorical) question: "whatever this may be"?

De Man takes the rhetorical question as his text because he reads it as an instance of figural language in which the "figure is conveyed by means of a syntactical device" (9) and "a perfectly clear syntactical paradigm (the question) engenders a sentence that has at least two meanings, of which the one asserts and the other denies its illocutionary force" (10). Perfect clarity of syntax is of no use to the de Manian interpreter; neither grammatical nor other linguistic devices will enable "us" to "read" this sentence. The analysis culminates in undecidability: "The same grammatical pattern engenders two meanings that are mutually exclusive" (9).

De Man interprets this situation as a strictly (literally) linguistic problem, in his terms, a rhetorical problem. The linguistic "pattern" is the source of two meanings, engendering aporia. His analysis does not produce a reading, but it does produce a particular kind of reader, a reader who doesn't take sides, indeed, a reader who cannot take sides. The aporia of the text thus positions its would-be reader in a kind of utopia. De Man's pluralist reader transcends the positions represented in this text; indeed, he transcends positionality itself, and retreats into a "suspended uncertainty that [is] unable to choose between two modes of reading" (16).

De Man sees, of course, that it is possible to settle on a reading, a position in relation to this "semiological enigma." But he rejects any such position because it can never be logically or epistemologically rigorous, and it can be achieved only if we lapse into an extralinguistic analysis.

The confusion can only be cleared up by the *intervention of an extra-textual intention,* such as Archie Bunker putting his wife straight; but the very anger he displays is indicative of more than impatience; it reveals his despair when *confronted with a structure of linguistic meaning that he cannot control* and that holds the discouraging prospect of an infinity of similar future confusions, all of them potentially catastrophic in their consequences. *Nor is this intervention really a part of the mini-text constituted by the figure* which holds our attention only as long as it remains suspended and unresolved. I follow the usage of common speech in calling this semiological enigma "rhetorical." The grammatical model of the question becomes rhetorical not when we have, on the one hand, a literal meaning and on the other hand, a figural meaning, but when it is *impossible to decide by grammatical or other linguistic devices* which of the two meanings (that can be entirely incompatible) prevails. Rhetoric radically suspends *logic* and opens up vertiginous possibilities of referential aberration. [*AR* 10, my emphases]

The opposition between the extralinguistic and the linguistic is critical here. Recourse to extratextual intervention is belittled because it shifts attention away from the area of "technical" interest—the figural potential of language, rhetoric. De Man defines the "tension" between grammar and rhetoric as a feature of language itself, which he believes works to limit the sphere of inquiry to logical and epistemological consequences. So-called extralinguistic analyses and explanations are symptomatic of either insufficient rigor or a kind of faintheartedness, an unwillingness on the part of the interpreter to remain uncomfortably suspended between meanings. Thus, de Man complains about the "detour or flight from language" which he believes characterizes literary studies (79). He suggests elsewhere that those who take refuge in extralinguistic, historical analysis are primarily seduced by comforting fictions or alibis. "The temptation is great to domesticate the more threatening difficulties by historicizing them out of consciousness"; "stating an epistemological tension in terms of a historical narrative . . . creates an appeasing delusion of understanding."[23]

[23]De Man, "Pascal's Allegory of Persuasion," pp. 3, 24.

My reading of the pluralist problematic suggests that the opposite is true. Historical explanation most threatens pluralism, in part because it questions the transhistorical status of consciousness and of reading: it remembers Edith. Because it privileges contingency and accident as determining and because, by emphasizing interests and conflicts, it resists the domestication that theory can seek to impose, historical explanation is always ultimately elided in pluralist discourse, assimilated to a general, normative model. For Hirsch, this model is logical, for Booth, ethical, for Fish, rhetorical, in the sense of polemical. In de Man's work, we find a second inscription of the rhetoric of general persuasion.

From the perspective of pluralist practice, then, de Man's rigid distinction between the linguistic and the extralinguistic in the case of the Bunkers is merely routine. But it is actually a rather spectacular instantiation of the strategy we have traced through other pluralist texts. Its appearance is dramatic in part because "Semiology and Rhetoric" opens with a discussion of the tension in literary studies between the demands of formalism and the temptations of reference, the linguistic and the extralinguistic, which is rooted in the metaphor inside/outside. De Man argues that the opposition itself spawns the longing to reconcile its terms:

> The attraction of reconciliation is the elective breeding-ground of false models and metaphors; it accounts for the metaphorical model of literature as a kind of box that separates an inside from an outside, and the reader or critic as the person who opens the lid in order to release in the open what was secreted but inaccessible inside. It matters little whether we call the inside of the box the content or the form, the outside the meaning or the appearance. The recurrent debate opposing intrinsic to extrinsic criticism stands under the aegis of an inside/outside metaphor that is never being seriously questioned. [*AR* 5]

This passage outlines a position that puts an often bitterly argued issue in perspective; the call to question the metaphor inside/outside implies that de Man has distanced himself from the terms of this argument and is therefore not likely to enter it on either side. His final observation—that the metaphor itself has never been seriously questioned—hints that such an interrogation may be about to begin.

De Man is cautious, as ever: "I certainly don't expect to dislodge this age-old model in one short try" (5). He never actually examines the metaphor, but tries primarily to elude it, "to speculate on a different set of terms, perhaps less simple in their differential relationships than the strictly polar, binary opposition between inside and outside and therefore less likely to enter into the easy play of chiasmic reversals" (5). The terms, as it develops, are grammar and rhetoric. De Man finally argues that "the couple grammar/rhetoric, certainly not a binary opposition since they in no way exclude each other, disrupts and confuses the neat antithesis of the inside/outside pattern" (12). But despite de Man's gloss on binarism and the legitimacy of his more general claim, the inside/outside opposition that he seems first to problematize and then to disrupt is reinscribed at other points in his text.

The couple inside/outside reappears most tendentiously in the text of *All in the Family*. A first reading of this example might leave the impression that the text consists of the entire exchange between Archie and Edith, from Edith's initial question to Archie's angry attempt to put her "straight." De Man reads the scene differently. He argues that the confusion produced by "a perfectly clear syntactical paradigm" "can only be cleared up by the intervention of an *extra-textual intention* such as Archie Bunker putting his wife straight" (10, my emphases). Archie's unrepresented remarks, doubtless to the effect that his wife is a dingbat, are *not* textual; the text does not include the entirety of the fictional scene: "Nor is this intervention really a part of the mini-text constituted by the figure" (10). The "mini-text" itself is entirely constituted by the "perfectly clear syntactic paradigm": "what's the difference." Everything else is outside this text. (Although my diction here echoes "il n'y a pas de hors texte," de Man's practice seems to me to differ significantly from Derrida's.) This analysis reasserts the inside/outside metaphor with a vengeance that parodies New Critical formalism. But the imperatives that force de Man to declare such limits to his "minitext" emerge immediately when one undertakes a reading of the so-called extratext.

There are two figures in this larger text, in addition to the rhetorical question. According to de Man's synopsis, they are Archie Bunker and "his wife." Edith is never named. The exclusion of Edith as a reader is the necessary beginning of de Man's reading and, in a certain sense, its end. Archie is inside and Edith outside the text. Anxious as he is to reach the pun that identifies a critic like Derrida as an arche De-Bunker who asks "what is the Difference?", de Man quite overlooks the other Bunker, a different Bunker, the difference within the Bunkers— Edith. Edith reminds us that Archie's difficulty is not solely linguistic, though it is certainly that. But if Archie is "confronted with a structure of linguistic meaning that he cannot control," he is also confronted by another uncontrollable figure, the figure of Edith. In fact, it is Edith who, not as an intention and certainly not as a psychology, but as a *reading,* a different reading, discloses the uncontrollable structure of language—to Archie and to de Man.

When "what's the difference" is placed within this larger text, two readings appear, and they correspond to the two readers in the text. Edith hears/reads this sentence as a question; in de Man's terminology, she reads it "literally." Archie, however, asks/reads a rhetorical question; for him, this is not a question that asks for an answer. As de Man puts it: " 'what's the difference' did not ask for difference but *means* instead 'I don't give a damn what the difference is' " (my emphasis). It means this, of course, to Archie, not to Edith.

Theoretically, de Man cannot afford to associate himself with either of these positions. As soon as he sides with one of these figures, reads from the position of Archie or Edith, he falls out of aporia; he passes into a position. He needs, instead, to remain suspended between these two figures, not taking sides. The phrase "these two figures" itself bears a double meaning, referring not only to Archie and Edith, but to the readings they give, the figuration each represents. Yet de Man characterizes Edith's interpretation as literal.

Archie is the central figure in de Man's analysis, and he quickly becomes a model for the general reader. Edith is Archie's wife; she is "patient"; she needs to be "put straight," which, ironically, means that she needs to be clued in to the rhetorical meaning of Archie's response, which she has mistakenly read "straight," "literally." De Man does finally see Archie's wife as a kind of reader, but one who reads with "sublime simplicity." Given that he regards reading as not simply complex, but as impossibly complex, this last epithet may be the de Manian equivalent of "dingbat." De Man assimilates Edith's simple reading to literalism and aligns her with Derrida's "followers," with those who mistake his historical figures for literal history. To take the grammatical pattern "what's the difference" literally is apparently to give a sublimely simple reading of it. In "common speech," the phrase "literal reading" indicates the absence of reading, no reading at all, or the refusal of interpretation; literal meaning is determinate, a core of determinate meaning.

But elsewhere de Man cites Nietzsche's view that language is essentially figural: " 'No such thing as an unrhetorical, "natural" language exists that could be used as a point of reference: language is itself the result of purely rhetorical tricks and devices. . . . Language is rhetoric' " (*AR* 105).[24] "What is being forgotten in . . . false literalism is precisely the rhetorical, symbolic quality of all language" (111). Only "false literalism" can oppose Edith's reading to Archie's reading as literal to figural. Once we refuse to oppose Edith's literal-mindedness to Archie's rhetoric, we can unmask the mechanism by which de Man tries simultaneously to exclude his context and read in it, too.

Edith's reading is no more "literal" than Archie's; it requires the same *kind* of interpretative activity, and it is equally com-

---

[24]De Man cites Nietzsche's *Gesammelte Werke* (Munich: Musarion Verlag, 1922), 5:300.

plex. There is, however, a sense in which Edith's reading is sublimely simple, in that simple means "having or manifesting little sense or intellect; silly."[25] It is probably safe to say that a portion of *All in the Family*'s audience reads Edith as a character with relatively little sense, a silly character. Edith is also sublimely "simple" to Archie. I would argue that de Man aligns himself unequivocally with Archie's position when he observes that Edith "replies by patiently explaining the difference between lacing over and lacing under, *whatever this may be.*"

Edith knows, though of course she who knows is only a fiction, a figure herself. Edith can and must—can only—give an apparently nonrhetorical reading of the question "what's the difference?" She, after all, must do the lacing, and from her position, lacing can *only* be done "over" or "under." What is more (and Edith does not need to know this, as de Man does not know it), Archie can only produce a rhetorical reading of "what's the difference" because he, like Edith, knows of the two ways of lacing and recognizes that they make no difference to the fulfillment of his desire.

When de Man offers his analysis, he identifies the aporia of his mini-text as rhetoric. That is to say, he chooses the term he has assigned to Archie; he agrees with Archie that the question "what's the difference?" is a rhetorical question. This choice might appear to be a superficial, terminological coincidence. De Man assures us: "I follow the usage of common speech in calling this semiological enigma 'rhetorical'" (10). But this gesture is not simply another pragmatic move, a technical convenience. De Man seems to redefine rhetoric, to give it a meaning neither Archie nor Edith anticipate, and thus to exclude both Bunkers. He tries to assert that his position participates in neither of the alternatives that compose his dilemma. That is one reason he

---

[25]*American Heritage Dictionary*. Simple also means: "not affected; unassuming or unpretentious; not guileful or deceitful; sincere; humble or lowly in condition or rank; not important or significant; trivial." All these terms might be applied by some readers to Edith. De Man observes that "as long as we are talking about bowling shoes, the consequences are relatively trivial": *Allegories of Reading*, p. 9.

insists on a reductive definition of the text. Nevertheless, essential affinities persist between Archie's position as a reader and the position de Man establishes for himself.

De Man initially glosses Archie's reading of the question "what's the difference?" as meaning "I don't give a damn what the difference is." As he parenthetically shrugs off this difference, he aligns himself with Archie and obscures the difference Edith's reading produces. Later in the passage, de Man glosses Archie's meaning again, but in slightly different terms. At this point, he claims that "the same grammatical pattern engenders two meanings that are mutually exclusive: the literal meaning asks for a concept (difference) whose existence is denied by the figurative meaning" (9). This reading clearly anticipates the puns below. This is the reading of Archie that de Man needs. But Archie's figure, as de Man himself shows us, does not "mean" to ask for the "concept" of difference or to deny that such a concept exists. Indeed, it has a much more circumspect, almost modest meaning: the difference, whose existence de Man's first gloss seems to concede ("what the difference *is*"), is not important to Archie: "*I* don't give a damn what the difference is." Archie's indifference to "what the difference is"—like the pluralist's indifference to the other reader—prevails because not he but Edith is positioned to lace the shoes, one way or another. It prevails by excluding the feminine reader.

Such a sublime and definitive indifference is precisely what de Man seeks to achieve by identifying his mini-text with the syntactic paradigm uttered by Archie: "what's the difference?" De Man makes his affiliation with Archie explicit, when he tells us that Archie's anger at his wife's "simplicity" is not mere "impatience." Rather, "it reveals his despair when confronted with a structure of linguistic meaning that he cannot control and that holds the discouraging prospect of an infinity of similar confusions, all of them potentially catastrophic in their consequences." This is de Man's catastrophe. He, like Archie, despairs of ever escaping aporia. Archie, anticipating de Man, is discouraged, even despairing, because he sees that this dilemma is not merely accidental, contextual, or historical; because the uncontrollable structure is language itself, error is infinite and inevitable. In de Man's reading, Archie doesn't realize that his despair requires the figure of Edith, that her uncontrollable intervention—her reading—produces the catastrophes of mis-understanding.

Aporia cannot, for de Man's purposes, be literal, a merely historical accident: "it is not so that there are simply two mean-ings, one literal and the other figural, and that we have to decide which one of these is the right one in this *particular situation*" (10, my emphases). Yet, because rhetoric is not, for de Man, the product of a (this) particular situation, but the deep structure of all language, he must claim to exclude what Archie and Edith both know about their positioning in their marital/rhetorical sit-uation and about the lacing of shoes. Only the rigorous exclu-sion of circumstance, extratextual interventions, and particular situations produces undecidability as a purely "rhetorical" fact.

The pluralism of this strategy is in some ways obvious. The alternative de Man brushes aside, the contextual analysis, is "simple" only in the bosom of an "interpretative community" already constructed within the pluralist problematic. The fiction of a homogeneous critical community of general readers is nec-essary to the view that any "particular situation" is similarly homogeneous and could therefore unambiguously guide us to the "right" meaning. The anti-pluralist position I have been sketching in relief insists that the community itself is irreducibly divided: not by knowledge (Edith and Archie share common knowledge), but by interests; not epistemologically, but politi-cally. If every "particular situation" is heterogeneous, the very possibility of the existence of any one "right" meaning is under-mined, and the question of the truth or falsehood of any reading ceases to be plausible. But de Man's commitment to general persuasion extends beyond his negative characterization of the analysis he refuses to perform.

De Man's analysis opposes the linguistic to the extralinguistic, the mini-text to its context, the rhetorical to the literal. These oppositions are all in the service of an analysis poised to read figurality as an effect that inheres entirely within a linguistic entity, for example, within a syntactic chain. In reading "what's the difference?" de Man stresses that the figure is conveyed by a syntactical device. He underlines the term "syntactical" to emphasize that this puts grammar and rhetoric into direct conflict. But the term "device" is equally critical. De Man excludes extratextual intervention and thus identifies his text with the syntactical device itself; this enables an analysis in which the designation of the sentence as a rhetorical question doesn't seem to rest on the specificity of Archie's reading. De Man claims to have excluded Archie's intervention, his reading, even as he claims not to be adopting Archie's position. He argues that this sentence is a rhetorical question because its linguistic character constitutes its rhetoricity. Rhetoric ceases to be a matter of reading, that is, a matter of conflict and discontinuity among readers; conflict exists only in the internal struggle and despair of the individual interpreter. Rhetoric is *in* the text itself. "The deconstruction is not something we have added to the text" (17).

This position is plainly pluralist. To begin, Fish's critique of the pluralist defense of the core of determinate meaning applies with equal force here. De Man imposes such a rigid boundary between the textual and the extratextual in order to control the possible interpretations that the text can elicit; he wants to exclude—as extralinguistic—the analyses that would *limit* meaning, what he calls elsewhere the paraphrase. Booth, in a similar situation, wants to exclude—as extralinguistic—the analyses that would *multiply* meaning.   De Man's mini-text must issue in aporia. To ensure the generality of his reading, he rhetoricizes it, that is, reduces it to a question about the epistemological traps of language. As Fish repeatedly demonstrates, this strategy requires an unacknowledged recourse to some contextual ground. De Man explicitly forbids such a move, but the undecidability that he designates as an effect of the syntactic device "what's the difference" is nothing but the effect of the context he claims to bracket. De Man defends rhetoric as the undecidability that is the effect of the clash of two meanings that he derives practically from a context. He excludes appeals to extralinguistic interventions only after he has made just such an intervention in order to assign any meaning whatsoever—not to mention two entirely incompatible meanings—to this particular "syntactical device." The aporia de Man's reading generates is the product of the kind of extratextual intervention he insists we must avoid.

It is possible to answer this criticism, at least up to a point. De Man might argue that his context is a different one, a third context, the context of a "technical" analysis of rhetoric, "rhetorically conscious reading." This claim assigns the literary critic a properly theoretical position, a position proof against feelings of "hostility" and "benignity," the position of the general reader in the pluralist problematic. Pluralist discourse is of course profoundly committed to the production of multiple readings. And, like de Man, pluralists are in no fundamental way discouraged by the fact that the various readings they generate may conflict directly with each other, either epistemologically or logically. Indeed, critical pluralism anticipates just such a conflict, and, although in a self-conscious pluralism such as Booth's, various ideological moves are undertaken in the hope of softening this blow to rationality, these efforts are never located at the level of an individual reading of a text, but always at the level of persuasion. When de Man addresses himself to the matter of the persuasiveness of rhetorical analysis, he repeats the characteristic pluralist gestures. Rhetoric—as a system of general tropes—serves as his ground.

Pluralism is precisely the effort to accommodate such conflicts without declaring relativism the victor, and de Man is not a relativist. In fact, "suspended uncertainty," the eternal condition of the de Manian reader, bears a startling resemblance to the pluralist's ultimate position. The pluralist constructs his suspended uncertainty on a foundation of lesser certainties, usually specific interpretations of texts, and, for a pluralist such as Booth, these interpretations designate determinate meanings. But this is entirely a question of content. Where Booth is sure of meaning, de Man is sure of tropes. His uncertainty is similarly grounded in his certainty about the literal and figural meanings between which he hesitates in permanent indecision. And as de Man cannot concede that these meanings are produced as the effects of extratextual intervention, he presents them, as every pluralist must, in the rhetoric of general persuasion. "The endless repetition of the same figure . . . . suspended between truth and the death of this truth" (*AR* 115) is the pluralist's dream come to haunt him as a nightmare. But it preserves the generality of persuasion. Indeed, it reasserts it in a new and less vulnerable form. This tropological rhetoric of general persuasion constitutes what is specifically pluralist in de Man's text.

When de Man identifies the trope that grounds his deconstruction and discloses the aporia of rhetoric, he "addresses" himself to a familiar figure, the general reader of the pluralist problematic. The figure he names is the rhetorical question, and, for him, it is the text itself. Undecidability thus figures the "inclusiveness" of de Man's analysis; it addresses the general reader in its assumption that when "we" read tropes, we are all seduced by undecidability, all equally undecided. The refusal openly to take sides is finally a refusal to admit the exclusion of any reader; again, "there seems to be no limit to what tropes can get away with." As in Booth's vision, there is no limit to the community of readers of tropes. The universality or generality of the trope is repeated in the figure of the reader. To assign any determinate qualities to this reader (other than the technical ability to recognize a rhetorical question when he reads one) is to impose a limit on the substitutability of tropes. Tropes are not read from a position limited by the discontinuities and conflicts of social relations.

Edith disrupts this model, for she represents the irreducible difference that disrupts not only the meanings that should unify and ground the critical community, but the tropes as well. She is necessarily excluded from the moment de Man announces that "what's the difference?" *is* a rhetorical question, but he cannot acknowledge that enabling exclusion. He conceives it, as Barthes observes, "in terms of inclusion," and thus "reinforces this relation of exclusion, . . . just when [he] thinks [he] is being most generous." For Edith, "what's the difference?" is *not* a rhetorical question. Her (historical) position—within the text— literally prevents her from seeing the figure as de Man and

Archie see it. Edith insists that it is not true that "one can always substitute one word for another" (*BI* 274). Substitution itself has limits that de Man's analysis dramatizes but is unable to theorize.

On the contrary, de Man argues that a failure to acknowledge the rhetorical aspect of a text, to call a rhetorical question a rhetorical question, is resistance: "once a reader has become aware of the rhetorical dimensions of a text, he will not be amiss in finding textual instances that are irreducible to grammar or to historically determined meaning, provided only he is willing to acknowledge what he is bound to notice. The problem quickly becomes the more baffling one of having to account for the shared reluctance to acknowledge the obvious" (R 18). In his effort to generalize the rhetoric of persuasion, de Man is baffled by the fact that different readers are "bound" to tropes differently and that this difference is essential to the process of reading. He argues that "technically correct rhetorical readings may be boring, monotonous, predictable and unpleasant, but they are irrefutable" (R 20), and he overlooks the fact that such an irrefutable reading is possible only if one assumes that every reader can agree on the "technical" question of what (or even if) the figure is. For de Man, such readings "are indeed universals, consistently defective models of language's impossibility to be a model language" (R 20).

Edith figures the "resisting reader," a baffling, feminine figure who can neither understand nor be persuaded to the apparently "obvious," technical reading. De Man misconstrues her, and she literally disappears from his audience; he thus obliterates the theoretical implications of her "sublime simplicity." Because he presumes that his analysis includes her reading, he has no theoretical or rhetorical interest in the suggestion that we might "learn to listen with re-trained ears to Edith Bunker's patient elaboration of an answer to the question 'what *is* the difference?' "[26]

---

[26]Barbara Johnson, "Gender Theory and the Yale School," *Rhetoric and Form: Deconstruction at Yale*, ed. Robert Con Davis and Ronald Schleifer (Norman: University of Oklahoma Press, 1985), p. 112.

6 THIS POLITICS WHICH IS NOT ONE

The greatest difficulties, theoretical or otherwise, which are obstacles to an easy reading of *Capital* Volume One are unfortunately (or fortunately) concentrated *at the very beginning* of Volume One, to be precise, in its first Part, which deals with "Commodities and Money." I therefore give the following advice: put THE WHOLE PART ONE ASIDE FOR THE TIME BEING amd BEGIN YOUR READING WITH PART TWO: "The Transformation of Money into Capital." In my opinion it is impossible to begin (even to begin) to understand Part I until you have read and re-read the whole of Volume One, *starting with Part II.* This advice is more than advice: it is a recommendation that, notwithstanding all the respect I owe my readers, I am prepared to present as an *imperative.* Everyone can try it out in practice for himself. If you begin Volume One at the beginning, ie. with Part I, either you do not understand it, and give up; or you think you understand it, but that is even more serious, for there is every chance that you will have understood something quite different from what was there to be understood.
        —ALTHUSSER, Preface to *Capital*, Volume One.

You cannot just write the truth; you have to write it *for* somebody and *to* somebody; somebody who can do something with it.
        —BRECHT, "Writing the Truth: Five Difficulties"

The "baffling figure" who both grounds and troubles de Man's rhetoric of general persuasion reappears in a most unlikely place—in Fredric Jameson's *Political Unconscious*. As in de Man's text, the scene is one of resistance, specifically of the "reluctance" of some readers to "acknowledge the obvious." But in Jameson's text, the situation is somewhat ambiguous: his judgment of his reluctant reader is peculiarly tentative, neither wholly dismissive nor genuinely forgiving. This contradiction is symptomatic of Jameson's unique historical and theoretical predicament, the dilemma of a "Marxist pluralism"[1] in the U.S. academy. Jameson struggles to "unearth" the political unconscious of general persuasion, to "restor[e] to the surface of the text the repressed and buried reality of [its] fundamental history" (*PU* 20), but he ends by rewriting that history in the discourse of pluralism.

Jameson's hesitation toward his readers is especially surprising, given that his tone of authority often rivals that of de Man. Consider this frequently cited formulation from *The Political Unconscious*, in which Jameson informs his readers: "This book will argue the priority of the political interpretation of literary texts. It conceives of the political perspective not as some supplementary method, not as an optional auxiliary to other interpretive methods current today—the psychoanalytic or the myth-critical, the stylistic, the ethical, the structural—but rather as the absolute horizon of all reading and all interpretation" (17). The absolutism here is unmistakable. But this passage also hints at some of the sources of Jameson's ambivalence toward his resisting reader(s). The inclusive list of critical methods is quintessentially Jamesonian, as is the unambiguous insistence on the possibility and the desirability of establishing a horizon, an "absolute" boundary, to contain and thus to enlist those methods, both critically and politically.

These features articulate Jameson's theoretical "respect [for]

---

[1]To my knowledge, this phrase is first applied to Jameson by Jane Marcus in "Storming the Toolshed," *Signs* 7:3 (1982), 626. Further references to this essay (ST) will be given in parentheses in the text. Marcus points out Jameson's pluralism and his "refusal to deal with gender" (626) only in passing; her critique centers on Annette Kolodny's celebration of the "playful pluralism" of feminist theory in "Dancing through the Minefield."

the methodological imperative implicit in the concept of totality or totalization" (57). This commitment to a "dialectical or totalizing, properly Marxist ideal of understanding" (10) is as absolute as the projected horizon of reading and interpretation. Many commentators have observed its intellectual roots in Lukács, whom Jameson calls "the greatest Marxist philosopher of modern times" (13) and in the Hegelian prehistory of marxist theory. It is the Lukácsian Jameson who argues:

> only Marxism offers a philosophically coherent and ideologically compelling resolution to the dilemma of historicism. . . . Only Marxism can give us an adequate account of the essential *mystery* of the cultural past, which, like Tiresias drinking the blood, is momentarily returned to life and warmth and allowed once more to speak, and to deliver its long-forgotten message in surroundings utterly alien to it. This mystery can be reenacted only if the human adventure is one. . . . These matters can recover their original urgency for us only if they are retold within the unity of a single great collective story; only if, in however disguised and symbolic a form, they are seen as sharing a single fundamental theme—for Marxism, the collective struggle to wrest a realm of Freedom from a realm of Necessity; only if they are grasped as vital episodes in a single vast unfinished plot. [*PU* 19–20]

The philosophical antecedents of this apparently single-minded line of reasoning are clearly in the Hegelian-Lukácsian tradition I have already invoked. But if marxism, armed with its totalizing dialectical method, is the only possible response to the "dilemma of historicism" (a formulation some pluralists would disparage as "monistic dogmatism"), at the same time, in Jameson's account, that marxism is itself an infinitely open sequence, "a single collective story," but one so "vast" as to be perpetually "unfinished," all-inclusive, but endlessly weaving episode upon episode and employing every conceivable weapon (psychoanalytic, myth-critical, stylistic, ethical) in its totalizing and collectivizing project.

This passion for inclusiveness, for an absolute horizon that excludes nothing, cannot be understood (much less dismissed) solely as an effect of Jameson's intellectual lineage. It must also be read as an expression of his commitment to or his inability to escape from a fundamentally pluralist model of political community. This model invades *The Political Unconscious* by way of Jameson's own difficult relation to his audience, and it persists despite his self-conscious efforts, as a marxist, to historicize and politicize that relation. The problematics of exclusion and inclusion are entangled at every level of Jameson's text; here, more dramatically than in any of the instances we have considered thus far, we find a potentially anti-pluralist discourse in direct confrontation with the pluralist problematic. Jameson's resistance to pluralism as such is more explicit and rigorous than that of any of the other theorists we have considered. But ultimately *The Political Unconscious* remains within the problematic of general persuasion, as the latter extends its field of play even to the once forbidding terrain of marxism.

Pluralism persists in *The Political Unconscious* insofar as Jameson allows himself to lose sight of the irreducibly partial operation of truths, that is, insofar as he allows himself to believe that a marxist hermeneutics can disclose a truth which is not, as Brecht puts it, for *some* body, some particular bodies, who will do *some* things with it, but for every body, an "absolute" truth. *The Political Unconscious* is an astonishingly heterogeneous text—in some ways, in spite of its author's totalizing project—and pluralism is only one of its important tendencies, but it ultimately exerts an overwhelming pressure on such crucial Jamesonian concepts as necessity, history, utopia, and the political unconscious itself. Pluralism persists in *The Political Unconscious* because Jameson retains a pluralist's model of audience and of the theoretical possibilities of persuasion.

Jameson rewrites Booth's concept of the "critical commonwealth" as a utopian space where political community, "achieved collectivity," appears (or more precisely, is read) as a trope: "all class consciousness of whatever type is Utopian insofar as it expresses the unity of a collectivity; yet it must be added that this proposition is an *allegorical* [my emphasis] one. The achieved collectivity or organic group of whatever kind—oppressors fully as much as oppressed—is Utopian not in itself, but only insofar as all such collectivities are themselves *figures* for the ultimate concrete collective life of an achieved Utopian or classless society" (290–91). Jameson's allegorical moment differs in telling respects from de Man's. When Jameson announces that "interpretation is here construed as an essentially allegorical act" (10), he means to challenge the anti-interpretative thrust of most contemporary post-structuralisms, including de Man's.[2] Furthermore, whereas de Man eschews politics, the appeal of Jameson's figural analysis is an explicitly political one: it is as an allegory of "collective solidarity" (291) that he offers the figure of utopia to his readers. These differences are of enormous theoretical and practical significance and should not be trivialized. Yet pluralism is the most tenacious and heterogeneous discourse of American literary theory; the fundamental divergences between de Man's text and Jameson's testify to that heterogeneity even as they allow us to isolate and examine an essential critical continuity. Jameson offers his readers a politics (or a political allegory) of reading, a rhetorical strategy of interpretation with a utopian aim. Critically speaking, "collective solidarity"—by which Jameson means the solidarity of the "human adventure"—is an effect of adopting the utopian as a ruling trope for interpretation. But the reader to whom this critical/political appeal is addressed is familiar to us: he is the reader of general persuasion.

[2]As he observes later: "Still, to describe the readings and analyses contained in the present work as so many *interpretations*, to present them as so many exhibits in the construction of a new *hermeneutic*, is already to announce a whole polemic program, which must necessarily come to terms with a critical and theoretical climate variously hostile to these slogans. It is, for instance, increasingly clear that hermeneutic or interpretive activity has become one of the basic polemic targets of contemporary post-structuralism in France, which—powerfully buttressed by the authority of Nietzsche—has tended to identify such operations with historicism, and in particular with the dialectic and its valorization of absence and the negative, its assertion of the necessity and priority of totalizing thought. I will agree with this identification, with this description of the ideological affinities and implications of the ideal of the interpretive or hermeneutic act; but I will argue that the critique is misplaced": *The Political Unconscious*, p. 21.

I

Jameson's position is an uneasy one, both theoretically and politically. Precisely because he is a marxist, pluralism raises especially acute problems for his argument. On the one hand, he unhesitatingly addresses both politics and history, topics that pluralists generally belittle or shun. As the passage above suggests, he is unambiguous about the privileged position he assigns marxist discourse; in fact, read together, the two passages I have cited indicate that the "priority of the political interpretation of literary texts" is, for Jameson, equivalent to the priority of marxist interpretation. As he argues in a reference that clearly reflects on his own political affiliations:

> Only an ethical politics . . . will feel the need to "prove" that one of [the] forms of class consciousness is good or positive and the other reprehensible or wicked: on the grounds, for example, that working-class consciousness is potentially more universal than ruling-class consciousness, or that the latter is essentially linked to violence and repression. It is unnecessary to argue these quite correct propositions; ideological commitment is not first and foremost a matter of moral choice but of the *taking of sides* in a struggle between embattled groups. In a fragmented social life—that is, essentially in all class societies—the political thrust of the struggle of all groups against each other can never be immediately universal but must always necessarily be focused on the class enemy. [*PU* 290, my emphases].

Here, as he does throughout his work, Jameson takes sides, acknowledging the political ground of his (and every) position. In this passage, argument is deemed "unnecessary" (if not inadequate) to the task of justifying political commitment, and the demand for proof is put aside as an ethical rather than a properly political concern. But we should recall that in his prophetic account of marxism's priority, history seems to replace "the political thrust of the struggle." Jameson focuses there on marxism's "philosophically coherent and ideologically compelling resolution to the dilemma of historicism" and its adequacy as an "account of the essential mystery of the cultural past." In this argument, the turn to marxism proves necessary to solve the problem of history.

Indeed, "Always historicize!" is the "slogan" that inaugurates *The Political Unconscious*. Jameson regards this commandment as "the one absolute and we may even say 'transhistorical' imperative of all dialectical thought" and observes that it, "unsurprisingly," "turn[s] out to be the moral of *The Political Unconscious*" (9). The category of the moral will be subjected to a thorough deconstruction by the conclusion of his text,[3] but it asserts itself unproblematically here, where the political appears in the guise of history, and Jameson seems to displace the slogan "Always politicize!"

The tension between history and politics, paralleling the tension between inclusion and exclusion, permeates *The Political Unconscious*. Finally, it seems that history is indeed the "moral" of Jameson's theoretical story, and that this is a direct consequence of the ambiguous or contradictory status of his concept of audience. Juggling history and politics, *The Political Unconscious* negotiates a remarkable series of displacements around the figure of the reader. Under the pressure of his effort to appeal to his theoretical audience, Jameson rewrites both history and politics in a pluralist idiom and thus constructs a new and persuasive pluralist politics, a politics whose enemy is reification and whose weapon is the totalizing strategy of utopia.

To interrogate the "baffling figure" of a reader's resistance is to confront Jameson's dilemma in concrete terms. *The Political Unconscious* opens with a masterly work of theoretical synthesis, transcoding, and speculation, "On Interpretation: Literature as a Socially Symbolic Act." It is no surprise to discover that this chapter begins with a lengthy discussion of Althusser and the problems of structural causality, mediation, historicism. As Jameson points out almost immediately, "the enterprise of constructing a properly Marxist hermeneutic must necessarily con-

---

[3]See Cornel West, "Ethics and Action in Fredric Jameson's Marxist Hermeneutics," for a very interesting critique of Jameson's reading of ethical problematics.

front the powerful objections to traditional modes of interpretation raised by the influential school of so-called structural or
Althusserian Marxism" (23). This "so-called" Althusserianism is
in many ways part of the anti-hermeneutical problem Jameson
hopes to solve, and his relationship to Althusser's *oeuvre* is particularly important. Indeed, *The Political Unconscious* represents a
major critical response—on one level, already noted, from the
position of Lukács, and, on another, equally determining, from
the perspective of the United States—to the Althusserian intervention in marxist theory.[4]

From this point of view, the hermeneutic Jameson develops
and refines throughout *The Political Unconscious* rests on the
force of the initial criticisms he offers of Althusser's views, and
he naturally gives them a prominent place in his discussion.
What is surprising—indeed, perhaps baffling—is the footnote
opening that discussion, barely half a dozen pages into the
chapter, a footnote addressed to the resisting reader.

> The issues raised in this section, *unavoidable* ones for any *serious*
> discussion of the nature of interpretation, are also unavoidably
> technical, involving a terminology and a "problematic" which
> largely *transcends* literary criticism. As they will *inevitably* strike
> *certain readers* as scholastic exercises within the philosophically
> alien tradition of Marxism, *such readers* may be advised to pass at
> once to the next section (below, p. 58), in which *we* return to a
> discussion of the various current schools of literary criticism
> proper. It should be added that not all the writers described as
> "Althusserians," at the level of historical generality which is *ours*
> in the present section, would accept that characterization. [*PU* 23,
> my emphases]

This is a note to give readers pause, "certain readers," at least. I
find it quite difficult to interpret, knotted as it is with conflicting
references to such readers, alien traditions, transcendence, the
proper, and, most important, an elusive "we." The complexity

---

[4]See Kavanagh, "The Jameson Effect," for a cogent analysis of the intertextual
relations between Althusser and the Jameson of *The Political Unconscious*. See
also William C. Dowling, *Jameson, Althusser, Marx: An Introduction to The Political
Unconscious* (Ithaca: Cornell University Press, 1984).

of Jameson's rhetoric makes what purports to be helpful (if somewhat obtrusive) advice puzzling to the point of obscurity. I want to offer a very close analysis of this passage; the gestures of inclusion and exclusion entwined here form an emblem of the persistence of pluralism, even in the anti-pluralist environment of a marxist text.

A glance back at de Man's treatment of his resisting readers may illuminate Jameson's reticence. The former's exasperation with those so contrary as to be "(un)willing to acknowledge what [they are] bound to notice" is not veiled, and de Man leaves no doubt as to his judgment on the reluctant. He dismisses the details of these readers' resistances and declines absolutely to make a polemical response. There is, from de Man's point of view, simply no point in trying to correct the misunderstandings and errors of such critics.

De Man's rejection of polemic grounds his pluralist rhetoric of general persuasion. Jameson's footnote seems to participate in a similar kind of anti-polemic, even to exaggerate it, insofar as he shies away from any straightforward criticism of (even some of) his readers. Yet unlike de Man, Jameson defends the polemical, at least, in principle. He insists that "the unavoidably Hegelian tone of the retrospective framework of *The Political Unconscious* should not be taken to imply that . . . polemic interventions are not of the highest priority for Marxist cultural criticism. On the contrary, the latter must necessarily also be what Althusser has demanded of the practice of Marxist philosophy proper, namely 'class struggle within theory'" (12). But rather than launching *The Political Unconscious* as an opening skirmish in the struggle Althusser demands, Jameson's apologia for the unavoidable accents of Hegel warns us that polemic is not to be the characteristic mode of his text. Indeed, he indicates that although *The Political Unconscious* might "appropriately" be recast as a "methodological handbook," "such a manual would have as its object *ideological analysis.*" Jameson unhesitatingly asserts that such analysis "remains . . . the appropriate designation for the critical 'method' specific to Marxism." But, he continues, "for reasons indicated above, this book is not that manual, which would necessarily settle its accounts with rival 'methods' in a far more polemic spirit" (12). Unthinkable as it is, this comment seems to suggest that Jameson's method in *The Political Unconscious* will not be "specific to Marxism"—or will not be simply that.[5] We shall consider his reasons for bracketing the operation of ideological critique in some detail in the coming pages, but first we must observe that he does not adduce as a reason one that may in fact be determining: his desire to avoid the polemical itself, with its inevitable exclusions.

Jameson's remarks about the necessary but (necessarily) bypassed polemic of ideological analysis precede a direct address to some of his readers. Having reiterated his allegiance to Althusser's view that "class struggle in theory" is the work of the marxist philosopher and that "polemical intervention" remains "the highest priority for Marxist cultural criticism," Jameson continues: "For the non-Marxist reader, however, who many well feel that this book is quite polemic enough, I will add what should be unnecessary and underline my debt to the great pioneers of narrative analysis" (12). This "non-Marxist reader" is rarely again so directly evoked, but he is a constant presence in *The Political Unconscious.* He is certainly the unnamed addressee of the footnote, and it seems in this passage to be for his benefit alone that Jameson underscores his intellectual debts to theorists including Northrop Frye and A. J. Greimas. Why should the other reader, the marxist reader, be less concerned with this indebtedness? Or, rather, what is the theoretical effect of Jameson's desire to reassure the non-marxist reader of his (non-marxist) intellectual debts?

Jameson avoids the style of a handbook of ideological analysis, in part, because this decision allows for a substantial lessen-

---

[5]Jameson states flatly that his "theoretical dialogue with [the great pioneers of narrative analysis] in these pages is not merely to be taken as yet another specimen of the negative critique of 'false consciousness' (although it is that too, and, indeed, in the Conclusion I will deal explicitly with the problem of the proper uses of such critical gestures as demystification and ideological unmasking)": *The Political Unconscious*, p. 12. While I would not endorse the category of false consciousness, my book is precisely a specimen of critique.

ing, if not the exclusion, of specifically marxist polemic, of the class struggle in theory. This exclusion is intimately connected to Jameson's rendering of his relation not only to Greimas and Frye, but to all the theoreticians and critics who crowd the pages of *The Political Unconscious*, and it lays the foundation for his largest methodological claims, as we shall see. The absence of marxist polemic allows Jameson to read (and to be read) as a marxist pluralist, theoretically (and politically) vulnerable to the persuasive force of every text he encounters. Just as important, it opens an avenue into *The Political Unconscious* for the reader of general persuasion.

This decision also affects the specific content of Jameson's theory, and he is not unaware of this fact. His concluding chapter, "The Dialectic of Utopia and Ideology," opens by acknowledging the relation between the absence of polemic and the theory: "The conception of the political unconscious developed in the preceding pages has tended to distance itself, at certain strategic moments, from those implacably polemic and demystifying procedures traditionally associated with the Marxist practice of ideological analysis. It is now time to confront the latter directly and to spell out such modifications in more detail (281). Although Jameson specifically cites the *concept* of the political unconscious, *The Political Unconscious* as a whole is distanced from implacable polemic and thus from one of marxism's traditions. Jameson here refers to this move as strategic and local, but it seems actually to be a systematic feature of his argument, and, in any case, the unforeseen theoretical consequences of strategic gestures can be considerable. Despite his reference to strategy, Jameson indicates that this distancing has been a controlled development in his theory, one leading directly to "modifications" in marxist practice, particularly as it concerns questions of ideology and utopia.

Jameson's disinclination to emphasize the explicitly polemical burden of marxism derives from his conceptualization of his audience. In the body of his text, Jameson tends, when he acknowledges his audience at all, to address an indeterminate reader, as, for example, when he warns "the reader what *The*

Political Unconscious is not" (10). The extraordinary difficulty (perhaps the impossibility) of establishing the political position of this indeterminate reader, who is finally the reader of general persuasion, produces the profound ambiguities both in Jameson's footnote and throughout his text. What, after all, does such a reader want? What are the theoretical grounds for his or her inclusion? Or exclusion? More to the point, what does he or she want from a "specifically" marxist critic?

It is perhaps not accidental that in his initial address to his readers, when he is establishing just what *The Political Unconscious* is not, the first expectation Jameson puts aside is one that could only be aroused in his marxist audience: "The reader should not, in the first place, expect anything like that exploratory projection of what a vital and emergent political culture should be and do which Raymond Williams has rightly proposed as the most urgent task of a Marxist cultural criticism" (10). This is a curious statement, conceding Williams's proposal as to the "the most urgent task of a Marxist cultural criticism" in the act of deferring it. Jameson offers a number of "good and objective historical reasons" for contemporary marxism's (and *The Political Unconscious*'s) failure to rise to Williams's challenge: the "sorry history of Zhdanovite prescription in the arts," a "fascination with modernisms and 'revolutions' in form and language," indeed, even the fact of "a whole new political and economic 'world system,' to which the older Marxist cultural paradigms only imperfectly apply" (11). But he neglects to cite the more local, historical, and political pressures of his positioning as a marxist critic in the Age of Reagan, or, to be less topical, of his legacy as an American academic, heir to one of the more virulently anti-marxist and resolutely (and inventively) pluralistic discourses in the West. Taking this situation into account, which is to say, taking the problematic of general persuasion, in all of its genuine diversity and cunning, as the immediate political and theoretical context for *The Political Unconscious*, allows us to begin to read Jameson's dilemma and its inscription in his unusual footnote.

To return, then, to the note. It is nothing short of perverse for a critic to suggest, a half dozen pages into his opening chapter, that some readers may (want to) just skip the next thirty-five-page section of his book. The most general effect of such a remark can hardly be in the service of persuasion. Reading for the traces of anti-pluralism, that is, for some challenge to the hegemony of the problematic of general persuasion, we might be tempted to cite this footnote as a startling instance of just the kind of rejection of general persuasion that we have been looking for. One might see Jameson as a critic more than happy to divide his audience explicitly into the included and the excluded, those who skip being the excluded, of course. Read in this way, Jameson betrays no pluralistic concern to persuade or even to encourage all his readers, much less to construct his audience within the theoretical confines of the problematic of general persuasion.

But this analysis takes the message of this passage at face value, smoothing over the contradictory movement of Jameson's prose in order to extract an unproblematic set of instructions for reading the text. In fact, even if we should accept this simplifying strategy, the message doesn't gloss easily. If, for example, we take Jameson to be trying to theorize the exclusion of certain readers, tracing out the limits of persuasion and inscribing those limits into his theory, we face an embarrassing contradiction. For far from excluding readers, this footnote goes to some lengths to include them, to reassure them that even if they do take its advice and pass on to page fifty-eight, they will *not* be excluded. On the contrary, they are specifically included, if on somewhat unusual terms. Whatever the subject matter of the thirty-five optional pages, Jameson's footnote claims that it is not necessary to entertain any aspect of it in order to be included, to be part of the intended audience of *The Political Unconscious*. Indeed, the solicitude of the note leaves open the possibility that the readers who will (or would prefer to) pass over pages twenty-three through fifty-eight are none other than that intended audience.

Everything I have said so far assumes that Jameson expects at least some readers to accept his blessing and cheerfully skip thirty-five pages. My own unscientific survey failed to uncover a single such person, although I did discover that numerous readers have no memory whatsoever of the footnote. One colleague argued that no one would even consider following Jameson's advice: "it would be like walking out of a room while everyone is talking—no one likes to be excluded." I have read "On Interpretation" without the (apparently expendable) pages and found that it is not an implausible exercise. Jameson sutures his elision convincingly, picking up the thread of his remarks about Deleuze and Guattari and the critique of hermeneutics and moving easily into his discussion of master codes and Freud. But I cannot say with certainty whether or not he actually intends his readers to take him at his word and skip well over a third of his first chapter. The footnote may be an ironic warning, simultaneously signaling that Jameson realizes some of his readers would like nothing better than to ignore part of the assignment and daring them to try it. This indeterminacy is itself revealing, symptomatic of the oblique and tentative gestures he makes toward his audience and, consequently, toward the theoretical problem of persuasion.

Generally, Jameson declines to make his readers a theme in the body of his text or a factor in his theory. The question of audience is acknowledged only in the note, placed to the side, insofar as that is possible. At the same time, the question apparently cannot be ignored entirely. Jameson is somehow concerned, but doesn't admit to being baffled by these readers, even though he seems to believe that they are unwilling to acknowledge the "unavoidable" importance of Althusserian theory for "any serious discussion of the nature of interpretation" (23). In purely intellectual terms, such recalcitrance is mystifying, as de Man points out, and this particular remark seems calculated to offend. If the issues to be raised are "unavoidable" for "any serious discussion" of interpretation, and not simply for a serious marxist discussion, then anyone who plays the truant for thirty-five pages is by definition a person who is not serious, someone whose discussion is unavoidably frivolous. And yet this is Jameson's prescription: that some readers should avoid the unavoidable.

Despite these equivocations and the space they open for implied disapproval, Jameson is rather too understanding of his readers' reluctance. He refuses to judge, much less to condemn or dismiss, any of his potential readers. Rather, he provides an apologia for their failure to meet the minimum requirements for serious discussion. He concedes that the thirty-five page section to come is "unavoidably technical," and, unlike de Man, he does not invest this technical language with the highest intellectual value. On the contrary, he admits that the technical discourse of a marxist involves a foreign "terminology" and a "'problematic' which largely transcends literary criticism," and that these drawbacks are serious barriers to reading (or at least, to some readers). Jameson genially assumes that literary critics are professionals with certain limited competencies, genuinely comfortable only with their own professional terminology, at home in "literary criticism proper." (As we shall see below, literary criticism is a category Jameson does not sufficiently disturb.) And he also accepts—in fact, he volunteers—the suggestion, really a cover story, that their resistance to marxism is merely practical, a matter of vocabulary and disciplinary problematics.

The reader who reads this alien section is understandably surprised when in the course of it Jameson endorses the view that Althusser's "notorious and self-serving attempt to reinvent a privileged place for philosophy proper" is "a renewed defense of the reified specialization of the bourgeois academic disciplines, and thereby an essentially antipolitical alibi" (38–39).[6] In his footnote, Jameson himself concocts just such a disciplinary

[6]Jameson is referring to Althusser's claim that "philosophy represents the people's class struggle in theory," serving "the master function of philosophical practice: 'to draw a dividing line' between true ideas and false ideas": *Lenin and Philosophy*, p. 21. Jameson ignores Althusser's claim to be struggling with "the beginnings of the ability to talk a kind of discourse which anticipates what will one day perhaps be a non-philosophical theory of philosophy" (ibid., 27) and apparently endorses at least part of E. P. Thompson's argument in *The Poverty of Theory* (London: Merlin, 1978), especially pp. 374–79.

alibi for certain of his readers. At the end of the optional pages, he refers to the section as a "lengthy digression" (58). Indeed, he claims that his technical analyses will *"inevitably* strike certain readers as scholastic exercises within the philosophically alien tradition of Marxism." "Inevitably" is a word that snares a reader interested in anti-pluralism, in the irreducible limits of general persuasion. But here the necessity expressed in that word is immediately undermined by the amorphous and contingent adjective "certain." A rejection of the "alien" and the "scholastic" is inevitable. Yet the readers who will act so decisively remain uncertain and unspecified, save insofar as they are proper literary critics. Who are these "certain readers"?[7] Jameson's answer is a tautology: they are readers who will certainly respond in "such" a manner to the "scholastic exercises" of an "alien tradition." These are readers who are at their ease with Derrida, but find Althusser "alien," who find the nuances of hermeneutics in Freud and Frye compelling, but the subtleties of the relations between mediation and structural causality "scholastic." Jameson is, of course, ventriloquizing his audience when he uses the epithets "alien" and "scholastic," but it is dismaying nonetheless to see him inscribe these charges in his text, to find him so tolerant of this parochialism (what Gayatri Spivak has called "sanctioned ignorance") and so reticent about discussing its fundamentally political significance.

Jameson's acquiesence to the proper literary critical view of the alien (un-American) marxist critic and his scholastic (dogmatic) quarrels becomes even more problematic when it develops that his diffidence works practically to excuse readers from attending to the portion of "On Interpretation" which addresses marxist theory as such. His footnote all but concedes that the most compelling debates in marxist studies are beside the point for ("transcend") literary criticism. Jameson provides an escape from the improper problematics that exceed the boundaries of

---

[7]They bear an uncanny resemblance—in their facelessness—to the anonymous figures Wayne Booth attempts to shrug off with the phrase "whoever they really are." De Man similarly lacks in any interest in naming names, and Hirsch gives only those that clearly stand as synecdoches for whole traditions.

literary criticism: "such readers may be advised to pass at once to the next section (below p. 58)." This is certainly not an unambiguous piece of advice. The passive voice removes Jameson from the scene: he doesn't address his readers directly. "May be advised" is a common idiom; "are advised" is available, but he chooses the less positive formulation. "Advised" is in any case an ambivalent verb. Jameson's tone is almost musing as he reflects on certain readers' predilections, their "inevitable" limits, and the strategic exclusions by which they may accommodate or, to use Jameson's term, "manage" them.

But perhaps it would be more accurate to say that Jameson is accommodating these limitations. This formulation recalls Raymond Williams's suggestion that pluralism often happily welcomes marxism as an "unruly guest." The generalizing imprecision of Jameson's references to "such readers" and "certain readers" is wholly within this accommodating pluralist idiom. In this reading, Jameson's footnote is a characteristically pluralist gesture, an invitation that arouses the anxiety of exclusion only to put it more soundly to rest. The excluded—certain readers— are finally not excluded. Instead, they are excused, and excused specifically from the burden of Jameson's marxism, from the specifically marxist polemic of his text. That burden is here rendered inessential; in effect, it is itself excluded. Jameson poses the dilemma of reading in strictly pluralist terms, as a pragmatic issue, just as Booth and Fish would, and he blocks any political analysis of the tensions between the literary critic and the alien, not unlike de Man. Ironically, Althusser, the polemics surrounding his work, and Jameson's own contribution to them are thus excluded, clearly marked off as an aspect of the text which is not irreducible or essential to Jameson's largest claims. This happens despite the latter's insistence that a marxist hermeneutic "must necessarily confront the powerful objections" of Althusserian marxism. The "polemic" that speaks unhesitatingly against the anti-hermeneutic of post-structuralism in general can apparently be offered to certain readers without a detailed analysis of that anti-hermeneutic's marxist instantiation: the figures of Deleuze and Guattari can stand in here for Althusser, a substitution that must give us pause.[8]

I will return to Althusser's place in *The Political Unconscious*, but first I want briefly to contrast Jameson's footnote with the superficially similar passage from Althusser's Preface to *Capital* that I have taken as an epigraph. Althusser also asks his (Marx's) readers to skip a portion of the text. He offers his opinion in the strongest possible terms: "This advice is more than advice: it is a recommendation that, notwithstanding all the respect I owe my readers, I am prepared to present as an *imperative*" (*LP* 81). Althusser gives reasons for advising an elliptical reading of *Capital* rather different from Jameson's apparent motives for warning off some of his audience. In Althusser's view, the elision is only a temporary one, but it is essential in order to understand Marx's argument. Eventually, the reader will return to Part One, "Commodities and Money," but to begin at the beginning is to take an enormous risk: "either you do not understand it, and give up; or you think you understand it, but that is even more serious, for there is every chance that you will have understood something quite different from what was there to be understood" (*LP* 81). Understanding, as we have seen, is the pluralist trope that grounds general persuasion and thus enables theoretical commitments to its operation to survive in the face of unremitting evidence of the practical failures of persuasive efforts. Jameson's footnote stays well away from the question of understanding, though his remarks enable us to speculate that any lapse or lack of understanding would be explained by reference to his alien terminology. He is careful not to suggest that his thirty-five-page discussion of Althusser's intervention in marxist theory might not be "understood" by some of his

---

[8]In another interesting note, Jameson enumerates the contributors to the "critical and theoretical climate variously hostile" to interpretation as such. The list names Foucault, Derrida, Baudrillard, Deleuze and Guattari, Lyotard and eight different texts, before concluding: "and last but not least, Louis Althusser, et al., *Reading Capital*" (21).

readers or that such failures—should they occur—might be neither accidental nor purely intellectual.

In the sharpest possible contrast, Althusser unambiguously
defines understanding—and thus reading—as both a theoretical and a political process. As he observes, citing one of the
difficulties of reading *Capital:*

> *Difficulty No. 1,* absolutely and massively determinant, is an ideo-
> logical difficulty, and therefore in the last resort a *political* difficul-
> ty.

> Two sorts of readers confront *Capital:* those who have direct expe-
> rience of capitalist exploitation (above all the proletarians or
> wage-labourers in direct production, but also, with nuances ac-
> cording to their place in the production system, the non-pro-
> letarian wage-labourers); and those who have no direct experi-
> ence of capitalist exploitation, but who are, on the contrary, ruled
> in their practices and consciousness by the ideology of the ruling
> class, bourgeois ideology. The first have no ideologico-political
> difficulty in understanding *Capital* since it is a straightforward
> discussion of their concrete lives. The second have great difficulty
> in understanding *Capital* (even if they are very "scholarly," I
> would go so far as to say, especially if they are very "scholarly"),
> because there is a *political incompatibility* between the theoretical
> content of *Capital* and the ideas they carry in their heads, ideas
> which they "rediscover" in their practices (because they put them
> there in the first place). That is why the Difficulty No. 1 of *Capital*
> is in the last instance a *political* difficulty. [LP 74]

Althusser's stark account of the politics of understanding, including the politics of understanding theory, contrasts with
Jameson's cautious and contradictory advice.[9] Althusser renders Marx's (and his own) audience(s) historically and politically

---

[9]To pursue Althusser's argument in its own terms would involve us in a
lengthy examination of Difficulty No. 2. He calls this the "theoretical difficulty"
and connects it to the claim that *Capital* is "a work of *pure theory*," rather than "a
book of 'concrete' history or . . . 'empirical' political economy" (76). I would like
to suggest, however, that he does not essentialize class positions; the difficulty
of grasping the argument of *Capital* is not the same as the impossibility of
understanding it; Althusser stresses that the problem/process of overcoming
these difficulties is always both political and theoretical.

concrete by specifying the terms of their relation to capital. The political limits or difficulties of understanding are acknowledged, and they carry both practical and theoretical weight. Jameson's footnote is a kind of revision of Althusser's warning to the readers of *Capital*, but it cannot address its pluralist audience as class actors.[10] Jameson's references to "such" and "certain" readers retain none of the dangerous political polemic that characterizes Althusser's comment. Whereas the latter concludes that readers with no direct experience of capitalist exploitation will have great difficulty understanding *Capital* ("especially if they are very 'scholarly'"), Jameson represents "certain" readers' disaffection from the tradition of an alien marxism as a problem of scholarship, that is, of insufficient scholarship and thus of unfamiliarity with marxist terminology and problematics. More scholarship might actually solve Jameson's dilemma. If "such readers" would acquaint themselves with the scholarly tradition of marxism, his footnote could be deleted.

Ironically, Jameson's representation of "such readers" defies his own insight into the urgency of constructing a "whole new logic of collective dynamics, with categories that escape the taint of some mere application of terms drawn from individual experience" (*PU* 294). Rather than address the theoretical question of his audience and its resistance in terms of the dynamics of class—or of some other kind of collective struggle—Jameson here thinks of his readers as individual literary critics who need to do more research. But they should begin somewhere other

[10]Althusser himself is revising Marx, specifically a letter Marx wrote, in March 1872, to Maurice La Châtre on the occasion of the publication of *Capital* in a French serialization. It reads, in part, "Dear Citizen, I applaud your idea of publishing the translation of *Das Kapital* as a serial. In this form the book will be more accessible to the working-class, a consideration which to me outweighs everything else. This is the good side of your suggestion, but here is the reverse of the medal: the method of analysis which I have employed, and which had not previously been applied to economic subjects, makes the reading of the first chapters rather arduous, and it is to be feared that the French public, always impatient to come to a conclusion, eager to know the connexion between general principles and the immediate questions that have aroused their passions, may be disheartened because they will be unable to move on at once." Cited in Althusser and Balibar, *Reading Capital*, p. 9.

than these thirty-five pages of *The Political Unconscious*. The practical shortcomings of individual readers are of course pluralism's category for understanding (that is, pluralism's alibi for) the recurring failures of persuasion. Hence the pluralist's lack of interest in theorizing the irreducible specificity of any group of readers in detail. If we hope to pursue Jameson's marxist hermeneutics beyond the boundaries of general persuasion, we must struggle to give his readers faces and names and political places.

II

The example of Jameson, of a "marxist pluralism," is especially important to my argument in part because the locution itself is nearly an oxymoron. As I observed in my opening chapter, marxism is one discourse that privileges exclusions; class is one of many potential limits to general persuasion. In this sense, marxist discourse is paradigmatic of the kind of critical intervention that most threatens pluralist hegemony, and, in the United States in particular, it has long served as the major target of pluralism's polemic. The fact, then, that a marxist pluralism is possible, that *The Political Unconscious* remains trapped within the problematic of general persuasion, alerts us, first, to the extraordinary flexibility and power of pluralism in academic discourse in this country, and, second, to the ambiguity of various theoretical discourses, including marxism, in relation to the opposition pluralism/anti-pluralism.

I have already discussed the way in which the colloquial meaning of the word "pluralist"—and its cold war political resonance—shadows every theory of pluralism. Jameson tries to turn this resonance back on itself, speaking of pluralism disdainfully, almost with contempt, in *The Political Unconscious*. The very appearance of the word in his discourse sets him apart from most of the other theorists we have considered. He criticizes the "various contemporary ideologies of pluralism" for their "unexamined valorization of the open ('freedom') versus its inevitable binary opposition, the closed ('totalitarianism')" (31). But Jameson's references are basically casual ones, and his use of the word pluralism often approaches colloquialism. Despite his suspicions about "the ideological climate of . . . contemporary American pluralism" and its "openness," the degree to which he endorses pluralism's account of its own character, even in the act of attempting to discredit it, is disturbing. Thus, he informs us that marxism "must compete in the 'pluralism' of the intellectual marketplace today" (10), and he stresses that "pluralism means one thing when it stands for the coexistence of methods and interpretations in the intellectual and academic marketplace, but quite another when it is taken as a proposition about the infinity of possible meanings and methods and their ultimate equivalence with and substitutability for one another" (31). While we must reject the notion of infinite meaning (here, as in Ken Newton's conversation with Derrida, the general absence of standards is identified as pluralism), it seems that Jameson finds pluralism's marketplace philosophy of intellectual discourse plausible and relatively benign. His concern to counter the anti-hermeneutic view of dissemination and free play distracts him from a critical consideration of pluralism's more mundane discursive proclivities. To agree to "compete" without first thoroughly deconstructing the field that pluralism calls us to is to concede the contest before it has begun. Pluralism certainly stands for coexistence, if "stands for" means "symbolizes" or "champions." But its concrete discursive effects are quite another matter. One consequence of Jameson's lack of systematic interest in pluralist discourse is the reinscription of its effects in his text. If we want to break with the pluralist problematic, we must interrogate its notion of competition and the operation by which methods and interpretations coexist in an academy conceived as a marketplace.

Jameson's willingness to employ the pluralist metaphor of the marketplace is symptomatic of his text's complicity with pluralist problematics. In fact, marxism cannot simply "coexist" in the intellectual marketplace except insofar as it is rewritten in pluralist terms; rather, marxism, in literary theory as in political economy, throws that market into radical question and interrogates its enabling conditions. That Jameson has not pursued this question very far is clear from his view that pluralism itself is primarily a brake on interpretative activity, rather than a constant incentive to interpret. He suggests that "the program to which the various contemporary ideologies of pluralism are most passionately attached is a largely negative one: namely to forestall that systematic articulation and totalization of interpretive results which can only lead to embarrassing questions about the relationship between them and in particular the place of *history* and the ultimate ground of narrative and textual production" (*PU* 32, my emphasis). Although I agree that pluralism is always anxious to block certain "systematic articulations," it is disappointing that Jameson evokes history here rather than politics. Historicism is not per se hostile to pluralism. As Terry Eagleton observes, "'Always historicize!' is by no means a specifically Marxist recommendation; and . . . though Jameson would no doubt gladly concede the point . . . , such a concession merely blurs the specificity of Marxism itself, which is not at all to 'historicize' (any more than ideology is always and everywhere naturalising), but, in a word, to grasp history as structured material struggle."[11] Jameson almost seems to take history as an unproblematic ground for marxism's challenge to pluralism. He might have demanded an inquiry, not into "ultimate groundings," but into the dirty secret of pluralism in the United States, which is class conflict. His twin concerns—to point out that pluralism blocks certain systematic analyses and to discredit what he sees as post-structuralism's self-indulgent fascination with the play of substitution —lead Jameson to overlook the fact that pluralism pursues positive projects as well and is not confined to the strategy of disarming systematic totalizations. The productivity of pluralist discourse is unlimited, and the problematic of general persuasion may even operate by projecting totalizations. That is in effect the strategy behind Booth's concept of the critical commonwealth and Fish's account of inter-

[11]Terry Eagleton, "Fredric Jameson: The Politics of Style," *Diacritics* 12:3 (1982), 19.

pretation as "the only game in town." And, in *The Political Un-conscious* as well, totalization is the vehicle of general persuasion.

If we are to pursue the special case of "marxist pluralism," the reading of the pluralist problematic I have offered so far must be extended somewhat in the direction of an "external" critique, a turn toward the larger social formation of which the pluralist problematic in literary studies is only one element. Such an investigation would ultimately seek to trace in detail the forms and the history of the affiliations that connect the critical plural-ism of literary theory and the university at large to the political and cultural pluralism that is such a powerful force in the United States. Jameson's remarks about the coding of pluralism and its other as "freedom" versus "totalitarianism" indicate that he is well aware of the relations binding the apparently innocent " 'pluralism' of the intellectual marketplace" to other social and political institutions. His persistent use of scare quotes around the word pluralism implies his distance from the term and from the ordinary politics of pluralism in the United States. But Jameson's adoption of that same marketplace imagery (and log-ic) indicates that he has not escaped the seductions of general persuasion.

Like most other commentators, including those who examine literary critical pluralism in considerable depth, Jameson doesn't address the discourse of contemporary political pluralism di-rectly; obviously, his focus is elsewhere. Many observers have remarked on the striking coincidences of imagery and narrative between Adam Smith's account of the operations of the market and the liberal democrat's account of the workings of his state; even the briefest comparison is illuminating. In both stories, the individual is the agent of all significant action, and his right to act is secured against all objections, save the direct claims of another individual's rights. Each narrative posits such individu-als as coherent, rational beings, acting "selfishly" in pursuit of their own interests (so long as the chase does not interfere with the rights of others) in a realm that is defined as a *market*. Garry Wills writes: "Laissez faire means, in effect, let the *other* man do

what he wants, and the whole point of liberalism was this de-
ference to others, the elaborate arrangement that made everyone keep "hands off" everyone else. The market, in order to
work, must invite people in, encourage (in that sense) participation, stimulate the widest possible competitive initiative. But all
those who enter the game must abide by its outcome" (333).
Booth almost seems to parody these terms when he urges us
both to pursue one chosen monism as best we can and to give
the other guy's monism a fair shake, and Fish's claim that "interpretation is the only game in town" all but does away with the
need to "invite" or "encourage" participation: he simply defines
everyone, willy-nilly, as part of the game, as does de Man, by
other means. Jameson implicates himself in the outcome of this
pluralist game when he accedes to the metaphor of the market.
As Gayatri Spivak suggests, pluralism operates precisely by "inviting [us] into the center at the price of exacting from [us] the
language of centrality" (S 106).

   That Booth's and Hirsch's strictures, their guidelines for right
reading, as well as Fish's therapeutic rhetoric, are necessary at
all reveals a certain perturbation in the critical marketplace. The
interference of the police function in this marketing apparatus is
ideally to be kept to a minimum. The beauty of the model of the
market is that it seems to work "all by itself," just as, according
to Althusser, the subjects of ideology work "all by themselves"
(*LP* 181). Indeed, tinkering (sometimes known as planning) is
regarded as a hubristic attempt to fix something that, by definition, can never be broken. (Current traditional polemics against
theory might be read in just this light.) As Wills observes, "the
claim of the Market is that actions undertaken for self-interest
are concatenated by Adam Smith's 'invisible hand' to bring
about universal benefit" (*NA* 230). In the political market, "the
'random' unpredictable act of altruism" baffles the system.
Robert Paul Wolff suggests, "it is essential to the success of this
proposal that everyone vote selfishly. If too many people, out of
a misguided concern for the general good, vote for what they
think will benefit society as whole, then the result will be an
opinion about the total happiness rather than a measure of it"

(*NA* 230). "Misguided" individuals who jam the system lose sight of the fact that a liberal state speaks for everyone, that is, "for the people," but listens to or recognizes those people only in the terms of their individuality, one at a time. In this way, liberalism blocks the very perception of significant differences among the people (of classes, for example), first, in order to generalize them in a homogeneous and unified whole, the better to represent them (pun intended), and, then, to prevent them from forming disruptive combinations, collectivities in pursuit of the general good, which would complicate if not destroy the essential, totalizing fiction of the unity of the people.

The parallel structures of the capitalist market and the liberal polity are repeated in the problematic of general persuasion. We can hear the echo of the declaration that government should be "of the people, by the people, and for the people" when M. H. Abrams insists, against the claims of what he calls deconstruction, that the reader interprets "determinably meaningful texts by, for, and about human beings" (*PR* 588). The metaphor of the market also clarifies Booth's difficulty in remaining a pluralist while actively defending pluralism's model of interpretation. The root of the embarrassment that surrounds any pluralist polemic lies in the knowledge that if pluralism's account of interpretation is correct, there should be no need for the authorities to enforce it. (Fish makes this point.) The trouble, both for the political system Wills and Wolff describe and for the interpretative model of pluralism, is dogma, that is, ideology and theory.

A dogmatic commitment to a program for the general good leads certain misguided individuals to vote unselfishly and, at the same time, self-consciously; both qualities are completely antithetical to the operation of the market. The "natural" sense of belonging to a national community, of being an American, is problematized by the very effort of thought that leads, on the one hand, to the rejection of individualism and, on the other, to the rejection of Americanism. Theory makes the same troubling double play against the reader of general persuasion. The theorist withdraws, self-consciously, from the natural practice of reading and dogmatically imposes a series of mediations that fragment the critical commonwealth (create "schools"). The anti-pluralist aggravates this disruption. In her practice, the rejection of innocent reading and the emphasis on system is focused by the question of exclusion; her double reading, the symptomatic reading that privileges the "break"—between reader and text and among readers—enables a critique of general persuasion. In a certain sense, this is the central project of marxist ideology critique, which explains its obsession with theorizing mediations. The intellectual market, as Wills calls it, resists such interventions because they expose discontinuities—resisting readers—in the apparently homogeneous field; suddenly, the reader sees that the market is made.

Wills's analysis of this intellectual market in *Nixon Agonistes* is superb. I have already invoked his observation that in the postwar years the American academy reached a consensus that excluded the "evil of system," that is, the dangerous and unnecessary dogmatism of theory, which threatens, because of its totalizing power, "to close the market." As I also observed above, marxism can stand as paradigmatic of the system that excludes and must therefore be excluded. Indeed, the broader historical analysis of pluralism of which this book is only a small part would have to trace the twentieth-century history of the theoretical and political confrontations between marxism and pluralism in the United States. We might follow the lead of political scientists who have been explicit about the importance of the exclusion of marxism to the constitution of pluralism. As Theodore J. Lowi puts it, pluralism "made a major contribution by helping to break down the Marxian notion of solidary classes and class-dominated government." Lowi also observes that "the strength of pluralism rest[s] in very great part upon the proposition . . . that a pluralist society frees politics by creating a discontinuity between the political world and the socioeconomic world."[12] Pluralists are committed to the mystifying proposition that critical pluralism frees interpretation by creating a discontinuity between the academic world and power. In both arenas,

[12]Theodore J. Lowi, *The End of Liberalism*, p. 36.

pluralists generally defend the view that persuasion can be insulated from the impurities of power. And in both, power is aligned with theory or dogma. The flight from theory is represented as an escape from power into community, from history into nature, from conflict and discontinuity into a critical "commonwealth" where "interpretation is the only game in town."

The persistence of anti-theoretical themes in pluralist discourse suggests a relation between the rise of pragmatism and the unrelenting pressure of the critiques confronting pluralism. It may be that an "anti-theory" position now seems the only one available to the defenders of pluralism. From the perspective of pluralism, pragmatism has the attraction of seeming to appeal neither to (special) interests nor to irrational desires, but to the critical community as an organic whole. Richard Rorty observes:

> of course the non-Kantian *is* a parasite—flowers could not sprout from the dialectical vine unless there were an edifice into whose chinks it could insert its tendrils. No constructors, no deconstructors. No norms, no perversions. Derrida (like Heidegger) would have no writing to do unless there were a "metaphysics of presence" to overcome. Without the fun of stamping out parasites, on the other hand, no Kantian would bother to continue building. Normal philosophers need to think, for example, that in forging the powerful tools of modern analytic philosophy, they are developing weapons to ensure victory in the coming final struggle with the decadent dialecticians. *Everybody needs everybody else.*[13]

These are the kinds of needs Wayne Booth can accommodate in his "critical commonwealth"; indeed, these are the very needs

---

[13]Richard Rorty, "Philosophy as a Kind of Writing," *Consequences of Pragmatism (Essays: 1972–1980)* (Minneapolis: University of Minnesota Press, 1982), p. 108, my emphasis. See also Rorty, "Postmodernist Bourgeois Liberalism," *Journal of Philosophy* 80:10 (1983), 583–89, and "Solidarity or Objectivity?" in *Post-Analytic Philosophy*, ed. John Rajchman and Cornel West (New York: Columbia University Press, 1985), pp. 3–19. Rorty has been criticized from the perspective of "cultural pluralism," by those who use the word "pluralism" in a very different sense from my own. See "Special Reports: Eleventh Inter-American Congress of Philosophy," *Proceedings and Addresses of the American Philosophical Association* 59:5 (1986), 747–59, and Cornel West, "The Politics of American Neo-Pragmatism," *Post-Analytic Philosophy*, pp. 259–72.

he needs. This is also a utopian vision. Rorty's logic recalls Jameson's claim that deconstruction's assault on totalization is in fact an ironic confirmation of the totalizing gesture itself.

> This negative and methodological status of the concept of "totality" may also be shown at work in those very post-structural philosophies which explicitly repudiate such "totalizations" in the name of difference, flux, dissemination, and heterogeneity. . . . If such perceptions are to be celebrated in their intensity, they must be accompanied by some initial appearance of continuity, some ideology of unification already in place, which it is their mission to rebuke and shatter. . . . We will therefore suggest that these are second-degree or critical philosophies, which reconfirm the status of the concept of totality by their very reaction against it. [*PU* 53]

Cornel West has observed that this "slippery" attempt to "disarm" the opposition is not persuasive argument but "a defensive recuperative strategy that co-opts the deconstructionists."[14] But what is most striking to me is the echo of the (non-marxist) Stanley Fish asserting the impossibility of discontinuity in literary studies; Jameson's totalizations are similar defenses against difference and discontinuity. What remains to be seen is why he perceives these interpretative (or anti-interpretative) strategies to be such a profound threat to the *marxist* enterprise—and how pluralism enables his defense. How does it happen that pluralism and the resistance to pluralism, for certainly *The Political Unconscious* participates in the latter, arrive at the same destination, even merge? How do Jameson's appropriation of the figure of the marketplace, his commitment to totalization, and his utopian allegory combine to implicate him in the pluralist problematic and bind him to the reader of general persuasion?

It would be a serious error—a characteristically pluralist mistake, as well—to read the crisis of pluralism solely as a moment in the history of ideas, to formalize it and thus obscure its contingency. The resistance to general persuasion includes the in-

---

[14]West, "Ethics and Action in Fredric Jameson's Marxist Hermeneutics," p. 126.

tellectual and political critique mounted from the margins of pluralism's own (allegedly) "common enterprise." The population of the university has changed in the last forty years; those once utterly excluded now form part of the audience pluralism seeks to generalize and discipline in the figure of the pluralist reader/critic. Questions of race, class, and gender have disrupted pluralism's complacency, and, as Jameson points out, these questions introduce notions of the collective which are quite heterogeneous to pluralism. This aspect of anti-pluralism threatens general persuasion much as any political discourse threatens a discourse seeking to confine itself to an ethical problematic. Most pluralists respond to this political intrusion by reading it as essentially extrinsic, as merely contextual; by trying to reduce the substance of its critique to a matter of ethics; and by displacing their anxieties about resisting readers into debates wholly devoted to the (im)possibility of reading at all. But these strategies meet more and more resistance. Anti-pluralisms bring the problem of politics *within* the confines of literary studies and thus force us to confront power, not as a polluting or compromising influence on our discourse, but as a enabling structure or economy internal to it.

Jameson's position in this conflict is different, as one might expect. His work is always explicitly aligned with the forces that threaten pluralism, and he has in fact contributed to the current crisis of pluralist discourse. Jameson is consciously reflecting on the political situation in the United States, and his reading of this situation informs both his understanding of his own political task and his theory. In *The Political Unconscious*, however, his discussion of these questions does not form part of the general argument of the book. It is largely confined to another footnote. Jameson argues:

> The critique of totalization in France goes hand in hand with a call for a "molecular" or local, nonglobal, nonparty politics: and this repudiation of the traditional forms of class and party action evidently reflects the historic weight of French centralization (at work both in the institutions and in the forces that oppose them), as well as the belated emergence of what can very loosely be

called a "countercultural" movement, with the breakup of the old cellular family apparatus and a proliferation of subgroups and alternate "life-styles." In the United States, on the other hand, it is precisely the intensity of social fragmentation of this latter kind that has made it historically difficult to unify Left or "anti-systemic" forces in any durable and effective organizational way. Ethnic groups, neighborhood movements, feminism, various "countercultural" or alternative life-style groups, rank-and-file labor dissidence, student movements, single-issue movements— all have in the United States seemed to project demands and strategies which were theoretically incompatible with each other and impossible to coordinate on any practical political basis. The privileged form in which the American Left can develop today must therefore necessarily be that of an *alliance politics*; and such a politics is the strict practical equivalent of the concept of totalization on the theoretical level. In practice, then, the attack on the concept of "totality" in the American framework means the undermining and the repudiation of the only realistic perspective in which a genuine Left could come into being in this country. [PU 54]

It is difficult to object to Jameson's suggestion that the American Left must privilege a politics of alliances. But *The Political Unconscious* offers us the theoretical equivalent of alliance politics, alliance theory, as it were, and the theoretical allies Jameson is willing to enlist are far more "diverse" than the political ones he lists here. Alliance theory is pluralist politics: a diverse and inclusive critical community, with a place in its structure for everyone, including the nominal marxist, struggling together for "our life together."

Even if there were not such a striking similarity between the pluralist ideal and alliance theory, Jameson's account would be problematic. In the first place, the relationship he describes between politics and theory is one of expressive causality; alliance politics is "the strict practical equivalent of the concept of totalization on the theoretical level." Structurally, the two instances are homologous, and Jameson is reasserting the very model of mediation that he works so brilliantly in the rest of his text to dismantle and complicate. The relations between politics and theory are in fact discontinuous, shifting, and unpredictable— not unlike alliance politics, in some ways. But this homology leaps over the complexity of the mediations at work, the better to assert the necessity of totalizing theories of cultural production.

Equally troubling is Jameson's diagnosis of the problems that continue to divide the so-called American Left. His explanation for the welter of interest groups and sects in the United States is rather terse. Given the importance of the decisions to be made, a fuller consideration would seem to be in order. "Social fragmentation" is at best an extremely limited explanation of a phenomenon that certainly also needs to be referred to such matters as the enormous size and strength of the U.S. economy, and, hence, of U.S. capital, and the violent and tremendously effective suppression of left activists and organizations, first in the thirties and (especially in the academy) again in the fifties.

Furthermore, had Jameson examined the practical situation of any of the various "'antisystemic' forces" he lists, he might have encountered a rather different analysis of their shortcomings and a different prescription for overcoming factionalism and division. To take the example of feminism: feminist theory and political polemic are currently alive with criticism, not of the left as a whole, for failing to achieve totalization, but of feminist theory and practice itself, precisely for practicing a premature (if not wholly unwarranted) totalization around the notion of woman. Feminists from all parts of the movement are offering critiques of the tendency in much of their critical and theoretical *oeuvre* and their organizing for "woman" to signify white, middle-class, and heterosexual and, thus, to obliterate the differences among women and erase the specificity of the lives of women who are black or working-class or lesbian.[15] In many of these texts, the failure of alliance politics is interpreted as the

[15]See, for example, Hazel Carby, *Reconstructing Woman* (London: Oxford University Press, 1987); Bell Hooks, *Feminist Theory;* Gloria Hull, Patricia Bell Scott, and Barbara Smith, eds., *But Some of Us Are Brave* (Old Westbury, N.Y.: Feminist Press, 1982); Cherríe Moraga, *Loving in the War Years* (New York: Kitchen Table Press, 1983); Cherríe Moraga and Gloria Anzaldua, eds., *This Bridge Called My Back* (New York: Kitchen Table Press, 1981); Tillie Olsen, *Silences* (New York: Delacorte, 1978); Lillian Robinson, *Sex, Class and Culture* (Bloomington: Indiana University Press, 1978); Gayatri Spivak, *In Other Worlds;* Alice Walker, *In Search of Our Mothers' Gardens* (New York: Harcourt Brace Jovanovich, 1983).

result of totalization; alliances have collapsed because the parties did not recognize one another's differences, or acknowledge the discontinuities between their stories, and thus failed to construct solidarity across those differences in the pursuit of specific ends. The very last thing that might enable feminist discourses to contribute to the construction of an effective alliance politics—by means, for example, of an intersection of the concerns of black and white women or working-class and middle-class women—would be a totalizing theory.

Jameson doesn't consider feminism or any other case in particular. The magic of expressive causality is that it saves one the task of investigating specific instances of social practice in their details. One can project back and forth across the social field, with a fair amount of confidence that one will find "strict practical equivalents." But Jameson's oversight may have been overdetermined. By not looking too closely into the internal politics of the actual constituencies that might be expected to form this alliance, Jameson can again bracket the problem of audience; this footnote, not unlike the earlier one, protects him from having to consider the precise nature of that audience, politically or theoretically, and enables him to continue to address a general (pluralist) reader.

III

Jameson's diagnosis of the fragmentation of the American left leads him directly to alliance theory. He produces marxism as a method of methods, a master hermeneutic that reveals History as a "single great collective story" (*PU* 19). The inclusiveness of *The Political Unconscious* is one of its most prominent formal features; it uncannily recalls the efforts of Wayne Booth, in a very different book, *Critical Understanding*, to allow his opponents to live on his pages. Of course this very gesture of inclusiveness can rewrite opponents as unwitting accomplices; but, for his part, Jameson does not acknowledge that any significant distortion is necessary to accomplish his appropriations. "Marxism subsumes other interpretative modes or systems; or, to put it in methodological terms, . . . *the limits of the latter can always be overcome,* and their more positive findings retained" (47, my emphases). This belief that limits "can always be overcome" extends from Jameson's reading of other interpretative modes to his reading of other readers and of himself as a reader. Limits are thus never really limits.

Jameson refuses, theoretically and politically, to exclude any interpretative strategy from the totalizing project of marxism. In his formulation,"positive findings" are not to be read symptomatically, to be interpreted as the trace of another class's interested efforts to construct history, but to be "retained." The "positive findings" of other methods are just that: positive and essentially accurate (accurate in their essence). They require the historicizing contextualization that (apparently) only marxism can provide, but Jameson seems to believe that no critical approach represents the historical forces ranged against marxism in such a way as to bar its effective appropriation by contemporary marxist readers. He gives no quarter to Bakhtin's suggestion that prior to any act of "appropriation, the word does not exist in a neutral and impersonal language . . . , but rather it exists in other people's intentions: it is from there that one must take the word, and make it one's own."[16] Bakhtin offers what I would call an anti-pluralist argument; in his view, "there are no 'neutral' words and forms. . . . All words have the 'taste' of a profession, a genre, a tendency, a party" (293), and there are limits to what tropes and forms can get away with. While no word or method has an essence, an unchanging meaning or effect, to take a word is not always possible: "many words stubbornly resist, others remain alien, sound foreign in the mouth of the one who appropriated them and who now speaks them; they cannot be assimilated into his context and fall out of it; it is as if they put themselves in quotation marks against the will of the speaker" (294).

[16]Mikhail Bakhtin, *The Dialogic Imagination* (Austin: University of Texas Press, 1981), pp. 293–94.

The question of method may seem to be a purely formal matter, but Jameson reveals that it always concerns readers. He writes:

> Marxism cannot today be defended as a mere substitute for such other methods, which would them triumphalistically be consigned to the ashcan of history; the authority of such methods springs from their faithful consonance with this or that local law of a fragmented social life, this or that subsystem of a complex and mushrooming cultural superstructure. In the spirit of a more authentic dialectical tradition, Marxism is here conceived as the "untranscendable horizon" that subsumes such apparently antagonistic or incommensurable critical operations, assigning them an undoubted sectoral validity within itself, and thus at once canceling and preserving them. [PU 10].

This concession to "undoubted sectoral validity" is an appeal to the general reader of the pluralist problematic. It refers to the process of preserving the positive findings of even antagonistic methods, but it goes further than that position in that it explains how validity is achieved. Non-marxist methods acquire their "authority" from "their faithful consonance with this or that local law of fragmented social life." This faithfulness is apparently not implicated in the class struggle; Jameson does not address the way in which politics and power are inscribed within theory, even within method, and thus within all efforts to read the local laws of the social. Indeed, his position amounts to an assertion that it is possible to escape politics and somehow be faithful to the literal fragmentation of the social.

Theoretically, this position returns to the model Althusser locates in the early Marx, to the transcendent myth of reading at first sight. The social text is fetishized as given, and alienation or fragmentation is simply present in social life to be read off. The politics of reading becomes something extrinsic. A properly marxist political orientation is appended to another method, one that has already "faithfully" rendered some "local law of a fragmented social life." The reader's, that is, the critic's political positioning does not enter into the calculation. But Jameson does acknowledge the problem of audience. He indicates that

"Marxism *cannot today* be defended as a mere substitute for such other methods" (my emphases). This remark doesn't refer to Jameson's argument as such, but to his readers; such a defense of marxism—one that "triumphalistically" consigned other methods to "the ashcan of history"—would not be persuasive to most of them "today." But Jameson doesn't pause over this insight into the theoretical significance of audience. He soon begins to sound eerily like the other pluralists in the marketplace, each accommodating the needs of others, each contributing to the general good by pursuing "sectoral validity."

The invocation of the "authentic dialectical tradition" works for Jameson much as the invocation of dialogue functions for Booth, or interpretation for Fish; it establishes a homogeneous field for the play of general persuasion. This is a marxist criticism so eager for alliances that it graciously includes all methods and thus makes a generous appeal to all readers. Jameson is unwilling to mark the exclusions that constitute his marxist audience in its particularity. He does argue that interpretation takes place on a "Homeric battlefield" and that "only another, stronger interpretation can overthrow and practically refute an interpretation already in place" (13). (One wonders if the Homeric reference stands in for a revolutionary one. In the *Iliad*, Athens and Troy share a cultural cosmos; the war is underwritten by the continuity between their social fields.) But when Jameson outlines the strength of marxist interpretation, he refuses to assign any significance to the limited and specific interests or desires of the audience that confronts it. The question of what constitutes "strength," and for whom, is addressed in the most general and metaphorical terms. Rather than cite the particular interests to be served — and thwarted—by a marxist hermeneutic, Jameson takes refuge in the metaphor of scales: "the metacommentary thus has the advantage of allowing us to measure the *yield and density* of a properly Marxist interpretive act against those of other interpretive methods—the ethical, the psychoanalytic, the myth-critical, the semiotic, the structural, and the theological—against which it must compete in the "pluralism" of the intellectual market place today. I will here argue the priority of a Marxian interpretive framework in terms of *semantic richness*" (10, my emphases). The form of the list reappears, reiterating Jameson's concern with marxism's relationship to all other forms of literary criticism. It is somewhat disconcerting to find Adam Smith's metaphor employed with no effort to unpack its ideological imposture. I do not want to question in absolute terms the "semantic richness," "yield" or "density" of marxist analysis. I hope it is clear by now that the possibility of any such "absolute" questioning is one of the objects of my critique. What must be put into question here is the existence of a scale that might measure such qualities. This scale represents the utopian aspect of Jameson's literary theory; the pluralist moment, outside politics, when marxism can establish its priority in quantifiable terms. The scale transcends the divisions between certain readers and the alien marxist reader. Now it is marxism's chance to claim a faithful consonance, not to local laws, but to the law of History itself.

Jameson asserts the "priority" of marxist interpretation as the politics of general persuasion, that is, he asserts its general priority, its theoretical persuasiveness, for every reader and every critic. He thus achieves a familiar pluralist indifference to the interests that must divide his audience. James Kavanagh has suggested that Jameson's discourse is "effective" precisely because "it continually produces a Marxism that is *recognized as something else*—as something that can comfortably digest (Jameson might say 'complete') and be digested by, any and every other discourse."[17] Jameson produces marxism within the problematic of general persuasion, and he conceals both the exclusions and the acknowledgment of exclusion that constitute the marxist audience as distinct and revolutionary. Instead, *The Political Unconscious* speaks in the pluralist marketplace to the "universal audience" it longs for. It respects the limits of general persuasion.

It is not surprising, then, that *The Political Unconscious* concludes with a utopian celebration of the utopian. The reader of

[17]Kavanagh, "The Jameson Effect," 27.

general persuasion is one who does not take sides, a general reader, a reader with no particular position, no place, as it were. When Jameson tells his reader that "all class consciousness of whatever type is Utopian insofar as it expresses the unity of a collectivity," he is, as he admits, offering an "allegorical" inter-pretation. As he puts it, "the achieved collectivity . . . of what-ever kind—oppressors fully as much as oppressed—is Utopian not in itself, but only insofar as all such collectivities are them-selves *figures* for . . . an achieved Utopian or classless society" (291). Cornel West reads this passage as "utopianism gone mad" and "Marxism in deep desperation." I read it as pluralism. It posits an audience of general readers for whom the figure of the Utopian can appear as figure, really as pure form, regardless of its historical content—fascism, for example—and without refer-ence to the politics of readings. Jameson makes no reference here to the politics of the readers of this figure—or to the possi-bility that figuration and politics are always mutually determin-ing. Uncannily like de Man, a figure who does not appear in *The Political Unconscious*, Jameson seems to assume an uncon-strained reader for whom the allegory cannot help but be legi-ble; limits can always be overcome. Utopian reading is for the reader of general persuasion.

In de Man's case, of course, figuration was the ruin of history. Taken as a group, the pluralist texts that we have considered suggest that the refusal of any "literal" history is one of the necessary effects of the problematic of general persuasion. To invoke the historical is not, however, sufficient as a critique of pluralism. The flight from history that characterizes pluralist discourse, whether it is viewed as a logic (Hirsch), an ethics (Booth) or a theory of rhetoric (Fish and de Man), alerts the critical reader to the significance of history in the pluralist prob-lematic and tempts her to press historical claims before all oth-ers. There is a certain level on which this temptation must be resisted. Jameson's account of history places him at a consider-able distance from other pluralists; and yet it seems that for him history, rather than signifying politics, actually replaces politics, just as the reader of general persuasion replaces the marxist and the potentially marxist reader. Suzanne Gearhart warns that a critique of de Man cannot be offered "from the standpoint of a theory of history that would claim to be the ultimate ground or context in which all events and objects, including literature, would be situated." She alerts us to the fact that a "theory of history that takes for granted its categories (time and space), its language, and its own metaliterary, metaformal (and ultimately metahistorical) status is not 'post-de Manian,' but 'pre-de Manian.'"[18] This warning is crucial. What Jameson calls the "necessity" of history must be approached cautiously if we are to avoid slipping into the very pluralist polemic I have been at such pains to describe.

Jane Marcus's critique of Annette Kolodny's feminist pluralism offers one model of the resistance to a pluralist invocation of history as ground. She charges:

> Kolodny's liberal relaxation of the tensions among us and the tensions between feminists and the academy reflects a similar relaxation on the part of historians and political activists. What this does is to isolate Marxist feminists and lesbians on the barricades while "good girl" feminists fold their tents and slip quietly into the establishment. There is a battle field (race, class, and sexual identity) within each one of us, another battlefield where we wage these wars with our own feminist colleagues (as in *Signs*), and a third battlefield where we defend ourselves from male onslaughts both on our work and on the laws that govern our lives as women in society. It is far too early to tear down the barricades. Dancing shoes will not do. We still need our heavy boots and mine detectors. [ST 623]

Marcus's invocation of an internal battlefield briefly echoes my analysis of de Man as a theorist who internalizes the warring forces of polemic and projects them into his text. But in her model, aporia is not only or even primarily a narrowly defined linguistic event; the warring forces meet in every conceivable textual instance. Her multiplication of overlapping and conflicting fields of struggle demonstrates her refusal of any homoge-

---

[18]Gearhart, "Philosophy *before* Literature," 73.

nizing or generalizing strategies and of any of the conciliatory tactics of pluralism. Marcus makes it clear that Kolodny's image of the minefield actually functions to conceal conflicts among women. This minefield is laid by men and external to feminism—the floor beneath our dancing feet or the ground of our discourse—and it is external to each woman. This totalizing figuration enables Kolodny to attribute unity to women by opposing them to men. Marcus exposes and refuses this strategy, both practically and theoretically. Marcus reiterates that the battlefield, irreducible difference, and the consequent conflicts are everywhere, within subjects, among women, between women and men; she thus prevents any single site from acquiring the status of an origin, the ultimate ground for all other battles. Her shifting sense of the place of battle is strategic; the ground is an effect of the struggle rather than a field that precedes and thus completely contains it.

Jameson's sense of the battle is less flexible. He argues that "history is *not* a text, not a narrative, master or otherwise" (*PU* 35). Rather,

> History is . . . the experience of Necessity, and it is this alone which can forestall its thematization or reification as a mere object of representation or as one master code among many others. Necessity is not in that sense a type of content, but rather the inexorable *form* of events. . . . History is what hurts, it is what refuses desire and sets inexorable limits to individual as well as collective praxis, which its "ruses" turn into grisly and ironic reversals of their overt intention. But this History can be apprehended only through its effects, and never directly as some reified force. This is indeed the ultimate sense in which History as ground and untranscendable horizon needs no particular theoretical justification: we may be sure that its alienating necessities will not forget us, however much we might prefer to ignore them. [*PU* 102]

Given the importance of the question of history and the controversy that surrounds it, this seems like an odd moment to assert that theoretical justification is beside the point. (This may be the only antitheoretical passage in the text.) Jameson's account of history gives up the terrain Marcus claimed by refusing to locate necessity on any single field. "Necessity," as Jameson describes it, is History, and History is understood entirely as the "inexorable form of events" which can never be eluded, though it may be ignored. History excludes no one from its Necessity.

The word "necessity" should arouse our concern. Jameson's use of the term resembles de Man's more than it does Althusser's or, for that matter, Derrida's. Rather than take necessity as the product of historical struggle, Jameson attributes to History the totalizing power to impose its Necessity as an Absolute. He leaves the critic the task, not of guiltily producing necessity, but of belatedly trying to comprehend it. Most important, this hermeneutic process is identical for every reader, just as necessity itself is. The reader of general persuasion appears in Jameson's text to register, in the sense of decode, the necessities of History and not to generate them. Thus every reader and every method is capable of generating "positive findings," able to uncover one of the "local laws" of historical necessity.

In the pluralist texts we have considered, the (implicit or explicit) invocation of the necessary is coupled with a view of interpretation and understanding that excludes genuine historical determinations, that is, politically conflictual determinations. For example, de Man cites Hölderlin to suggest:

> "what is true is what is bound to take place." And, in the case of the reading of a text, what takes place is a necessary understanding. What marks the truth of such an understanding is not some abstract universal but the fact that it has to occur regardless of other considerations. It depends . . . on the rigor of the reading as argument. Reading is an argument (which is not necessarily the same as a polemic) because it has to go against the grain of what one would want to happen in the name of what has to happen; this is the same as saying that understanding is an epistemological event prior to being an ethical or aesthetic value. This does not mean that there can be a true reading, but that no reading is conceivable in which the question of its truth or falsehood is not primarily involved. [*DH* xi]

De Man's position is repeated in some form by each pluralist we have considered. E. D. Hirsch defends the "logic of inquiry" on the grounds that the epistemological problem of understanding as such precedes all the ethical and political questions privileged in the "sociology of knowledge." Wayne Booth excludes the accidental matters of race and class and sexuality because they are contingencies, "irrational forces," that "kill criticism," blocking the act of "critical understanding." Stanley Fish sees all of us as obliged to practice the art of persuasion, to work polemically, "argu[ing] for a way of reading which if it became accepted, would be, for a time at least, the *true* one" (F 16). But de Man's remarks also echo with Derrida's comments on pluralism and deconstruction. Derrida's rejection of that label was linked to his rejection of the problematic of truth:. "I am not a pluralist, and I would never say that every interpretation is equal, but *I* do not select. . . . I would not say that some interpretations are truer than others, I would say that some are more powerful than others. The hierarchy is between forces and not between true and false." Derrida's refusal to conceive his readings in terms of truth and falsehood critically distinguishes his position from de Man's and, simultaneously, aligns him (roughly to be sure) with Althusser and Barthes on the questions of power and reading.

De Man never claims that truth is marked by an abstract universal; rather, truth is "what is bound to take place," "a necessary understanding" which "has to occur regardless of other considerations." Althusser also cites "necessity" in his account of reading. Yet in his case, necessity is linked, not with truth, but with crime, with guilty as opposed to innocent reading. The guilty reading is not absolved—as it would be if it stood in the guise of truth. But the guilty reading is "justified" and theorized by the "necessity of its contingency" (*RC* 45).

Necessity, for Althusser, is historical, whereas for Jameson, History is Necessity. In *The Political Unconscious,* the "Homeric battlefield" within which interpretations struggle is again externalized and grounded; it resembles Kolodny's minefield rather than Marcus's range of uneven displacements. And this battlefield, despite the conflicts within it, is a homogeneous space; Necessity reigns unchallenged there, and Necessity "hurts" us all equally as readers, imposes on us all equally as critics.

I have argued that to defend the infinite substitutability of one signifier for another is to elide the historical limits on what "tropes can get away with"and thus to obscure the resisting reader. Jameson criticizes substitution, the anti-hermeneutic play of differences, from the perspective of Necessity. History's Necessity operates for him as the ground that limits possible meanings and thus imposes on all of us a story that, as Samuel Weber notes, could "not be told otherwise, could not be changed, altered, or modified, without being falsified and losing its necessity."[19] But in his account of History as the experience of Necessity, Jameson once again displaces the political. He allows a generalizing history to elide the discontinuities in his audience, the uneven play of limits. As Neil Lazarus has pointed out, it is not "History" which "hurts" or "refuses desire"; it is unequal power, tyranny. But Jameson avoids this polemical position; it threatens to involve him in the kind of exclusions the pluralist problematic cannot support. Only History conceived as Necessity allows him to put aside the task of theoretical justification and to assert that we are all inscribed within "the unity of a single collective story."

This is precisely the crux where Althusser would insist that there are many necessary—and necessarily guilty—readings; history is their conflict with one another and the discontinuities among them. The outcome of their struggle awards one the appearance of an absolute necessity but that appearance is a posture of false innocence, a naturalizing appropriation of truth. For Althusser, the guilty reading takes responsibility for its operations by acknowledging its historical necessity, and, thus, its power. The historically necessary reading of a marxist declines the posture of innocence, which always refers its necessity to truth or falsehood. Rather, it points to the play and hierarchy of powerful forces, and it confesses that its reading is the reading it *needs*. The historically necessary reading can never be understood as what is bound to take place because it has abandoned the problematic of general persuasion. What is bound to take place is a matter of struggle.

[19]Weber, "Capitalizing History," p. 51.

EPILOGUE

> Within the enclosure, by means of indirect and always
> perilous maneuvers, risking constantly a relapse back
> into what one intends to deconstruct, our task is to
> encircle the critical concepts with a prudent and
> scrupulous discourse, to note the conditions, the
> context, the limits of their effectiveness, to indicate in
> a rigorous manner their adherence to the mechanism
> which they themselves will enable us to deconstruct.
> —DERRIDA, *Of Grammatology*

The identifying mark of a symptomatic reading is that it works
to disclose an unacknowledged problematic, a structure that is
precisely not the essence of a thought. Insofar as a problematic
is constituted in part by the absence of problems, concepts, and
questions, this structure cannot be uncovered by an empirical,
generalized reading but only by means of a symptomatic analysis. This practice of reading rejects the notion that the text itself
can tell us how it should be read. On the contrary, as Macherey
argues, "we must go beyond the work and explain it, must say
what it does not and could not say." The very possibility of a
symptomatic reading depends on the view "that although the
work is self-sufficient, it does not contain or engender its own
theory; it does not *know* itself" (M 77, 83–84).

Most of the theorists I have examined do not identify themselves as pluralists. It has not been part of my exposition to offer
synoptic accounts of their careers or to summarize the pluralist
"content" in each critic's work. Rather, I have tried to isolate the
concrete pluralist effect of each text and to trace those effects
back to the problematic of general persuasion. The pluralist

problematic constitutes the enabling conditions for the logic, ethics, politics, and even the competing rhetorics we have read in works by Hirsch, Booth, Jameson, Fish, and de Man; the obvious diversity of its instances is both a sign and a cause of its hegemony, and, as I indicated when I began, these five theorists could easily have been replaced by others.

Pluralism's history is one of spectacular success in enforcing its limits upon the discourses of literary studies. Pluralists have rarely drawn back from their opponents; indeed, pluralist discourse may still succeed in containing its critics, quite literally by including them, with some adjustments, of course, much as Booth will accommodate the "deconstructionists" and "mysreaders" as untidy guests in his critical commonwealth, provided he can disregard their polemic against understanding. But the resistance to pluralism is ongoing and perhaps even growing in some critical traditions. Some strains of feminist criticism have been fairly consistent in their wariness of the blandishments of general persuasion. Gayatri Spivak, for example, has warned:

> to embrace pluralism (as [Annette] Kolodny recommends) is to espouse the politics of the masculinist establishment. Pluralism is the method employed by the *central* authorities to neutralize opposition by seeming to accept it. The gesture of pluralism on the part of the *marginal* can only mean capitulation to the center. It is not a question of the choice of methodologies but rather of who is officially in power. However pluralist its demeanor, American liberal masculism (alias humanism) will never declare that it is merely one of many plausible choices.[1]

For Spivak, the question of pluralism is primarily a question of power: a pluralism of the margins is a kind of oxymoron, and feminist criticism must insist on the place of margins despite the promises of the "central authorities."

Spivak's criticisms, like Jane Marcus's, are directed at Annette Kolodny's essay "Dancing through the Minefield." Kolodny argues that feminist discourse should take up the pluralist model

[1]Gayatri Spivak, "A Response to Annette Kolodny," unpublished ms., p. 2.

of M. H. Abrams and "initiate nothing less than a playful pluralism, responsive to the possibilities of multiple critical schools
and methods, but captive to none. . . . Only by employing a
plurality of methods will we protect ourselves from the temptation of so oversimplifying any text—and especially those particularly offensive to us—that we render ourselves unresponsive
to what Scholes has called 'its various systems of meaning and
their interaction.'"[2] Kolodny's accommodating, unifying, and
apparently inclusive, pluralist view of feminism has been the
subject of several sharp critiques.[3] Spivak's rejection of her position is unambiguous and practical: pluralism is a strategy of
power, for the powerful. And like all the strategic or pragmatic
gestures we have considered, this claim has theoretical significance. Spivak doubts the possibility of a successful feminist pluralism (save as a capitulation to the authorities) because she
envisions feminist criticism, in part, as the effort to expose the
phallocentric movement by which "all explanations . . . claim
their centrality in terms of an excluded margin." She argues that
feminists will be invited into the center only at the price of
adopting the language of centrality, the language of general
persuasion.[4]

The conflict between Spivak and other critics of "playful pluralism" on the one side and Kolodny and her defenders on the
other reveals the ambiguity of feminism's relation to the problematic of general persuasion and raises the question of whether
pluralism can in fact ever be a strategy of the margin. Can the

[2]Annette Kolodny, "Dancing through the Minefield: Some Observations on
the Theory, Practice, and Politics of a Feminist Literary Criticism," *Feminist
Studies* 6:1 (1980), 19.

[3]See Judith Kegan Gardner, Elly Burkin, Rena Grass Patterson, and Annette
Kolodny, "An Interchange on Feminist Criticism: On 'Dancing through the
Minefield,'" *Feminist Studies* 8:3 (1982), 629–75. Kolodny's essay was awarded
the 1979 Florence Howe prize by the women's caucus of MLA and reprinted in
Elaine Showalter's influential anthology of feminist criticism, *The New Feminist
Criticism: Essays on Women, Literature and Theory* (New York: Pantheon, 1985). See
also Lillian Robinson, *Sex, Class and Culture*, and Spivak, *In Other Worlds*, for
criticisms of pluralist feminisms.

[4]See Spivak, *In Other Worlds*, pp. 201–6 and passim. It is important to recall
that the feminist figure here is also a deconstructive critic.

power of pluralist discourse (to exclude, silence, and objectify its others, as well as to produce, adapt, and incite those very others to discourse) be run in reverse, turned, in a Foucauldian figure, against its apparent masters? Or are the effects of general persuasion always in the service of hegemonic discourses? Would a feminist pluralism be, as Peggy Kamuf has asked, just another such discourse of power, "reverting to the very terms of opposition which feminist theory has sought to undo?"[5]

Feminist criticism presents a particularly rich field for investigating a *positive* inscription of anti-pluralism, the obverse of the negative critique I have presented here, and for exploring the relations between pluralist and anti-pluralist instantiations of a "single" discourse. Feminist literary studies are extremely diverse; pluralisms and anti-pluralisms, each in several forms, contend for authority even as they question the possibility (and the desirability) of a definitive feminist discourse. The special status of the concept of difference within feminism seems to me to work as a brake on its assimilation to the hegemonic pluralist problematic. But this is not to say that feminist theory is essentially anti-pluralist. Indeed, it is the recurring problem of essentialism that draws feminists to the problematic of general persuasion.

Naomi Schor has recently observed that women in feminist theory persistently return to the possibility of a "femininity beyond deconstruction"; she points out that "no feminist theoretician *who is not also a woman* has ever fully espoused the claims to feminine specificity, an irreducible difference."[6] The assertion of irreducible difference is, in my terms, an anti-pluralist strategy, a strategy of the break or of discontinuity. The problematic of general persuasion requires a general reader, and that reader, despite the formal neutrality of his gender, is in fact a masculine reader; the feminist critic responds by insisting on her "difference of view."

At the same time, the assertion of specificity frequently threat-

[5]Peggy Kamuf, "Replacing Feminist Criticism," *Diacritics* 12:2 (1982), 42.
[6]Naomi Schor, "Dreaming Dissymmetry: Barthes, Foucault and Sexual Difference," *Men in Feminism*, p. 109.

ens to lapse into a new pluralism, ever so slightly more local than that which characterizes the problematic of general persuasion, but largely recuperated by pluralist models, especially by a pluralist essentialism; the disruptive "difference" of woman is asserted, only to be essentialized in turn. Feminism then threatens to become another humanism, reinscribing pluralist strategies and a pluralist model of the general woman reader within its boundaries. Elizabeth Berg warns against this tendency, urging feminist critics to "insist on the partial nature of sexual identity, to [remember] that gender is not the only difference among people, nor even the essential difference, that the move to privilege gender as the primary defining characteristic of people participates in the same logic of oppression as the masculine philosophy one criticizes."[7]

The hegemonic discourses of feminist theory and women's studies have been challenged in turn by the differences among women. Bell Hooks, in *Feminist Theory: From Margin to Center*, points out that the white, heterosexual, middle-class feminist all too often makes "her plight and the plight of white women like herself synonymous with a condition affecting all American women. In so doing she deflect[s] attention away from her classism, her racism, her sexist attitudes towards the masses of American women."[8] In the terms I have been developing in this book, Hooks exposes the process by which feminist discourse reinscribes pluralism, even in a contestatory concept of difference such as sisterhood: "the vision of Sisterhood evoked by women's liberationists was based on the idea of common oppression. Needless to say, it was primarily bourgeois white women, both liberal and radical in perspective, who professed belief in the notion of common oppression, [which] was a false and corrupt platform disguising and mystifying the true nature of women's varied and complex social reality" (43–44). The assertion of difference seems all too easily recuperated by the seductions of a pluralist center.

---

[7]Elizabeth Berg, "Inconoclastic Moments," p. 220.
[8]Bell Hooks, *Feminist Theory*, p. 2.

Schor points to the tendency essentialisms and anti-essential-
isms have of attracting each other and suggests that feminists
abandon their polemics against essentialism, not in order to
embrace it, but to try to understand its persistence and its inti-
mate relation to anti-essentialism; to ask, for example, "how and
why a Cixous and an Irigaray deconstruct and construct femininity at the same time". Simultaneously, she calls for the "multiplication of all differences—national, racial, sexual and class".[9]
It is in such a practice that feminist criticism might develop án
exemplary discourse, or exemplary discourses, of anti-pluralism. As Biddy Martin and Chandra Mohanty point out, this
multiplication of differences as a strategy for undermining pluralism's essentialism can be as politically and theoretically powerful as the "vigilante attacks on humanist beliefs in 'man' and
Absolute Knowledge" mounted "from the ranks of antihuma-
nist intellectuals."[10] They describe Minnie Bruce Pratt's auto-
biographical narrative in *Yours in Struggle: Three Feminist Perspectives on Anti-Semitism and Racism* in these terms: "the perspective
is multiple and shifting, and the shifts in perspective are enabled by the attempts to define self, home, and community that
are at the heart of Pratt's enterprise. The historical grounding of
shifts and changes allows for an emphasis on the pleasures and
terrors of interminable boundary confusions, but insists, at the
same time, on our responsibility for remapping boundaries and
renegotiating connections. These are partial in at least two senses
of the word: politically partial, and without claim to wholeness
or finality" (193). Like Elizabeth Berg, Martin and Mohanty emphasize partiality, the insistence on limits which is impossible
within the problematic of general persuasion. They privilege
Pratt's text over some of the "more abstract critiques" of anti-
humanists because of "the political limitations of an insistence
on 'indeterminacy' which implicitly, when not explicitly, denies
the critic's own situatedness in the social, and in effect refuses to
acknowledge the critic's own institutional home" (194). We observed the political limitations of this denial of situatedness in

[9]Naomi Schor, "Introducing Feminism," *Paragraph* 8 (1986), 98–99, 101.
[10]Biddy Martin and Chandra Mohanty, "Feminist Politics: What's Home Got
to Do with It?" in *Feminist Studies/Critical Studies,* p. 193.

de Man's inability to acknowledge Edith's exclusion. But in my analysis of de Man, I left the question of sexual difference in suspense. What is the connection between the problematic of general persuasion and the effacement of femininity?

Seductive Reasoning is a book written by a feminist. But is it a feminist book? And what is the relation between its feminism and its desire for anti-pluralism? In the opening pages of *Reading Lacan*, Jane Gallop asks a similar question about her own work in the course of a reflection on the ambiguity of the genitive: "women's studies": "I was at work on the present book, a book on Lacan. Not a recognizably feminist project, since Lacan is not a woman, nor have I been concerned in this book explicitly to address Lacan's relation to feminism or women, which I have already done in another book. Perhaps naively, I had not considered this a feminist project but had thought of it as a 'straight' book on Lacan, a study that addressed the general question of how one could possibly read Lacan's text."[11] While I was at work on *Seductive Reasoning*, my naiveté ran in the opposite direction from Gallop's. I thought of my book as an obviously feminist project, in that my critique of pluralism seemed to me to draw consistently on what feminism had taught me. Feminist theory and practice introduced me to the critique of humanism and the hermeneutics of suspicion, to the politics of interpretation and the inevitability of theoretical entanglements, to theories of the subject and the interestedness of academic discourses, the disciplines, the canon, theory, advertising, fashion. You see. It appeared to me as I wrote that this book was unthinkable without my training as a feminist critic.

Yet Gallop points out that Lacan is not a woman, and the same must be said of Stanley Fish, Wayne Booth, Fredric Jameson, and so on. (I have nothing fancy up my sleeve.) But while none of the pluralists I centered my attention on are women, my break with the problematic of general persuasion seemed to assume my positioning as a feminist. Feminism thus appeared to me in the form of an anti-pluralism.

Gallop began to rethink the status of her "straight" book after

---

[11]Jane Gallop, *Reading Lacan* (Ithaca: Cornell University Press, 1985), p. 18.

receiving a report from a referee who objected both to her use of a generic "she" and to her refusal to claim a position of mastery over Lacan's text: "the main objection was that I was not in command of the material *and* I admitted it." These two practices may seem of a different order, but Gallop writes: "Thanks to their joint appearance in my reader's report, I have come to consider that they are, theoretically, the same gesture" (19). This connection in turn engenders Gallop's questions about what constitutes feminist criticism: "Extremely attracted to the notion of women's studies as a force that could revolutionize the very structures of knowledge, I wish to pose the question of what a feminist practice of study might be, beyond the recognizable themes: women and sexual difference. For example, what would be a feminist criticism that neither read women's texts nor read for the representation of women? If women's studies involves an epistemological revolution, how would it effect realms other than those in which women are already the object of knowledge?" (18). Gallop's reasons for considering her Lacan book a straight study and her subsequent questions suggested to me the possibility that some readers would not view *Seductive Reasoning* as a feminist essay. Although in fact my referees were less dismissive than the one Gallop invokes, each called for an extension of my remarks on feminist discourse and a clarification of the place of feminism in what one reader saw as the primarily Althusserian frame of my book. In revising my work, I realized that I had tacitly offered two feminisms to my readers: the anti-pluralist feminism I "assumed" in my own analyses and a potentially pluralist feminism that was unrepresented but might indeed have taken its place alongside the pluralist figures I critique here. I have not belatedly attempted to exfoliate this double reading.[12] Rather, I have aggravated this doubleness in order to dramatize the question of anti-pluralism.

[12]Schor has suggested that "the most active site of the feminine resistance to the discourse of indifference is a certain insistence on doubling, which may well be the feminine mode of subverting the unitary subject: mimeticism (Irigaray and Kolodny), the double and even double double identification of the female film spectator (Mulvey, Doane, De Lauretis), women's writing as palimpsest (Gilbert and Gubar), female fetishism (Kofman, Berg, Schor), the foregrounding of the 'other woman' (Gallop)": "Dreaming Dissymmetry," p. 110.

Anti-pluralisms are "subversive," that is, they offer resistance to a powerful discourse of domination; the fields for their subversions are multiple without being infinite. But I am still seeking to specify the limits of those fields. At a certain point in my work, it occurred to me that anti-pluralism was really nothing but my umbrella term for everything I saw as subversive (or at least potentially subversive). My analysis of the limits of pluralism is finally a kind of negative inscription of the deconstructive potential of anti-pluralisms. The temptation was strong, given the nature of my reading, to conclude it by establishing pluralism and anti-pluralism as binary opposites, antagonists facing off across the discursive discontinuities I have tried to produce. But an unusual and absolutely critical feature of anti-pluralisms, which once made plausible the thought that they were nothing but a grab bag of resistances, renders such specular drama impossible.

Anti-pluralisms are inflections or versions of discourses that can also be spoken—in fact, often are spoken—in nonsubversive forms, that is, in pluralist forms. This is the meaning of the claim that the pluralist may be a member of any faction in the critical field, so long as she practices a contentious criticism founded on the theoretical possibility of general or universal persuasion. Thus, marxism can be a pluralism or an anti-pluralism, depending on its relationship to the problematic of general persuasion. Feminism can be a pluralism or an anti-pluralism; indeed, in the United States today, it is both. *Any* discourse can take up a place within the problematic of general persuasion.

This is a radically anti-essentialist view of theory. I would like to invoke Edward Said's phrase, "traveling theory,"[13] because it captures the importance of locale, of the determining force of location, on theory, and, of course, on resistances. This form of anti-essentialism can complicate the process of marking limits, both the limits of pluralism and the limits of anti-pluralisms. If anti-pluralisms are subversive, they are subversive only in particular places, and it is crucial to name those places. Both subversions and compromises must be localized, tied to specific

[13]See *The World, the Text and the Critic*, pp. 226–47.

audiences, and recognized as mortal—always already in the process of breaking down or reaching their limits. These limits do not have to be identified because we are perverse, or committed to a kind of formal pessimism; we are not forced to find them as a matter of principle, given our knowledge that limits exist as logical or structural necessities (no matter what the cost in terms of our own political and theoretical demoralization).

On the contrary, we need to identify the limits of local subversion in order to find the place of the subversion of subversion, the point at which we need to shift strategies, to disrupt the game. Delineating this limit, then, might be an optimistic project, implying, as it does, a certain confidence that we can play more than one game, that we have more than one option: anti-pluralisms. But whatever its mood, this process is especially difficult when localities themselves lose their stable boundaries and seem to merge and run together, as they inevitably do. This problem is particularly acute in the case of pluralism in the United States, especially when the question at hand concerns the relation between pluralism and heterogeneous feminisms. This is because feminisms combine a critique of essence and a deconstruction of the stereotypes of sexual identity with the assertion of woman's difference and the constant temptation to "risk" essentialism. The appeal of general persuasion is always an appeal to the essence of critical community.

Thus, while in certain locations or inflections, feminism is an exemplary anti-pluralism, in others, the process of accommodation and recuperation is very far advanced, and feminists stand among those issuing polemical calls for pluralism.[14] From this perspective, *Seductive Reasoning* is both feminist and not feminist: feminist insofar as feminism articulates a position outside the problematic of general persuasion and not feminist in that it resists (even as it hopes to intervene in) the movement of some feminisms into the pluralist community.

It would be an unwarranted anticipation of a certain historical

[14]For a recent example, see Nina Baym, "The Madwoman and Her Languages: Why I Don't Do Feminist Literary Theory," *Feminist Issues in Literary Scholarship,* ed. Shari Benstock (Bloomington: Indiana University Press, 1987), pp. 45–61.

process (that is, it would be wishful thinking), for me to risk a prediction as to the configurations of theory, reading, and critical community that will characterize either literary or feminist studies in the future. The problematic of general persuasion, as I have tried to show, is as flexible and innovative as it is pervasive. At best, one can only propose that the struggle to recognize discontinuity plays across a critical field of difference and is one that admits of no closure. Audre Lorde warns that the price of belonging to the pluralist's community may be the fortification of those very structures feminism names as the sites of oppression: "The master's tools will never dismantle the master's house." The conditions that nurture anti-pluralisms are as shifting as our own alliances and conflicts; thus, our efforts to dismantle pluralism cannot adhere to a single plan, and they are constantly besieged and tempted by the promise of persuasion. To resist is first to refuse homage to those who hope to master otherness in the figure of persuasion; conceiving knowledge as productive work, we can then undertake to fashion our own tools.

INDEX

Said, Edward, 172, 249
Scholes, Robert, 40, 97, 243
Schor, Naomi, 38–39, 244, 246–48
Scott, Patricia Bell, 229
seduction, 55–63, 162–63, 174
Shaviro, Steven, 31
Showalter, Elaine, 8, 243
Smith, Adam, 46, 48, 50, 221–22, 234
Smith, Barbara, 229
Smith, Paul, 38
Spivak, Gayatri, 6, 38, 213, 222, 229, 242–43

theory, 10–13, 24–25, 33–37, 187, 195, 216, 223–25, 241
Therborn, Göran, 43
Todorov, Tzvetan, 155–56

undecidability, 159, 170–74, 181, 185, 196, 246

understanding, 101–2, 105–10, 113, 215–17, 230–32, 238
misunderstanding, 102–9, 113, 116, 136, 159, 169, 171, 184

Walker, Alice, 229
Warren, Austin, 96, 98, 111
Weber, Samuel, 29, 240
Welleck, René, 96, 98, 111
West, Cornel, 7, 204, 225–26, 235
White, Hayden, 34, 72, 133
Williams, Raymond, 78, 82–84, 86, 89, 93, 114, 144, 149, 209, 214
Wills, Garry, 27–30, 36, 62–63, 221–24
Wittgenstein, Ludwig, 138
Wolff, Robert Paul, 222–23
Wordsworth, Ann, 138

Library of Congress Cataloging-in-Publication Data
Rooney, Ellen, 1957–
    Seductive reasoning.

    Includes index.
    1. Criticism—Philosophy.   2. Rhetoric.   3. Persuasion
(Rhetoric)   4. Pluralism.   I. Title.
PN81.R66   1989   801'.95'01   88-47917
ISBN 0-8014-2192-6 (alk. paper)